Discourses of Authority in Medieval and Renaissance Literature

*edited by Kevin Brownlee
and Walter Stephens*

Discourses of Authority in Medieval and Renaissance Literature

*Published for Dartmouth College
by University Press of New England*
Hanover and London

© 1989 by the Trustees of Dartmouth College

Printed in the United States of America
∞

Library of Congress Cataloging in Publication Data
Discourses of authority in medieval and Renaissance
 literature.
 Based on the proceedings of the Fifth Darmouth Colloquium on Medieval and Early Modern Romance Literatures,
held in Hanover, N.H., in Oct. 1985.
 Bibliography: p.
 Includes index.
 1. Literature, Medieval—History and criticism. 2. European literature—Renaissance, 1450–1600—History and criticism.   3. Authority in literature. I. Brownlee, Kevin.
II. Stephens, Walter, 1949– .   III. Dartmouth Colloquium on Medieval and Early Modern Romance Literatures
(5th : 1985)
PN671.D57 1989   809'.02   88–40346
ISBN 0–87451–471–1

5   4   3   2   1

In Memoriam
Lawrence E. Harvey
1925–1988

Contents

Preface

The present study grew out of the fifth Dartmouth Colloquium on Medieval and Early Modern Romance Literatures, held in Hanover in October 1985. Each Dartmouth Colloquium has examined a key literary question concerning the continuity and gradual evolution of the European Romance literatures from the Middle Ages to the early modern period. The colloquium series has consistently taken two courses in its contributions to literary study: first, to transcend the conventional compartmentalizations of literature along historical and national lines so as to facilitate a dialogue among scholars who would otherwise rarely come into contact with one another. Second, to provide an arena for the sometimes difficult reconciliation between criticism grounded in literary history and the linguistic, philosophical, psychoanalytic, and anthropological theories of literature that came to prominence in North America during the 1960s and 1970s. Since its inauguration in 1981, the Dartmouth Colloquium has contributed significantly to the progressive integration of scholarship, criticism, and theory within studies of medieval and early modern romance literature, as attested by two previously published volumes. The first of these, *Mimesis: from Mirror to Method, Augustine to Descartes*, eds. John D. Lyons and Stephen G. Nichols (Hanover, N.H.: University Press of New England, 1982), examines literary representation. The second, *Romance: Generic Transformation from Chrétien de Troyes to Cervantes*, eds. Kevin Brownlee and Marina Scordilis Brownlee (Hanover, N.H.: University Press of New England, 1985), explores the status (and the problematics) of literary genre.

The present volume focuses on the question of authority, of central importance to the medieval and Renaissance literary enterprise, which examined its parameters in a strikingly self-conscious manner. At the same time, the specific textual processes of self-authentication, which medieval and Renaissance writers manipulated to establish their credibility, have provided fertile ground for investigation by contemporary scholars, given our own intense preoccupations with the origin, nature, and function of authority. This collection of essays adopts this double perspective—at once contemporary and historical—to present a coherent treatment of medieval and Renaissance "discourses of authority" on their own terms. The individual essays range from the twelfth through the sixteenth centuries (from Chrétien de Troyes to Tasso and Montaigne), with an excursus to Vico as mediator between Renaissance and later developments. Contributions come not only from specialists in French, Italian, and Spanish literature, but also from two historians of philosophy. Each essay constitutes a close reading of one or more literary or philosophical texts, and each is strongly representative of contemporary methodological concerns as outlined in the Introduction. However, there is no easy methodological uniformity among contributions, which were instead solicited by the editors with a view towards exploring the range of concrete manifestations possible within an optic defined by the problem of authority. Each contribution explores the deployment of discourses on authorship, intertextuality, and/or counterfeit within literary or philosophical texts, and confronts these thematizations with congruent developments within contemporary literary theory. Nor does any contribution necessarily subscribe to a canonical "state of the art" definition of intertextuality or authority; indeed, since all contributions are grounded both in literary history and in literary theory, they point variously to the limits of one or the other discipline in relation to specific texts.

Hanover, New Hampshire   K. B.
                                                             W. S.

Discourses of Authority in Medieval and Renaissance Literature

Introduction

Over the last decade, the question of authority has reemerged as a central critical preoccupation, the result of a series of inter-related developments in literary theory that have both proble-matized the very notion of authority and redefined its constitutive terms. On the one hand, there has been a serious critique of the notion of Author. Indeed, since the arrival of Structuralism, we have witnessed a widespread reaction against traditional scholarly dependence on the notion of the (invariably male) Author as the determining criterion of literary evaluation. Structuralism and the various disciplines of Poststructuralist theory have tended to de-value the Author, the plenitude of whose originating presence in, behind, and underneath the literary work had been the funda-mental tenet of literary scholarship since the rise of modern phi-lology and literary criticism in the Renaissance. To the recuper-ability of the Author's intentions, his personality, and his society, the Structuralist and Poststructuralist disciplines have opposed an emphasis on language as a potentially infinite system of interpe-netrating signs largely beyond the control of the individual enun-ciating subject.

Second, there has been a critique of the notions of Text and Source, a serious rethinking both of the status of the literary artifact and of the way in which literary texts are functionally related to each other and to nonliterary texts. This development should be seen in part as a reaction against a previously dominant ideology of literary practice. Although the Author was the orig-inator of the work according to traditional medieval and early modern scholarship, he himself was not characterized by origi-nality. Behind the Author stood his Sources: by a largely conscious process of imitation, adaptation, and quotation, the Author molded his new work, patterning it after the most excellent examples of diction, structure, or theme in a canon of exemplary models. Like the notion of the Author, that of Sources and filiations implies a controlled genealogical evolution of literature and presumes that a work of literature can be adequately explained by the identification, isolation, analysis, and recombination of its constituent elements, that is, that we can recuperate the fullness of an Author's conception by retracing his composition in reverse. To this definition of the work as a finite linguistic embodiment, modern theory has opposed the notions of the Text and intertextuality. While the work assumed a closure imposed by the completion of the Author's activity, the Text presupposes an ongoing, unfinished *working* of language in which, since reading and writing are inseparable, the reader's interpretation cannot be completely subordinated to or determined by the Author's intentions. Taken to its logical conclusion, the notion of the Text defines the Author as a linguistic predicate formed by the workings of a text, rather than its originating subject. Similarly, the reader is not "empirical," identifiable with a particular person, but is also inscribed within the workings of the text. Finally, since a text functions within a potentially unlimited field of language, it is necessarily intertextual, traversed by other texts in ways that are neither predictable nor controllable.[1]

The present volume attempts to historicize, or more accurately to re-historicize, these matters—to reconsider the question of authority in terms of and by means of literary history. Our primary focus is thus on that period of literary history during which the standard modern notions of Author and Text, authority and authenticity, were first established: the Middle Ages and the Renaissance.

Our collective point of departure is an examination of the central importance of authority to the medieval and Renaissance literary enterprise, considered on its own terms; for the entire period was characterized by a highly self-conscious awareness of the necessity of establishing authority as a precondition to writing. The responses to this imperative of course varied over time, in accordance with changing historico-literary circumstances and with changing perceptions of the nature of authority itself. The result was a series of diverse "discourses of authority" rather than any single, monolithic authoritative discourse. The overall structure of the volume reflects our awareness of this discursive diversity. At the same time, it results from a methodological commitment to close textual analysis as the most effective means of exploring questions of theory.

Our overall approach involves three interrelated questions: first, regarding the status of the Author as originating referent—the problem of authorial representation and representability; second, regarding the functioning (and the limitations) of the controlled praxis of intertextuality, at the heart of medieval and Renaissance literary activity; and third, on the notion of counterfeit, both as a "legitimate" means of medieval and Renaissance text production (*contrafactum*) and as a discursive mode that privileges self-conscious (often playful) treatment of the question—the problematics of authorship.

Whereas the importance (and the interrelationship) of the first two questions are obvious, the third requires further elaboration in terms of traditional and contemporary critical practice. The figure of the Author and his relation to his Sources determined the traditional concept of counterfeit, along with its specular antithesis, plagiarism. Traditional scholarship relied upon the recuperability of the Author through the recognition of his intentions, as partially revealed by the prior identification of his Sources. Thus the verdict of counterfeit was tantamount to verifying the lack of an authenticating presence within the work, while plagiarism amounted to the identification of unacknowledged sources, presences other than the Author who diminished his own presence. Once the Author's irrelevance had been proclaimed, the work was effectively orphaned, excluded from the Canon or register of authenticated names. Having no single originating "referent," the work became illegible, deprived of all reference outside the realm of words.

Curiously, modern theory has paid little explicit attention to the phenomenon of counterfeit. However, because of a preoccupation with problems of authority and intertextuality, many theorists and critics continue to analyze counterfeit indirectly and, as it were, allegorically. This is especially true of such synoptic pronouncements as Michel Foucault's "What Is an Author?," which defines the Author as a function or projection of texts and posits the "author-function" as "a certain mode of being of discourse" that empowers an artificial and repressive delimitation of meaning.[2] The implication of such definitions is that "counterfeit" and "authentic" discourses are not inherently differentiated one from another. Rather, "counterfeit" is a mode of discourse that preempts and internalizes the author-function, placing the text's referentiality at issue by intensively thematizing the question of authorship.[3]

By its conceptualization of the problem of authority in relation to authorial self-representation, intertextuality, and counterfeit, the present volume undertakes to combine historical and theoretical perspectives. We do not attempt a comprehensive survey of the evolutionary development of these concepts and practices in medieval and Renaissance literature; rather, we focus on a series of what we view as "privileged cases" in literary history. At the same time, we remain keenly aware of the issue of authority as a surrogate of power, manifested by the text's possibilities in interacting with the extraliterary world of political and social action.

The volume thus opens with a section that deals with the "definition" of authority for two key authors: Dante and Vico. In this context, authority is intricately connected to the idea of a canon. If the canon is that body of works a culture accepts as central to its discourse about itself and the world, then this "centrality," the frequency with which a text is printed (or transcribed), quoted, alluded to, repeated, interpreted, is in turn the index of its authority. Authority, however, is a mysterious quality. Like success, nothing succeeds like it. Literary history can discern its presence, describe it once it is in motion. But what *sets* it in motion? Are there mechanisms that can be described in textual terms whereby the process of authorization can be discerned as it begins?

In the first essay of this collection, Albert Ascoli suggests that the process of authorization can be discerned by a process of reading that mimics it. In a move that owes something to Deconstructionism, Ascoli begins his analysis with an examination of a moment in Dante's *Convivio* (c. 1304–1307) that is "structurally pivotal and yet thematically marginalized" (25). However, Ascoli's essay does not seek to "deconstruct" the text in any orthodox way but rather to demonstrate how Dante's text exploits overt mention of received notions about the constitution of authority in order to move its own discourse—and therewith a figuration or representation of Dante the Author—from marginality to centrality. Ascoli presents the *Convivio* as a complex of strategies whereby the speaking "Dante" first strips himself of authority and then recreates that authority. Specifically, the *Convivio* proceeds by inducing a crisis in the traditional notion of textual authority as the product of time and then by contaminating it with a discourse whose overt theme is a refutation of the notion that nobility—the authority of a living person—can derive from genealogy, or historical continuity (36).

This contamination effects an implicit analogy that resituates the origin of authority within "the Author," making the self the origin of both nobility and authority. Ascoli shows how authority arises within the *Convivio* "while we aren't looking" by demonstrating the analogous roles played by two marginal moments, one "digressive" and one dismissive, at opposite ends of the *Convivio*.

Ascoli shows how Dante's self-induced crisis, in which he overtly denies himself both the "impersonal" authority of historical continuity and the personal authority that is endangered by speaking about oneself, allows him covertly to "have it both ways," since his text makes "Dante" both author (poet) and canonizer (commentator or writer of prose glosses). At the same time, his choice of the "unauthoritative" Italian vernacular enables his Italian definition of the *autore* to subsume three separate concepts from Latin, the language of authority, "thereby allowing Dante as author the ambiguous role of being either 'mere' poet or philosophical authority; either the *actor* who writes but cannot guarantee the truth of his writing or the *autor* [/*auctor*] who is the transcendent guarantor of his own words, who summons up absolute *fede* and *obedienza* almost as if his language approximated the perfect intersection of truth and power that God's Word alone should and could effect" (41).

Ascoli's conclusion has important implications not only for the study of the *Convivio* but for that of the *Divine Comedy* and for the study of pre-Enlightenment literature in general. For Ascoli, the project of the *Convivio* is to create an Author capable of writing the *Convivio*; that the text remained unfinished is thus not a sign of its failure but rather of its success. By creating an author capable of writing itself, the text essentially made its own completion otiose, for at the same time it created an author capable of writing the seminal text of European vernacular literature, the *Divine Comedy*.

Ascoli shows how a text situates its authority in relation to "shifting human discourses of knowledge and power" (45), or philosophy and politics. Another sort of tension among poetry, knowledge and power half a millennium later is the subject of Donald Verene's essay on Vico. Verene finds that although Vico's *Scienza nuova* (1730/1744) proposes itself as a *philosophy* of authority, it is particularly unloquacious—at least in modern terms —about authority, especially regarding its own authority. Vico's project might at first strike us as more medieval than modern, since he attempts to define authority by seeking to return to the originary moment, when it was first made manifest in the world. His method is based on the postulation of a necessary resemblance between the structure of inquiry and its subject: it attempts to recuperate the origin of the civil world by recuperating its principle of origin, which Vico locates in imagination or *fantasia*, the "common sense" that creates human culture. He can propose to endow his own text with intellectual authority by knowingly employing *fantasia*, because it is not only the principle of poetry and the foundation of myth, but for him it is also the "science of the Muses," the same thing as memory. Vico's new critical art is thus a rejection of reason in favor of "a recasting of the art of the muses into modern philosophical form" (56).

Vico's intuition, at bottom the same as that of modern ethnologists, was that culture is not "structured" by reason; if anything, the reverse is true in the Vichian scheme since "intellectual and philosophical formulation" is the "highest"—latest—stage in the formation of cultural authority. Thus, there is no rational *basis* for authority. Authority is instead "dominion, or power" and, specifically, "the power to give title" (50). Like the poets he emulates, Vico maintains that this power was originally external to humans. His project is thus informed by a sort of enlightened reaction to the Enlightenment view of human culture: although he agrees that Galileo correctly approached Nature as a text written in the language of number and accessible to reason, he declines to approach the text of human cultures expecting it to speak the same "language." He hopes to bridge the gap between the universal (or the true) and the particular (or the certain)—to wed philosophy and philology (52). Yet this process must not proceed through reason and abstraction but rather through "the formation of images" (53). Verene maintains that Vico outdoes Plato at his own game: although Plato, "the quarreler with poets," employs myth when reason proves an inadequate means to knowledge, this "noble lie" is the very foundation of Vico's method. He "gives us a new version of how philosophy is poetry and poetry philosophy" (58).

Both Dante and Vico present us with overt self-portraits of the author at work. The account of the attempt to constitute a method whereby the work can be written is an overt, thematic component of both the *Convivio* and the *Scienza nuova*. This volume's second section focuses on the related question of the reading process as a key component in authorial self-fashioning. The four essays in this section each examine how different kinds of intertextual strategies are used to confront textual closure and fragmentation, coherence and incompleteness, elements commonly viewed as functions of textual authority. In every case, the process of continuation is central. François Rigolot's article on Ronsard's *Franciade* (1572) explores an author's explicit "autopsy" (etymologically, an eyewitnessing) of his literary corpus from the outside. In this case, autoexegesis is in fact less an anatomy of the work than an attempt to confect a convincing genealogy of the Authoring Self, an effort that will be seen in other texts in this collection. Like Dante in the *Convivio*, Ronsard constitutes an autoexegetical self that discusses the origin of its unfinished poetic corpus in order to fashion an authoring self that can complete the corpus. Like the *Convivio*, the *Franciade* remained unfinished, but for reasons that appear quite different.

The problem confronting the autoexegete in this case is not the novelty of the enterprise so much as its perilous resemblance to an authoritative original, the *Aeneid*. As has long been acknowledged, Vergil seems to have blocked Ronsard rather than "guiding" him past himself in the way Dante pretended for the *Divine Comedy*. The theoretical problem facing Ronsard in the prefaces is to define imitation so as to stress its excellence rather than its lack of originality. Like Dante, Ronsard is also necessarily concerned to disprove the accepted causal relation between temporal anteriority and authority, a problem that calls into question not only the relation between the *Franciade* and the *Aeneid* but also both their relations to the *Iliad*. Furthermore, it reaches out into the political arena as well, since the ideological premise of the *Franciade* is that "French rulers were meant by destiny to be greater than their Roman predecessors" (66). Here again, however, the peril of derivation makes itself felt, for such had been Vergil's exact project vis-à-vis Greek civilization.

Rigolot shows that Ronsard discovered his expedient in somewhat the same way as Dante, by attempting to differentiate among authorities on the basis of a criterion distinct from anteriority; in this case, the criterion chosen was *mode* of composition. A distinction between Homer's "natural facility" and Vergil's "careful diligence" enables Ronsard to skirt the issue of his own lateness by inverting the cognitive sequence of two forms of imitation, the *mimesis* of nature and the *imitatio* of other discourses. If the imitation of other texts is *methodologically* prior to the imitation of nature, then one can compete directly with Vergil, having conveniently placed Homer in a timeless, ahistorical realm that is qualitatively different from one's own and therefore nonthreatening.

In other words, by differentiating between Homer and Vergil, one can eliminate the hierarchizing effect of historical succession.

Homer is unique, but flawed; Vergil is neither free from error nor a father: he is a contemporary because of his mode of composition. Ronsard's treatment of Homer has much in common with that of Vico, since it makes Homer available as a timeless "source." But whereas Vico proposed Homer as a source of method, Ronsard delegated that function to Vergil. Like Dante, Ronsard attempts to "have it both ways" by dividing his "fathers" against each other. Rigolot thus refers to his *démarche* as the creation of a "counterfeit" authority. Rigolot's conclusions accord with those recently put forward by David Quint in *Origin and Originality*,[4] with the exception that Rigolot examines "autopsies" performed by a self-named Author from outside the text rather than looking at the emergence of a discourse on the production of meaning from within a text.

The relation of the "unfinished" work to the creation of an author-figure continues in David Hult's examination of Chrétien de Troyes's *Chevalier de la charrete* (c. 1177–1181). Hult begins by challenging the historicity of a "continuator" of Chrétien, one Godefroi de Leigni. Somewhat like Ascoli, Hult discerns an attempt to constitute authority through a division of the text. In this case, the division is not formal (text and commentary) but rather sequential (fragment and supplement) and personifying (author and continuator). Hult defines the question of presence as the means whereby the definition of the text as divided against itself both creates a double authority and comments upon several episodes in the plot of the *Charrete*. The naming of the absent *auctor* (*autor*) by a present continuator is doubled by scenes in which the narrating voice appears to divide against itself, to observe the movement of the plot as an "outsider," from the vantage point of the reader. Hult therefore explores the possibility that an "unfinished" text might have been "a part of Chrétien's intention" and considers what such an intention might be. "Godefroi de Leigni's" statement may well point to a motivation for protecting the authority of "Chrétien" by allowing "the luxury of two endings, two voices, and thus a highly nuanced, unlocalizable intentionality" (88).

One might wonder at this point just how important the criterion of a text's wholeness or completion is to the constitution of artistic authority, whether literature might not have its own constitutive myths of "unfinished symphonies," and whether or how much they might contribute to literary hagiography, from Vergil onward. How important is the *frustration* of our desire for such wholeness to the authority of a text? Does this frustration locate authority within discourse rather than within the bounds of a closed, perfect masterwork?

Nancy Vickers's contribution explores the relation between hopeless desire and the postulation of fragmentary or incomplete texts in Petrarch and Dante. Dante's *Vita Nuova* (c. 1292–1293) is, like the *Convivio*, an autoexegetical text, composed of lyric poetry and prose commentary. Like the *Convivio*, its ideal unity is supposedly both more and less than the sum of its parts, the product of prose meditation on lyric discourse. As with the later text, the covert aim of the *Vita Nuova* is the creation of an autobiography (or a biography of the Author); this time, however, the overtly stated purpose of the text is not the merging of philosophy and poetry but rather the biography of the poetic "subject." Vickers concentrates on a point of rupture in the text, where the inversion of discursive structure purports to mimic the transformation that takes place when the object of desire and the referent of language are no longer merely absent but definitively lost.

Dante's gesture of "widowing" his song, which is a "revisionary system of composition" (97), becomes an object of imitation when Petrarch divides the structure of his *Canzoniere* (c. 1366–1374) against itself by separating poems written "during the life of Laura" from those written *in morte*. Dante connects the experience of widowing in his life and poetry to the concept of widowing in the liturgical structure of the calendar and history via references to the "widowed city" of Jeremiah. Petrarch's much more overt references to the liturgy in his Good Friday "anniversary" poems, like his imitation of the "widowed words" of Dante, serve not to associate the poet to a community of mourning but rather to perpetuate the originary and solipsistic experience of Laura. Petrarch's collection already plays upon the concept of fragmentation, personal and poetic failure, and incompleteness in its official title, *Rime sparse* or *Rerum Vulgarium Fragmenta*. What is perhaps most interesting about Vickers's article in the context of this volume is its implication that such failure is the condition for poetic success. Vickers's analysis demonstrates how Petrarch was able to create the kind of consummately self-referential verbal universe John Freccero described in "The Fig Tree and the Laurel" by emulating one of the most intensely authoritative, liturgical moments of Dante's lyric *oeuvre*.[5]

Marina Scordilis Brownlee recalls the saying of Borges to the effect that every writer creates his own predecessor. Her own study of texts about texts about texts in Ovid, Boccaccio, and Juan de Flores presents a series of inscribed readers whose adventures tend to blur the boundary between reading and writing, character, empirical person, and reader. Boccaccio's *Elegia di Madonna Fiammetta* (1344) presents an avid reader of Ovid's *Heroides*, while Juan de Flores's *Grimalte y Gradissa* (1480s) introduces two readers of Boccaccio's reader of Ovid. Both texts introduce characters that either enact or attempt to enact their preferred texts. Although comparisons with Don Quijote and his narratological progeny necessarily impose themselves, Brownlee discerns other, very different interfaces between reading and action in the earlier texts she examines. Boccaccio "remotivates" Ovid's metalinguistic preoccupations but collapses the Ovidian distinction between character and reader, fusing them into a single figure, Fiammetta, who echoes, but inadequately enacts, the paradigmatic figure of Medea.

The "continuation" of Boccaccio's *Fiammetta* by Flores, like the continuation of Chrétien's *Charrete* by "Godefroi de Leigni," allows for, among other things, an alternate ending in which Fiammetta is forced to enact, "to suffer in *actions* the *words* of malediction which she had so deceptively articulated" in Boccaccio's text (126). Brownlee's analysis of the "tension between uniqueness and exemplarity" (114) in Fiammetta and her readers goes beyond thematics to establish an intriguing discursive itinerary: from the collective, "objective" presentation of external action (Ovid's *Metamorphoses*), to the interior monologue of a suddenly subjectivized mythic personage (Ovid's *Heroides*), to a failed attempt at reenacting the "personal" experience or ethos of a mythic personage, which is the experience of lyric (Boccaccio's *Fiammetta*), to a failed attempt at literally revising the plot and closure of the "original" by entering and participating in them, which approximates novelistic experience (Flores's *Grimalte y Gradissa*). The experience of the reading character can trope the experience of authoring, since the problems of Boccaccio's and Flores's characters have to do with the slippage between speech and action, "the truth-status of speech" (125). Apparent contradictions between the words and actions of both characters and authors expose "one of the mechanisms of deception inherent in language" (112).

The third section of this book focuses on the complex relation between authority and gender, especially on the notion of (personal and/or textual) genealogy as authorization. In this context, the gendering of the authorial self is linked to the instability (and mutability) of canonical literary genres.

Kevin Brownlee's article addresses the same intersecting crises of political and personal authority that François Rigolot examined in Ronsard; but aside from occurring a century and a half earlier, the case of Christine de Pisan's *Ditié de Jehanne d'Arc* (1429) is further complicated by the issue of gender. Like Ronsard, Christine sets out to define her personal genealogy as Author; unlike him, she must face the problem of authorizing a writing self and an epic subject who are both female. How this text changed both strategies and themes of authorization from Christine's earlier work is Brownlee's subject. By relating Joan to Christian and pagan tradition, Christine succeeds in turning women's "natural" lack of military aptitude into definitive proof of divine intervention and thus divine authorization. But the structures of repetition and foreshadowing (*figura* or typology), intended to prove the divine authority behind Joan of Arc's decisive intervention in the French military and political crisis of the late 1420s, also create the epistemological basis for Christine's self-presentation as Author. Christine's act of prophesying in verse inscribes her in a continuum or genealogy of Sibyls, whose double authority bridges the dominant discourses of Christine's day. The Cumaean Sibyl is especially important, since she both guided Aeneas to a vision of the greatness of Rome and prophesied the coming of Christ. Thus Christine, the new feminine *vates*, and Joan, the "divinely sanctioned military leader with a mission that is at once religious and political" (146), "collaborate" as contemporaries in a synergistic historical process unavailable to Vergil and Aeneas, Vergil and Augustus, or Vergil and Dante. By constituting herself and Joan as *auctores* in the sense discussed by Ascoli—"originators or authenticating witnesses to an act"—Christine proposes woman as a political subject rather than erotic object of literary art.

The problem of gendering the *auctor*, of enfranchising the feminine voice, returns to the fore in William Kennedy's study of Petrarchan textuality in the Renaissance. The complementarity of imitation and exegesis as acts of rewriting is implicit in several studies of this volume and is an explicit concern of Ascoli, Vickers, and Rigolot. Kennedy views both activities as having been "gendered masculine" by Renaissance tradition, not only in historical terms but in rhetorical ones as well. The originality of Kennedy's approach lies in his investigation of the means by which the highly foregrounded instability of the Petrarchan text is accommodated to the competitive, male-gendered norms of Renaissance debate. Kennedy's suggestive study juxtaposes his own modern rhetorical and historical explication of a Petrarchan text with the exegeses of Petrarch's early commentators, thereby showing how commentaries consistently "locate Petrarch's poetry in a world of aggressive rhetorical action," conceptualizing it as a dialectic of power associated with the issue of gender. It would be logical to suppose that this dialectic, common to Kennedy's reading and those he examines, would be thematized in Renaissance imitations of Petrarch's poems. But in his readings of poems by Louise Labé and Shakespeare, Kennedy concentrates on variations in the way texts displace the locus of conflict. Labé's approach to rhetorical action involves not only a reversal of gendering between speaking subject and desired object but also a displacement of aggression onto—and back again from—the lute that metonymically figures the process of poetic composition.

Some of Shakespeare's sonnets, those addressed to the young man, carry the processes of gendering and displacement into a quasi-Girardian sphere of "rivalry," wherein the male speaker concentrates his energies not upon feminine reluctance to love but on another male's reluctance to wed. Here, however, the process of displacement becomes potentially rich as the speaker displaces his own erotic message onto the "voice" of music, leaving some doubt as to the sexuality of the relation between speaker and addressee. It is this instability of Petrarchan discourse that constitutes its paradoxical authority, somewhat like the incompleteness of other texts seen thus far. As Vickers showed, Petrarch's collection of "fragments" created an author figure who could use the words and conceits of a predecessor to define himself through a play of sameness and difference, a process of "differential imitation" (somewhat like the Oedipal struggle of Bloom's poetic fathers and sons) that Claude-Gilbert Dubois associates with outdoing and subversion.[6] For Kennedy, the typographical convention of printing discordant commentaries side-by-side mimes not merely the "climate of controversy inherent in Renaissance rhetorical practice" but also the "iridescent" quality of Petrarchan textuality, which gains "distinctive shades and tones with each performance" (153, 151). As iterability and variability, this unstable quality of Petrarchan textuality provides both for its authority and for its imitability.[7]

Walter Stephens's essay on *Gerusalemme liberata* closes the third section with a look at the aspect of Tasso's poem (1575, 1581) that has most intrigued generations of readers—its portrayal of women. Stephens takes the portrayal of a minor and "insignificant" character as the place where, somewhat reluctantly, the poem reveals profound connections among forms of authority—domestic, political, and literary. What all three forms have in common is "a nostalgic idealization of marriage and a profound anxiety about the human body" (176). On the one hand, Stephens opposes deconstructive approaches that, while zealously describing slippages and allegories about the impotence of writing, fail to move beyond a catalogue of what the text does not authorize or sanction. On the other hand, he takes issue with feminist approaches that seek to discern in the text a hidden "desire" to sanction the oppression of women. Arguing that neither approach really reads anything but the surface level of plot, Stephens seeks out those moments when different levels of inconsistency or inappropriate consistency align themselves, where the "desire of the text" is more plausibly revealed.

Stephens explains such convergences by recourse to those "too obvious echoes" of canonical texts that have disturbed generations of critics. The plot at such moments is often a covert enactment of yet other texts, especially the discourse on marriage and the body in Saint Paul's epistles. This "meta-thematics" of the body, an enactment of themes imported from Paul and other texts that are never overtly acknowledged, actually seduces the reader into constructing those kinds of closure that it does not explicitly sanction and that are otherwise susceptible to deconstruction. The point, Stephens maintains, is not that Tasso's theoretical works and declared intentions for the poem are "fulfilled" by it, but rather that both the overt themes of the poem and Tasso's theoretical pronouncements are "partial truths," which only indirectly and obliquely address the real concerns of the poem. His theory is not an "adequate" version of his narrative praxis; it *is* a version. Like some of the other studies included here, Stephens suggests that a text can be characterized by a "hidden agenda." But in the case of *Gerusalemme liberata*, the "hidden agenda" is recognizably related to the apparent one.

James Burke's study of two early fourteenth-century Spanish texts opens the final section of our volume, which focuses on the strategies by which texts seek to enter the arena of personal and political interaction. Burke reads *Conde Lucanor* (1335) and the *Libro de buen amor* (1330, 1343) as manuals of interpretation; like Marina Brownlee, one of his concerns is the way in which texts confront the problematic relation between speech and action. Burke explicitly poses this problem in terms of counterfeit, which has drawn the attention of several other critics thus far in the volume. Again like Marina Brownlee, Burke opposes a text dependent upon the *exemplum* to another in which the dominant discourse is one of desire, a textual difference that translates into a difference between faith in the ultimate powers of language and interpretation and in what Malcolm Read calls the "crisis of language" in the *Libro de buen amor*.[8] The possibility of a fissure between language and reality, signifier and signified, creates what might be called the menace of counterfeit, or, as Burke says quoting Cassirer, the "curse of mediacy."[9] The possibility that language might not be a "medium" of communication, verification, control, and construction but rather the vehicle of deception and delusion is rather neatly embodied in the differences between these two early texts.

All the essays thus far in the volume reflect a contemporary view of authority as "serious business," because they presuppose a relationship between literature and social and personal interaction. Giuseppe Mazzotta's article provides a new perspective, however, by suggesting that in some texts the issue of authority as power might be grounded instead in a metaphysics of play. By play, Mazzotta does not imply any frivolity of purpose but rather describes a refined notion of the gratuitous act. Mazzotta discerns in Dante's thematization of play in the *Divine Comedy* (c. 1320) "his vision that play is the activity that best uncovers God's deepest being," and further that poetry and theology are unthinkable either without play or without each other (218). The authoritative nature of an act is related to its freedom from any necessity, its status as the expression of fundamental autonomy. This ultimate significance of play for the *Divine Comedy* stems from its implicit reformulation of a basic tenet of Christian doctrine: that the world and humanity were not created because of necessity but rather through God's exercise of free will, that Creation is the product of "free, spontaneous choice" (221). Because it is an activity of divinity expressing free choice, play is therefore also an attribute of those beings closest to the divine, because their will is free: man, the Giants, the angels, and the devils.

Closely related to play is esthetics, which also aims at pleasure; but like play, esthetics has implications that are paramount for the theology of the *Divine Comedy* and its historical period. Esthetics is the criterion of God's act of creation, and only the language of esthetics can account for the likeness between God and the universe. Since play and pleasure depend on free will, however, they also define the area in which sin takes place (231). From another standpoint as well, as the grounding principle of creation, pleasure—esthetics and play—is necessarily coextensive with both ethics and metaphysics (224). Dante harmonizes a number of disparate philosophical and theological sources. If for Tasso the dominant enacted metaphors are incorporation and marriage, however, the metaphoric coincidence of ethics and music as *harmonia,* or the accord of disparate components, "[bears] the brunt of Dante's *theologia ludens*" (228). Thus the comedy of the devils, which in itself is repulsive and degraded, is the necessary obverse of the *angelici ludi,* the angels' music and play that is both worship of God and movement of the heavenly spheres.

This doubleness, which is essential to all cognitive activity, brings to the fore the danger of representation. Since esthetics is "the faculty that transforms essences into images" (228) the danger of play for human activity is a danger of counterfeit, the danger of pure appearance without substantive value. In itself, counterfeiting has the same origin as mysticism—in the conviction that appearance is fallacious—but the two activities diverge because appearances may be freely embraced or else rejected. The perilous double nature of esthetic and ludic activity thus leads "to the unavoidable conclusion that whereas God plays, man is enjoined to work" (233) so as to shun the slide from mysticism into counterfeit. The further consequence of this problem is the status of verbal art, especially poetry, which is play and music—sheer appearance. The ideal solution, Mazzotta implies, is that adopted by Dante; to fuse work and play, to attempt to encompass "the most diverse contradictions" of human experience.

Nancy Struever's study of Machiavelli and Montaigne closes this series and to some extent brings its survey of discourse full circle. We began, in the studies of Ascoli and Verene, with examinations that concentrated upon the constitution of an authoritative figure of the author or an authoritative ground of method within the text. Struever's essay, however, concentrates on changes in ethical inquiry as "changes in the ethics *of* inquiry" (236). If the ethical imperative of literary discourse is to provide "good counsel," how is this best done? How does a text best address itself to readers? Struever provides a history of the problem of ethical discourse in the Renaissance and finds that, with the exception of *The Prince* (1513, pub. 1532) and Montaigne's *Essais* (1580–1595), the "artful prose" of the more famous texts of "good counsel" diagnoses their "social dysfunction." Her approach is all the more interesting since, along with Tasso, Machiavelli and Montaigne are probably among the most notorious cases of confusion between the character of the text and that of the Author.

Struever reads both texts as an application of rhetoric to the problem of distinguishing between "proper moral work and moralism" (250). Like texts examined by Burke and Marina Brownlee, both Machiavelli and Montaigne adopt the *exemplum*, but for correspondingly different reasons. Struever argues that Machiavelli adopts the *exemplum* in order to problematize political choices, much as Boccaccio's *novelle* problematize morality by rewriting the *exemplum*. According to Struever, Machiavelli's project is thus not historical but philosophical: the famous exemplary narrative of Cesare Borgia is "not proto-scientific or pseudohistorical, but has a status like that of the hypothetical cases of philosophical discussion" (240). The unsatisfactory nature of Machiavelli's narrative, its "inconsistency," derives from modal and generic choices that are "deliberate interventions, tamperings with the rules and conventions of Classical-Christian advice literature" (243). Struever thus concludes that Machiavelli's importance to the history of ethical inquiry is "meta-discursive, meta-critical," and that its analysis is centered on the relation between texts and their users.

Struever's contribution to the analysis of Montaigne's *Essais* is essentially the obverse of her examination of Machiavelli. It begins from her conviction that too much analysis of "Montaigne's skepticism" has led to "anachronistic attributions to Montaigne of twentieth-century literary-philosophical interests in self-subversion, deconstruction, and destabilization" (244). Montaigne's text does not so much constitute "an impregnable skeptical position" as reconstitute "a proper set of beliefs." Self-presentation is here not a strategy of *mise en abîme* but rather of circumscribing flux.

Struever's approach culminates several tendencies shown by essays in this volume, the most important of which is the vigilance to maintain a balance between historicism and literary theory. Any scruple about methodological purity would have destroyed the article since, on the one hand, it argues against a modern, deconstructive reading of Montaigne and, on the other, it argues against any substantial premodern understanding of the Machiavellian project. Struever finds numerous methodological and ethical points of contact between Machiavelli, Montaigne, and recent developments in rhetoric, linguistics, and ethical inquiry, but she also situates the sixteenth-century texts with respect to previous intersections of rhetoric and ethics.

1. Defining Authority

Albert Russell Ascoli

The Vowels of Authority
(Dante's *Convivio* IV. vi. 3–4)

Questo vocabulo, cioè "autore," . . . può discendere da due principii: l'uno si è d'uno verbo molto lasciato da l'uso in gramatica, che significa tanto quanto "legare parole," cioè "auieo." E chi ben guarda lui, ne la sua prima voce apertamente vedrà che elli stesso lo dimostra, che solo di legame di parole è fatto, cioè di solo cinque vocali, che sono anima e legame d'ogni parola . . . A, E, I, O, U. . . . E in quanto "autore" viene e discende da questo verbo, si prende solo per li poeti, che con l'arte musaica le loro parole hanno legate: e di questa significazione al presente non s'intende.

[This word, to wit *auctor*, . . . may spring from two principles; the one is that of a verb, dropped very much out of use in Latin, which signifies as much as "binding words," to wit *auieo*. And whoso regards it well, in its first form, will clearly perceive that it shows its own meaning, for it is made of nought save the bonds of words, that is to say of the five vowels alone, which are the soul and juncture of every word . . . A,E,I,O,U. . . . And in as far as "author" is derived and descends from this verb, it is understood only of poets, who have bound their words with the art of music: and with this significance we are not at present concerned.]

DANTE, Il Convivio[1]

Some years ago, Etienne Gilson pointed to a curious feature of Dante's attitude toward authorities in a number of different fields or institutions—notably the political, the philosophical and the ecclesiastical—which he dubbed the "aporia dantesca."[2] What Gilson remarked upon is a consistent doubleness in Dante's treatment of human authorities, a desire at once to make an individual absolutely authoritative within his domain and yet to define clearly the limits of that domain, beyond which this individual possesses no special authority. Obviously, Gilson was thinking first of the attempt in the *De Monarchia* to free imperial rule from any subordination, in temporal matters, to the papacy, whose field was exclusively spiritual. But the *Convivio*, at the beginning of Book IV, offers a related and equally clear example. The general context is Dante's definition and discussion of human *nobilitas*. The specific moment in the argument is Dante's attempt to show that the apparent support for an opposing definition by two different authorities (*autorità*)—the Emperor Frederick II and *the* Philosopher, Aristotle—is either not authoritative in this field or not actually in opposition to Dante's claims at all. This he does, in part, by a very careful definition and delimitation of the areas of philosophical and imperial competence.

What Gilson does not remark upon, in this context, is that during the brief transition between delimiting and paying homage to imperial authority, on the one hand, and, on the other, defining the philosophical *autore*, personified by Aristotle, as "dignissimo di Fede e d'obbedienza" [most worthy of faith and obedience (IV.vi.9)], Dante introduces the short and rather odd discussion of the poetic *autore* quoted at the beginning of this paper. In the *Monarchia* the question of the authority of Dante's own discourse is not considered in any great or problematic detail.[3] In this section of the *Convivio*, however, it is precisely the relation of Dante's arguments to the other authoritative discourses, specifically those of knowledge and of power, that is at stake. The *aporia dantesca*, the little gap between the emperor's and the philosopher's domains is, presumably, where Dante's own authority subsists. Since the *Convivio* is a text composed of poetry—philosophical *canzoni*, to be precise—attended by extended, explicitly subservient (I.v–vii) commentaries, which are said to expound the "allegory of poets" hidden in the obscure verses (II.i), one might suppose that the position of the poetic *autore* between the political and the philosophical might imply an equation between that "binder of words" and Dante himself. The first of several curiosities in the passage is that this is not, at least not explicitly, the case. In fact, Dante baldly dismisses this derivation of *autore* from his consideration immediately: "e di questa significazione al presente non s'intende" [and with this significance we are not at present concerned].

In the balance of this essay I will suggest that the passage in question, structurally pivotal and yet thematically marginalized, is in fact a key to understanding the *Convivio* as a text bent on constructing its own authority, one which both appropriates and criticizes traditional medieval concepts of *auctoritas*—poetic, philosophical, political, and, as we shall finally see, theological as well. In addition to revising notions of how the *Convivio* is structured (and why it remained incomplete), my arguments will lead me two steps beyond to (1) some suggestions about the relation of the *Convivio* to the *Commedia* that modify current claims that the "theological" poetics of the latter effect a complete rejection of the former and (2) a few observations of a methodological and theoretical character about how one should approach the general question of "poetic authority" in the Late Middle Ages and Renaissance, using Dante as an instance both typical and extraordinary.

Let me begin by suggesting just what it is that makes Dante's etymological derivation of the poetic *autore* from *auieo* at once so quirky and so crucial. As M. D. Chenu has shown, and others have confirmed, there was a long medieval tradition for defining the word *auctor* in relation, conceptual and etymological, to two other words: *actor* and *autor*.[4] *Actor* comes from *agere*, "to do," and refers to the one who makes a work, without reference to the authority or veracity of that work. *Auctor* comes from *augere*, "to augment or make grow," and refers to one who is at once the originator of and the authenticating witness to an act (for instance, of composition). In many medieval texts, but not all, as we shall see, *auctor* is used interchangeably with *autor*, derived from the Greek *autentim* and defined as one "worthy of faith and imitation" (anticipating the *second* of Dante's two definitions). The basic conceptual distinction is between *actor*—the creator of a work—and *auctor/autor*—those who confer authenticity (truth and binding force) upon their works. Now, Dante's two etymologies of the Italian *autore* (from *auieo* and from *autentim*) are

taken from Uguccione da Pisa's *Magnae Derivationes*, an influential etymological dictionary of the early thirteenth century. Uguccione, otherwise known as Hugutio, was a bishop of Ferrara
and a leading scholar of canon law, one of Dante's best known
predecessors in the attempt to keep Church and State separate
and "equal."[5] I will return to Uguccione's full discussion shortly.
For now it is important to note that he adds *auieo* to *autentim* as
an alternate etymon of *autor* (as far as I know, for the first time
and without much later echo beyond Dante).[6]

The etymology is innovative, if not original, with Dante, and
thus constitutes a deliberate and particularly significant statement
on his part. What is most striking about the definition, especially
as Dante contextualizes it, is how it is at once remarkably sweep-
ing and extremely restricted. In effect, it equates the poet's art
with the very constitution of language itself, built out of the
constituent letters and bound together by the vowels (just as, at
another level, the poet "binds together" words with rhyme and
meter). On the other hand, as I have already suggested, poetry
is contextually severed from the domains of either power or knowledge—it is an activity "only" of the poets, and it is ruled irrelevant to any discussion of emperors and philosophers. Dante's
etymology is, in fact, almost a perfect allegory of the paradoxical
status of etymology for the Middle Ages—on the one hand, it
suggests how "words follow things" (to echo Dante's own phrase)[7]
in a precisely motivated way since, again as Dante says, the word
auieo acts out the linguistic binding that it signifies ("a figurare
imagine di legame," IV.vi.3). On the other hand, the "thing" of
which the word is a consequence is precisely language itself, words
tied together by vowels. Explicitly, the passage exalts the power
of language, above all of poetic language, to unite and express
the totality of meaning; implicitly and resignedly, it seems also
to suggest something like the modern critique of the doctrine of
"nomina sunt consequentia rerum" as an arbitrary and purely
linguistic game, a producer of signs without any reference or consequence but that of their own signhood.[8]

Since we are accustomed to thinking of Dante as the most
"authoritative" of all poets, at least in the *Commedia*, what is

most noticeable here is the clear tendency to marginalize poetry, especially in relation to philosophy. To account for this trend, we should look at several other aspects of the *Convivio*: (1) the crisis of Dante's authority and the attempts to resolve it, which are the matter of the first, introductory book of *Convivio*; (2) the relation between the excursus on authority in Book IV and the discourse on nobility to which it is only apparently ancillary; and finally (3) the problematic relation between poetry and philosophy, *canzoni* and commentary, throughout the treatise. First of all, however, I need to review the traditional view or views of the *auctor* and of *auctoritas* both against and within which the *Convivio* is positioned.

The concept of *auctoritas* is usually traced back to a *locus classicus* in Cicero's *Topics* (XX. 73 ff.), where it is discussed at length as that quality in a (juridical) witness, the *auctor*, that inspires faith in his testimony.[9] For Cicero, authority of this kind is clearly a matter of appearance rather than of essence, of politics and law rather than of philosophy and theology.[10] According to Curtius's brief account, St. Jerome subsequently applied the term to the Bible as verbal witness of God's work in history.[11] As an obvious consequence, medieval concepts of *auctoritas* shift away from the rhetorical notion of authority as the persuasive *appearance* of truth and toward the theological idea of an original, essential, and transcendent truth and power behind appearances from which all circumscribed human authority ultimately derives.[12] In the Holy Trinity, the Father's absolute Power is linked to the Son's absolute Wisdom by the Holy Spirit's perfect Love (cf. *Convivio* II.v.8): God is the *Auctor* of *auctores* because what he knows is what he willed into existence, which is everything. His authority is complete because he is subject and object and copula of every sentence in his own Book of Creation. As Chenu points out, then, the most obvious path of derivation of human authority is in the theological-ecclesiastical field. In fact, in the *Monarchia* Dante specifically traces the descent of divine *auctoritas* through the Scriptures to the Fathers and the Church, down to the Decretals.[13]

There are other fields, however, where the term is applied, even though the derivation from God is not as immediately obvious—specifically in (classical, pagan) philosophy, Roman political institutions, and poetic composition. The traditional etymologies of *auctor/autor/actor* and the modern scholarship that discusses them focus on the authoritative texts used in the schools and in intellectual compositions of all kinds. Uguccione's variant, however, contrives to display side-by-side these three distinct fields of authority—since here *auctor*, from *augere*, refers specifically to the political ruler who expands his realm, while *autor* in one derivation refers to the poet and in the other to the philosophers and the "inventores artium."[14] In Dante's book, the etymology of *auctor* is omitted, but the emperor remains, side by side with poet and philosopher, all referred to by the one Italian word *autore*, which has replaced the two (or three) Latin nouns.

In each case, theological or otherwise, medieval *auctoritas* seems as far as can be from Cicero's witness, whose credibility and political effectiveness depend upon his own special character and upon the unique set of historical circumstances that define him to those before whom he testifies. Medieval *auctoritas* grows stronger the further it recedes into dim antiquity, the closer it comes to a quasi-divine transcendence in which the speaking (or governing) person disappears and a timeless truth or power takes the stage.[15] This exaltation of the *auctor* and the authoritative text has a paradoxical double effect. On the one hand, moderns are reduced to mere commentators or compilers of the texts of the true ancient *auctores*. On the other hand, because the *auctor* is treated as if transcendent, impersonal, and absolute in truth, commentators and compilers have the de facto license to reinterpret, even rearrange, their texts so as to produce normative, orthodox results that obscure the individual, historical nature of the human author and his texts.[16] The author is thus simultaneously divinized and banished.[17]

To justify assigning such inhuman authority to human and often non-Christian *auctores*, explanations were often constructed linking them to divine authority. For instance, the alleged Donation of Constantine was often construed as putting imperial rulers under papal and, ultimately, divine supervision. Just so, St.

Thomas Aquinas and others carefully positioned the philosophical reasonings of Aristotle in a relation of support and subordination to theological revelation.[18] Inevitably, however, such explanations were also liable to basic Christian critiques and demystifications. Attempts to valorize the political could be countered by an Augustinian insistence on the radical separation of the glorious City of God from the irredeemable City of Man.[19] Neo-Aristotelian theologians were faced with neo-Pauline attacks on the blindness and madness of pagan philosophy.[20] And the list of conceptual and historical dilemmas could be multiplied. Apparently, the problem of the authority of origin can, in theory, be resolved by a single act of Christian faith, but that explanation soon dissolves into a far less soluble series of cruxes regarding the derivation and mediation of divine and transcendent authority by human agents. Moreover, there are no end of practical problems regarding the relationship between the mediating human authorities, who are often in veiled or open conflict; as, for instance, were a long series of popes and emperors.[21] In every serious attempt to reduce the origin of authority back to God's power and truth, then, the Ciceronian problem of rhetorical appearance and political interest reemerges, de facto and historically.

It is precisely within this display and attempted reconciliation of multiple impersonal authorities, as well as within these continuing crises of authority, that Dante's *Convivio* situates itself, and not only in the few chapters dedicated explicitly to *autorità* in Book IV. The stated aim of the *Convivio*, or rather one of two stated aims, as we shall see, is to transmit the truths of Lady Philosophy to those who, because they lead active lives outside the authoritative intellectual culture of Latin, are in need of her guidance. Dante specifically aims his discourse at secular rulers and other "nobili" who exercise authority in the community (I.x.5). Within the domain of philosophy, which is that of human reason unaided by theological revelation, Dante takes the unusual step of setting ethics above metaphysics. In fact, had the projected fifteen books of the *Convivio* actually been completed (only four exist) the last eleven would in all likelihood have been expositions of the eleven active virtues enumerated by Aristotle and recalled explicitly by Dante in Book IV.[22] In other words, Dante focuses on the branch of philosophy that is meant to shape the conduct of life in this world and to have direct formative authority over those who possess political power, from the emperor on down. Thus, the whole *Convivio* sets out to effect the necessary bridging between knowledge and power posited in Book IV when, after conceptually delimiting philosophical and imperial authorities, Dante insists on the latter's need for the former to govern wisely and the former's need for the latter's powerful support in making his wisdom count (IV.vi.17–20).[23] Finally, and most obviously, the form that this ethical project takes is an introductory treatise followed by extended commentaries on three of Dante's *canzoni*; the point being that poetry, at least a certain poetry, is the bearer of hidden philosophical content. Poetry, philosophy, power: the *Convivio* projects their intersection from the first.

Also from the first, however, the *Convivio* puts in jeopardy its own, and its author's, ability to carry out such a project. The whole of the first book is a confession of his own and his work's apparent lack of *autorità*, with a series of interwoven attempts to acquire or reacquire it. The very first words of the treatise are: "Sì come dice lo Filosofo nel principio de la Prima Filosofia, tutti li uomini naturalmente desiderano di sapere" [As the Philosopher says at the beginning of the First Philosophy, 'All men by nature desire to know' (I.i.1)]. In afterward defining his work as an intellectual banquet for curious members of the vulgar culture, he refers to himself as one who does not sit at the table of the philosophers but rather "a' piedi di coloro che seggiono ricolgo da quello che dà loro cade" [at the feet of them who sit at meat, (I gather) of that which falls from them (I.i.10)]. The name and words of Aristotle are so often invoked throughout the four books that Dante appears as a second-degree *compilator* or commentator rather than as an *auctor* in his own right.[24] He does, in fact, explicitly take on the role of commentator, but he is expounding *canzoni* he himself composed several years earlier (a gesture, we shall see, that can also be read as the extreme opposite of self-effacement) (I.iii.2). In addition to setting himself up as divulger or vulgarizer rather than as philosopher or theologian proper,

Dante specifically circumscribes his own authority in several other ways. He writes not in Latin, the official language of ecclesiastical, philosophical, and political-legal authority, but in Italian, which he himself initially defines as less *nobile* than Latin (I.v.7).[25] He is a disenfranchised political exile who wanders from city to city throughout Italy.

Perhaps most striking of all is Dante's attempt to explain why he feels called upon to speak about himself (extending the first person singular of his lyric verse into philosophical prose) in a context where such a reference "pare non licito" [seems unjustifiable (I.ii.2)]. Curtius has actually shown that the later Middle Ages did not so thoroughly discourage self-reference and self-naming as Dante's discussion, and the arguments of modern scholars like Zumthor, seem to suggest, even though the prohibition seems apt in a culture of ancient authoritative names and self-effacing modern commentators.[26] In fact, Dante's subsequent treatment of the question reveals that he is worried precisely about the loss of the authority that grammatical impersonality and "objectivity" confer. When one speaks of oneself, he says, it is always either to praise or to blame. But self-praise is self-defeating because it always implies that one is *not* well thought of and thus actually amounts to self-blame in the ears of one's listeners (I.ii.7); while *open* self-blame is even worse because it reflects that one recognizes failings without willing a real change in them (I.ii.5–6). Above all, we are simply in no position to refer accurately and objectively to ourselves since "non è uomo che sia di sè vero e giusto misuratore, tanto la propria caritate ne 'nganna" [there is no man who is a true and just measurer of himself, so (much) does our kindness to ourselves deceive us (I.ii.8)]. On the other hand, he goes on to say, it may after all be permissible to speak of oneself for either of two reasons: (1) if, like Boethius in the *Consolation of Philosophy*, one thereby escapes danger or "infamia" (I.ii.13); or (2) if, like St. Augustine, one thereby benefits others by setting a positive model for imitation (I.ii.14). The Augustinian model corresponds to the basic ethical-political project of the *Convivio* discussed earlier. The Boethian model of self-justification by self-reference defines, I would argue, a second and

parallel project that actually dominates the first book and continues unabated, though less apparent, throughout the next three
as well.[27]

At first he says he is trying to dispel the *infamia* deriving from
the general impression that his *canzoni* tell the story of his subjection to *passione,* when he can reveal that they actually, allegorically, express a pure love of wisdom (I.ii.15–16). But we soon
discover that there is another issue that troubles him far more;
one that makes him, indeed, like Boethius who "sotto pretesto
di consolazione escusasse la perpetuale infamia del suo essilio"
[under cover of consolation (wished to) ward off the perpetual
infamy of his exile]—that is, his fall from the favor of Theodoric,
barbarian king of Rome, and his metamorphosis (à la Pier delle
Vigne) from political and judicial authority into condemned prisoner (I.ii.13). To justify the fact that his expository commentaries
sometimes create more questions than they resolve (I.iii.1), Dante
explains that, because of the circumstance of his own exile, he
feels the need to adopt a "higher style" in order to acquire "mag-
gior autoritade" [greater authority (I.iv.13)]. And the primary reason for the *loss* of authority is that, in the course of his wanderings
after banishment from Florence in 1301, "sono apparito a li occhi
a molti che forsechè per alcuna fama in altra forma m'aveano
imaginato, nel conspetto de' quali non solamente mia persona
invilio, ma di minor pregio si fece ogni opera, sì già fatta, come
quella che fosse a fare" [and I have seemed cheap in the eyes of
many who perchance had conceived of me in other guise by some
certain fame; in the sight of whom not only has my person been
cheapened, but every work of mine, already accomplished or yet
to do, has become of lower price (i.e., the *Convivio* itself, if not
the *Commedia*) (I.iii.5–6)]. This powerful and pathetic effect of
personal presence, which demystifies disembodied fame, has three
causes. The first two belong to those who are perceiving Dante:
(1) most are too ready to judge by external appearance alone,
while (2) others have their judgments distorted by envy. The last
cause is in Dante himself and in any man (any writer)—the fact
that no human is without defect or stain (*macula*) (I.iii.iv). The
human stain, which appears inevitably in Dante when he repre-

sents himself, reminds us that he is trying to purge this and other stains (*macule*—the word is the same) from his work by these self-justifications (I.ii.1–2). In short, Dante localizes the crisis in his authority around the questions of self-presentation (to the Italian courts) and of self-representation (in his work). He must take the risk of re-presenting himself in words, thereby diminishing his *auctoritas*, because his human presence has already compromised it even further. Authority is clearly diminished by personalization and subjectivization—but it is partly recovered by the same route.

What is really most striking in this discourse is how Dante brings together, around his own authorial figure, the opposed concepts of vulgar *fama*, opinion based on mere appearance and dangerous passions, and of *auctoritas*, the impersonal and transcendent name that inspires faith and guarantees truth.[28] In his extended account of how both evil and good *fama* work, Dante relates how the biased report of either friend or enemy gives rise to a series of exaggerations that gain force as they recede in time and space from the man whose name is repeated (I.iii.6ff.). And a malicious modern reader might see figured there an account of the creation of *auctoritas* itself. Moreover, Dante's discussion of the operations of *fama* and *infamia* in relation to his own exilic predicament suggests both that impersonal, distanced accounts lose sight of the person to whom they purportedly refer (I.iii.6–11) *and* that the *presence* of the person also leads inevitably to mistaken evaluations (I.iv. esp. 12). In effect, there seems to be no way left to guarantee that a person, an author, will be taken for what he really is—no grounds for accepting either traditional impersonal bases of authority or for creating a new and personalized concept of authorization.

In spite of this seeming dilemma, the balance of *Convivio* I is dedicated to reclaiming the authority of which Dante has systematically stripped himself. His attempts to (re)acquire it are, as we have begun to see, evenly divided between subjecting himself to the traditional canons of impersonal (though nominal) authorization (e.g., submitting himself to the higher authority of Aristotle; writing in a generically "higher style") and making new virtues out of his lack of such authority (e.g., speaking of himself in the first person; writing in Italian precisely because it is his *own* native tongue [I.x.6] and because it will open up philosophical culture to those who have been excluded from it [I.ix.2–4]; even insisting on the novelty, the originality, of his language and his enterprise [I.ix.10]). We have seen that Dante himself points to the obvious slippage between the adoption of a difficult but authoritative style and writing in a more accessible language (I.iii.1). But, if he is aware of the tension, he is clearly not in full control of it. The wild swings between "new" and "old" modes of authorship, as well as between Dante's self-proclaimed lack of authority and his large claims upon it, can be measured between the opening image of a doglike collector of the crumbs of others and the parallel that closes the first book—between Dante's intellectual banquet for his readers and Christ's multiplication of the loaves (I.xiii.12, from John 6:5–13, traditionally allegorized as the dispensing of divine Wisdom).[29]

Perhaps the most powerful evidence for Dante's rejection of traditional models of authority while in the act of embracing them can be seen in the very structure of the *Convivio*. He certainly seems bent on following the basic pattern of authoritative text paired with normalizing commentary.[30] Here, however, as before in the *Vita Nuova*, Dante's use of the model is almost unique in that he assumes *both* roles: that of author and of commentator.[31] What results, reinforcing at the structural level what I have already shown on the thematic level, is a *personalization* of both roles, a foregrounding of the historically determined author/reader that demystifies, in effect if not in intent, both the impersonality of the transcendent *auctor* and the self-effacing deference of the commentator. At the same time, of course, by virtue of treating his own poetic works as worthy of commentary, Dante assigns them unprecedented *auctoritas* for "modern" works and expresses his specific desire to exercise a control over our understanding of them, which is, as we saw earlier, denied in practice if not in theory to the ancient *auctores*. The special, ambiguous status of these poetic texts can be seen in Dante's argument that they are the "signori" of servant commentaries, but that the latter cannot be written in Latin since "servant" would then become "master" (I.v–vii).

The three books that follow the introduction continue to be profoundly concerned with constructing an authority-conferring ethical-intellectual history of the self. Book II gives an account of how the rhetorical charms of Cicero and Boethius won Dante from the love of "quella gloriosa Beatrice" to that of Lady Philosophy (II.xv.1ff; cf. II.xii.2ff.); while Book III describes the nobility of Dante's new beloved (II.xv.3), who ennobles the human nature of her lovers (including Dante) by leading it to the perfection of its highest faculty, reason. In each case, the lesson offered to the reader is coupled with an account of the author's own experience, the "history" of his ascent toward the position from which he can look back and offer his own knowledge as a guide to others. In Book IV this "autobiographical" troping seems to have ended (though he does give an account, to which I will return, of the circumstances of the poem's production), as if he had now achieved the authority necessary for writing the *Convivio*. In fact, the canzone "Le dolci rime d'amor ch'i' solia" [The sweet rhymes of love which I was wont] is by its author specifically named "Contra-li-erranti mia" [my Against the Erring Ones] after Aquinas's *Summa Contra Gentiles*, because it assumes a privileged position of philosophical insight to dispel the errors of willful ignorance about the nature of true nobility (IV.canzone 141,xxx). As we are about to see, however, this new "impersonality" of Book IV is only apparent. What Dante "personally" has at stake is precisely the nobility and authority that allows him to write Book IV, though we can only discover this by carefully examining the implicit parallels between his central topic, nobility, and the "digression" on *auctoritas* to which I have already alluded several times.

The plan of the Book, is, first, to refute a complex of erroneous, though generally held, definitions of human nobility and, then, to offer a counterdefinition, which is the true one. The errors Dante wants to erase are encapsulated in a phrase here attributed to Emperor Frederick II—that nobility consists in "antica richezza e belli costumi" [the ancient possession of wealth, with gracious manners (IV.canzone 21–24, iii.6)], with the added implication that nobility is derived genealogically, by birth. From this account stems the ignorant "vulgar" opinion that wealth and high birth equal nobility (IV.iii.7; xiv–xv). Finally, Aristotle himself is brought into question, not because of an errant definition of nobility but because he says, or rather Aquinas says he says (*Comm. in Ethic.* VII lect. 13, n.1509), that something believed by many cannot be entirely false. Aristotle thus seems to lend his *autorità* to the truth of this or any other popular belief or opinion (IV.iii.9). In contradistinction, Dante offers a definition of nobility as an entirely individual or personal attribute, as the ground or root out of which all the active virtues grow, as the heaven in which the starry virtues shine (IV.xviii.5; xix.1ff.).[32] Since he defines virtue as an "elective habit," nobility becomes the basis for free and autonomous acts of will, unconditioned by personal possessions, ancestry, or standing in society (IV.xvii.1–2, 7–8; xx.5). Moreover, *nobiltà* is derived from a combination of the disposition of the individual body/soul complex with God's direct gift to that individual (IV.xx–xxi). Finally, Dante is careful to reject Uguccione's etymological definition of *nobilis* as deriving from *notabilis* ("well known") and favors the innocuous *non vilis* ("not vile or ignoble") of Isidore (*Etym.* X.184; in *Convivio* IV.xvi.6). He thus insures that nobility is not dependent upon *fama* or opinion but is rather an intrinsic quality.

This argument is by no means original with Dante, despite a claim to that effect (which actually seems to be an echo of St. Thomas) (IV.xvi.6). The theoretical opposition to it is certainly not as widespread or potent as he indicates—although in *practical* terms the feudal order, to which Florentine mercantile republicanism was a radical challenge, contradicted it flatly.[33] What is more interesting is the straightforward analogy one can draw between the "objective" philosophical discussion of *nobiltà*, on the one hand, and, on the other, Dante's struggle to acquire an *autorità* that is not dependent on genealogy or antiquity, impersonality, general reputation, or acceptance and promulgation by authoritative institutions; rather, this *autorità* is *individual*. Although Dante does not quote Uguccione's discussion directly equating *autenticus* (the adjectival companion of *autor* from *autentim*) with *nobilis*, he could hardly have overlooked it, for I believe that equation structures Book IV.[34] Dante, in fact, makes the link, and shows its relevance to him personally, when he prefaces his discussion of philosophical *autorità* by saying that in this treatise "di nobilitade trattando, me nobile e non villano deggio mostrare" [treating of nobility I am bound to show myself noble and not churlish (IV.viii.5)]. There is still, however, a problem, because when he says he wants to show himself noble it is not, at least not explicity, in the sense of demonstrating intellectual autonomy but rather of proving his perfect respect for the authorities of Frederick and Aristotle. If we look more closely at his treatment of the two, nonetheless, we will see how this superficial subservience and self-effacement is actually aimed at establishing his independence from them.

The treatment of Frederick seems relatively straightforward—as an attempt both to honor one kind of authority and to delimit it.[35] The Empire and its Emperor have great *autorità* conferred directly from God, not subordinate to other earthly authorities as regards its own field of competence; but it is also a specific kind of authority, over the human will and its expressions in the active civic life on earth, not over intellectual truth at all, since only God has uncircumscribed authority (IV.ix). For the intellectual understanding of the realities over which he presides, the Emperor requires the aid that only Aristotle (or perhaps Dante) can provide (IV.vi.17). By contrast, the treatment of Aristotle's authority is not so simple, since it does not directly concern nobility at all but rather the philosopher's claim for the veracity of popular opinion. This matter is clearly crucial, because we have already seen that, in the *Convivio*, opinion or *fama* (unfounded belief) is the antithesis and enemy of authority; but it is also its parodic double, for both are versions of *fede*, faith or belief, in a name.[36] Thus Dante deliberately entertains the notion that Aristotle authoritatively sets forth a view that radically undercuts hierarchical authority, subjecting truth to whatever the greatest number of people happen to think at the present moment. Dante's solution to the problem is equivocal—he simply says that Aristotle must have meant opinion based on rational understanding rather than on deceptive sensory appearances (IV.viii.8). One might argue that this is a typical tactical device for conserving *auctoritas* when it becomes problematic, just as Dante conserves Frederick's authority by circumscribing it.[37] On the other hand, it might suggest how *auctores* become whatever their interpreters want them to be.

The matter does not end at this rather uncertain point, however. It gets more complicated, but also clearer, if one recognizes a rather startling fact: that the opinion attributed to Frederick, and then to the vulgar herd, that nobility comes from ancient wealth and good manners ultimately derives not from Frederick at all but rather directly from the *Politics* of Aristotle (IV. viii.1294ᵃ.20–21). In fact, in the *Monarchia*, written several years later, Dante actually quotes this passage directly and openly (II.iii.3–4).[38] The fact has not gone unnoticed by commentators, but it is always assumed (with a view to protecting Dante's reputation for candor, one supposes) that he remained ignorant of the Aristotelian source until well after writing *Convivio* IV. I, by contrast, am persuaded that Dante knew the passage already and was thus playing a subtle game indeed in Book IV.[39] By attributing the idea to Frederick, he compassed at least two important ends: first, he was able to structure a triad of complementary and rival authorities for reasons already partly discussed and soon to be taken up again; and second, he was thus allowed to have it both ways with Aristotelian authority. He could both draw upon it, appropriating it to himself as humble mediator, *and* attack it obliquely, opening the way for his own redefinition of an autonomous and personal *autorità.*[40]

Dante's stated agenda in the first chapters of Book IV is to defend the authority of his discourse on nobility against apparent attacks on it by political and philosophical authorities, without at the same time being irreverent towards either the Emperor or the Philosopher. As I have just shown, he plays this game agilely, while adding to it an implicit parallel between his attack on nobility as genealogically derived from antiquity, as mere name assigned by popular opinion, and his critique of the concept of *autorità* based on the same grounds. If time does not confer no bility (IV.xiv–xv), why should it bring authority? Carried to its logical and explicit conclusion, which of course does not appear in this text, this line of argument reveals that every *autore* is in the same position as the Dante of the first book—a historical and fallible ("stained") person who must prove and/or construct his authority from the ground up, or who must receive it directly from God.[41]

What, then, does Dante's positioning of his own (individual, contemporary) authority between, and implicitly above, those of Frederick and Aristotle, between power and knowledge, have to do with my original questions about his concept of poetic authority in the *Convivio*? And what does it have to do, finally, with the relation of poetic to theological authorship raised briefly at the beginning of Book II and echoed endlessly in criticism of the *Commedia* and its relationship to the *Convivio*? The structure of the *Convivio*, as we have seen, deliberately highlights a comparison and contrast of philosophical and poetic writing, much like Boethius's *Consolation*. In fact, Book II tells the tale of Dante's abandonment of the love lyrics of the *Vita Nuova* and their object, Beatrice, for the study of philosophy and a new kind of verse (II.xii). The structuring movement from *canzoni* to commentary itself has an odd double effect on our perception of the status of poetry in the new project. On the one hand, it clearly reflects an attempt to show that poetry is, or can be, philosophy, the conduit of intellectual truth. Hence Dante's famous discussion of the "allegory of poets," positing the concealment of allegorical truths under the "bella menzogna" of fiction (II.i.3). But this same discussion tends to trivialize poetry per se, just as the later etymology of *auieo* does. Without prosaic philosophical commentary, Dante argues, the poem's content is unintelligible—it can only be understood by the angelic intelligences of the Third Heaven (II.canzone 1–3, 53–55; iii–vi; xii.8). The human audience, as he says in the *congedo*, can only remain at the level of pure "aesthetic" delight in artistic beauty (II.canzone 61; xi). This trend reaches its climax in the canzone, "Le dolci rime d'amor," which opens Book IV. From its opening stanza, the poem is an explicit rejection of poetic delight in favor of a philosophical style, "aspra e sottile" [harsh and subtle (IV.canzone 14)]. As the first chapter of the commentary makes plain, Dante has tacitly abandoned the "allegory of poets" for a *literally* philosophical canzone, where the precepts are on the surface (IV.i.10–11). The desire to convert poetry directly into philosophy is then hammered home by the name he gives the canzone, *Contra-li-erranti mia*, which, as already noted, reflects a Dantean aspiration to follow in Aquinas's footsteps.

This is the context into which Dante inserts his brief discussion of the poet's seemingly limited role as "binder of words," whose domain, language, pales by comparison with the emperor's charge (human will and the active life, IV.ix.4–10) and the philosopher's arena (human reason and the contemplative life). Dante, in effect, recapitulates the long-standing tradition of marginalizing or even rejecting poetry precisely at the moment when the dream of uniting knowledge and power comes to the fore. In Plato's *Republic*, the utopian figure of a Philosopher-King is famously linked to the banishment or exile of the poets.[42] But Dante, the poet of exile par excellence, finally refuses the simplicity of Plato's solution. Instead, he insists on the necessary historical separation of philosopher and prince, even though the only remedy to the disastrous political scene in early Trecento Italy would be their collaboration and mutual reinforcement (IV.vi.18–20). Nor is Book IV so absolute in its trivialization of the poet as I have just argued. There is a subtle countertrend whose most crucial moment is the implicit qualification of Aristotelian authority. That qualification is itself anticipated by a curious and generally unremarked feature of Dante's account of the genesis of his polemic on nobility—that he describes it as the product of a period of difficulty, even of *failure*, in the harmonious relationship with Lady Philosophy described in Books II and III (IV.i.8). Moreover, as Ulrich Leo has shown, the end of Book IV seems to have been shaped by an extremely productive rereading of classic poetic *auctores*—Statius, Ovid, Lucan, and, above all, Virgil.[43] That same Virgil, as Leo stresses, will become Dante's "maestro e autore" (cf. *Inferno* I.85) for almost the first two-thirds of the *Commedia*, a role commentators have often thought would have been better suited to Aristotle, the "maestro e duca de la ragione umana" [master and leader of the human reason (*Convivio* IV.vi.8)].

There is, finally, the etymological definition of the poet as "binder of words," a definition whose abstract, "objective," and dismissive character undergoes a surprising change if we look back carefully at the end of Book I. There, even as Dante defines an Italian language striving for a unity, a *perfezione*, to rival Latin, he alludes to his own continuing part in that struggle, his incessant efforts to "bind together" his native tongue in a series of works—obviously including the *Convivio* itself (I.xiii.6–7). In brief, the "impersonal" discussion of Book IV, chapter vi, alludes specifically to Dante's personal and original project of writing poetry and/or philosophy in Italian, a project that clearly continues through Book IV.

To summarize and focus: Dante's *Convivio* is in the business of constructing a "new," an "original," "language of authority" and is also creating a newly authoritative language. The climactic point of this dual project is the philosophical and etymological definition of three types of *autorità* in the first chapters of Book IV. In this language, Italian, the Latin trio—*actor, auctor, autor*—is reduced to a single word, *autore*, thereby allowing Dante as author the ambiguous role of being either "mere" poet or philosophical authority; either the *actor* who writes but cannot guarantee the truth of his writing or the *autor* who is the transcendent guarantor of his own words, who summons up absolute *fede* and *obedienza* almost as if his language approximated the perfect intersection of truth and power that God's Word alone should and could effect (since the Christians have long since rejected the Platonic hope for a human and terrestrial union of the two). A little detour into the *Commedia* will suggest that the "mere" authority of the poet in *Convivio* IV.vi is actually expressed in terms surprisingly close to those of the theological authority of God. As others have already noticed, in the upper reaches of *Paradiso* Dante figures God as the "Alfa e O" (XXVI.16–18), the constitutive and totalizing alphabet that composes all Creation, and then, later, portrays him as the Author of authors whose creations are "legato con amore in un volume" (*Paradiso* XXXIII.86), *bound with love* in a single volume.[44] The same binding vowels of authority that define a seemingly impotent and ignorant poet in the *Convivio*, then, figure the theological unification of absolute Power and absolute Wisdom in the *Commedia*. I suspect, in fact, that Dante's focus on vowels is ultimately related to their deliberate omission from the Tetragrammaton, the Hebrew representation of the unutterable name of the unrepresentable God. For Aquinas, in his crucial and lengthy consideration of the names of God, the Tetragrammaton is the most proper of all human designations of Deity because it paradoxically expresses his incommunicability.[45] Thus, to make the poet "master of the vowels" is precisely to make him a theologian; to make him, indeed, more than Aquinas's theologian since he then seems uniquely capable of "filling in the blanks" in our knowledge and representation of God. And with this elision in mind, one may find it hard to sustain the Dantean distinction, so often reiterated, even reified, by his scholarly readers, between the *Convivio*'s "allegory of poets" (which has broken down by Book IV) and the "allegory of theologians" apparently adopted in the *Commedia*—that is, Dante's evident imitation in his greatest work of God's own mode of writing in the Bible, as read according to the fourfold interpretive scheme of the theologians.[46]

It is usual these days to posit a radical break between the *Convivio* and the *Commedia*, partly because of this apparent shift in modes and partly because of a related rejection of the former's reliance on philosophical wisdom as a means to human happiness in favor of the latter's turn toward faith and the theological order. This thesis, advanced tendentiously and tenaciously by Luigi Pietrobono in the first half of this century, has been given more substance by the elegant work of John Freccero on *Inferno* I and XXVI, as well as on *Purgatorio* II.[47] In *Purgatorio* II, the minstrel Casella sings one of the *canzoni* from the *Convivio* and becomes thereby an obstacle, rather than an aid, to the souls' ascent of the blessed mountain. This account of why the "humanistic" *Convivio* was abandoned and the "theocentric" *Commedia* begun is not at all mistaken, though it does tend to overlook clear tendencies within the *Convivio* to qualify and question its own philo-

sophical humanism; such tendencies are seen in a distinct preference for ethics over metaphysics, as well as in a strange oscil-
lation, especially throughout Book III, between proto-humanistic
exaltations of man's language and intellect and an equally clear
sense of the narrow epistemological and expressive limits of human minds and words.[48] On the other hand, it seems clear to me
that because the thesis of a radical break between the works is
developed from the retrospective, palinodic point of view of the
Commedia, it overlooks elements of continuity and logical progression that can be seen if one looks forward from the *Convivio,*
especially as I have just read it. In my reading, the *Convivio* is
certainly incomplete from the perspective of an Augustinian project of teaching "virtute e canoscenza" [worth and knowledge],
but as far as the "Boethian" goal of self-authorization is concerned, it is finished by the end of Book IV. And what has been
discovered or invented by that point is precisely a writer of suffi-
cient autonomy and authority to write the *Commedia* in the manner of the allegory of theologians; one who has, at least linguistically and poetically, removed himself from subjection to the
authorities of temporal power and rational truth and has thus
opened the way for the theological poetics of *Purgatorio* XXIV. 52–
54: "quando / Amor mi spira, noto, e a quel modo / ch'e' ditta
dentro vo' significando."[49] In other words, his poetry is unmediated by any authority but that of the Author of authors.
And that possibility is already potentially in place by *Convivio,*
Book IV.

The other side of this argument, and one that I can only adumbrate here, is that the *Commedia,* for its part, never quite gets
beyond the problematic figure of the poet sandwiched uncom-
fortably between imperial power and intellectual tradition; it is
never fully confident in its role as "allegory of theologians." Daniel
Ransom has shown that already in *Convivio* I Dante attempts to
shore up his natural poetic-philosophical authority with recourse
to Biblical language and Christological analogies, such as the
earlier noted image of the multiplication of the loaves. He aptly
notes, however, that such levies simply signal all the more clearly
the defects and weaknesses in the "allegory of the poets" that

they were designed to remedy. He then asserts that only the *Commedia*'s turn toward theological allegory and authority solves the problem.[50] For me, the problem remains even then. Singleton's famous phrase defining Dante's use of theological allegory, "the fiction . . . is that it is not a fiction," means for me (as I suppose it would have for Dante) "the 'allegory of poets' of the *Commedia* is that it is an 'allegory of theologians.'"[51] It is not that I disagree with Singleton's formulation; rather, I believe it creates more problems, poetic and theological, than it solves both for us and for Dante. It signals a protracted tension in the poem between the imagining of a possible "authorization" by divine inspiration and the lingering suspicion of origination in an "autonomous" human imagination.

In the *Convivio*, Dante defines the "allegory of poets" as "una verità ascosa sotto bella menzogna" [a truth hidden under beauteous (lying) (II.i.3)]. In *Inferno* XVI he describes his representation of Geryon, the very image of fraud and deceitful fiction, as "ver c'ha faccia di menzogna" [truth that has the face of a lie (124)] and swears to the truth of that representation by "le note / di questa comedìa" (127–128). Robert Hollander reads these lines as Dante's assertion that even when his discourse seems furthest from literal-historical verisimilitude, appearing to be as fraudulent as Geryon himself, it is nonetheless literally, theologically, *true*.[52] Given the clear intertextual echo of *Convivio*, however, this interpretation is clearly only one of two possible meanings; the other being that Dante knowingly constructs here an "allegory of poets" whose fictive, figurative "faccia" *lies* over its hidden truth.[53] As his self-reflexive, self-authorizing, oath upon the "notes" of his *sacro poema* suggests, he knows that our faith in and understanding of his authority rests as much upon our reading of his mediating vowels, and the words and verses he binds together out of them, as upon an unmediated act of belief in the powerful truth of a transcendent Author-God.

I would like to conclude my speculations by pointing to certain implications of Dante's treatment of authority in the *Convivio* (or, rather, to my understanding of that treatment) for assessments of the changing status of poetic authority between the Middle Ages and the Renaissance; assessments in which Dante's text often plays a pivotal role. The relationship between theology and literature, between God's writing and the poet's, has been *the* outstanding theme not only of Dante criticism but also of the most important literary histories of the twentieth century.[54] The theme has recently returned in an especially efficacious incarnation with David Quint's study of the relation between *origin* and *originality* as opposed and intertwined canons of poetic authority.[55] For Quint, the medieval theological model of *auctoritas*, which is derived from a divine origin or source, is translated into a poetics of "origin" founded on imitation of ancient authoritative models. In the Renaissance, then, this poetics gives way, slowly, to one of "originality" where the historicity and novelty of a modern poet's work takes precedence over its derivation from authentic sources. The most typical result is an attempt to have both originality and origin at the same time, as for example in Milton's novel retelling of the Biblical myth of origin and "original sin" in *Paradise Lost*.[56] I have shown the same double desire in Dante's (much earlier) need to appropriate and supersede Aristotle's authority in the *Convivio*. The same could be argued for his "imitation" and appropriation of Virgil in the *Commedia* and perhaps even for his imitation of God's way of writing in the "allegory of theologians."

Nonetheless, if this reading of the *Convivio* has shown anything, it has shown that the poetry-theology axis is only part of the question, that even in a poetics of divine "origin" and authority, problems of human mediation and of the relation between language, knowledge, and power continually intrude upon and precede the "divine analogy," whose presence at center stage is as much the work of Romanticism as of the Middle Ages. More than just a problem of tracing sources, in other words, the constitution and dissolution of poetic authority is a matter of positing language in relation to shifting human discourses of knowledge and power —their practical disjunction, their utopian intersection. By juxtaposing poetry's desire to mime or become the Bible with its more historically pressing needs to fend off and to appropriate surrounding intellectual-cultural disciplines and necessary-but-

oppressive political institutions, we move away from idealized accounts of pseudo-divine poetic authority and toward an understanding of how poets and poetry are forever painfully recon-
structing those sheltering and enabling ideals out of the lies and
the violence, the truths and the law, of the historical scene.

Donald Phillip Verene

Vico's New Critical Art and the Authority of the Noble Lie

Vico claims that his new science has seven principal aspects. The second of these he calls "a philosophy of authority" (*una filosofia dell'autorità*).[1] Vico's major work, the *Scienza nuova*, is first and foremost a science of the civil world, the world of civil things—*cose civili*. Vico's aim is to bring together in one-text all the principles that govern humanity's power to make a world for itself separate from nature and that govern the divine power of providence to make itself manifest in this human world. From Galileo forward, the new sciences of nature have shown that nature can be read as a divine book once its principles are known to the human intellect. What Vico attempts in the early eighteenth century is to read the world of nations as a total book, discovering the principles by which it has been made and showing how this world, like that of nature, has a divine providential structure. Vico, like Hobbes before him and Hume after him, wished to make a science of the civil or of custom, but he would distinguish himself from both Hobbes and Hume owing to his conception of providence, Hobbes's conception of the social covenant, and many significant matters of detail of both philosophies.[2]

The first principal aspect of his science Vico calls "a rational civil theology of divine providence" (*una teologia civile ragionata della provvedenza*) (385). Vico wishes to create, using reason, a civil theology that shows the ultimate structure of history to be the work of divine mind. This theology is a counterpart to the natural one derived from the new sciences of nature. As Vico states: "Our new Science must therefore be a demonstration, so to speak, of what providence has wrought in history" (342). Vi-

47

co's science in its first aspect, then, is a rational theology built from history rather than from nature.

The second principal aspect of this science is that it is "a philosophy of authority." The third is that it is "a history of human ideas" (*una storia d'umane idee*) (391). The fourth is that it is "a philosophical criticism" (*una critica filosofica*) that grows out of it being a history of ideas (392). The fifth, that it is "an ideal eternal history" (*una storia ideal eterna*) (393). The sixth, that it is "a system of natural law of the gentes" (*un sistema del diritto natural delle genti*) (394), which relates to Vico's criticism of the natural-law theories of Grotius, Selden, and Pufendorf. The seventh, that it presents the "principles of universal history" (*principi della storia universale*) (399). Of these seven principal aspects of Vico's science, that of authority is the most curious. The first, the idea of a rational civil theology, makes general sense once it is seen in contrast to the more common project of a natural theology derived from the science of nature. The third through the seventh make general sense just on the common knowledge that Vico is the founder of the philosophy of history and thus has a total conception of human history. These aspects clearly describe elements of that conception. But to the reader of the *New Science*, his claim that this science is "a philosophy of authority" is an odd element that immediately raises the question, What does Vico mean by this claim? Most commentators have said very little about its meaning. They repeat it and recall Vico's explanation, but they do not offer much interpretation of it. This was, in fact, my own approach in my book, *Vico's Science of Imagination*;[3] but I wish here to rectify my own quite slight mention of it there.

I wish to raise two questions concerning the idea of authority and Vico's new science: (1) In what sense is Vico's science a philosophy *of* authority? and (2) In what sense is Vico's science itself an authoritative philosophy? On what authority does the truth of Vico's science rest? The first of these questions leads in part to the second, and both together define the role of the idea of authority in Vico's philosophy. I wish to confine my analysis to the text of what Vico himself called *La Scienza nuova seconda*, with his revisions that were to make up a third edition (1730/

1744).[4] As is well known, Vico saw this text as the definitive version of his thought.

The major places of discussion in Vico's text of "una filosofia dell'autorità" are: in his introduction to the idea of the work (7); in the section on "Method" (350); as the corollaries to "Poetic Metaphysics" (385–99); and in the short section entitled "Three Kinds of Authority" that is one of the lists of threefold characteristics of the first course of nations at the beginning of Book 4.

In his mention of authority in his introduction and in sections on method, Vico connects this idea to his claim that his science is based on the discovery of a new critical art (*nuova arte critica*). Thus the idea of authority is connected to the very conception of knowledge and method upon which the work rests. In the other two places he explains, but only in the briefest terms, what authority is. I wish to begin with this explanation and then return to the new critical art.

In explaining "a philosophy of authority" as the second principal aspect of his science in his list of seven (385–99), Vico says he takes "authority" (*autorità*) in its original sense as "property" (*proprietà*) and from those *autori* from whom, in Roman civil law, we derive the title to property. Authority has three forms that follow the three ages of Vico's ideal eternal history—divine, heroic, and human. The first form of authority is divine and was manifested when the divine as Jove instilled fear in the giants and caused them to take up the three fundamental practices of humanity—religion, marriage, and burial. These first humans are the property of the divine as Jove. Jove has authority over them through his power to instill fear (*spavento*) in them. They begin to take auspices, retreat into their caves and marry, and bury their dead.

This divine authority (*l'autorità divina*) is followed by human authority (*l'autorità umana*). This human authority is the free use of will (*il libero uso della volontà*). At this point, humans begin to exercise freedom of choice. They act as free agents and establish the things of human society. Choice is a power within the human being. It is as Vico says "the property of human nature which not even God can take from man without destroying him" (388).

The authority of human nature (*autorità di natura umana*) is followed by the authority of natural law (*l'autorità di diritto naturale*). In this stage, what was accomplished in practice by the power of will to exercise choice and to found human institutions is given intellectual and philosophical formulation. Correct actions performed out of the authority of human nature are now given intellectual authority in the conception of natural law. The authority of right action is supplemented by the authority of right principles. Right action is given rational justification.

The pattern present here in broad terms is this: The power to give title is originally external to humans. Jove's power lies in his ability to instill fear in the giants and cause them to settle in particular places in which to take the auspices of this power above them. Once they grasp this divine power, the power within them as humans—the power to control their bodies and senses, to certain ends, the power of choice—becomes available to them. As a reflection of their own human nature, they form the world of human customs over which they hold dominion or title. This power or authority is achieved only because these humans could respond to the divine authority originally manifest in the thundering sky of Jove. Their power to establish their human nature in social terms through the actual creation of customs and institutions by their actions is finally given form by reason, through which the meaning of their actions or choices becomes statable as intellectual principles or natural law. Authority is now philosophical in form and rests on the power of the intellect and on the eloquence of speech to justify action. Knowledge, one might say here with Plato, is power, and power is a kind of knowledge. Authority takes the form of knowledge.

In describing what Vico says in his corollaries of "Poetic Metaphysics," I have taken liberties of interpretation, principally in my use of the term "power," which is not Vico's term but which seems necessary to describe what authority is. It is dominion, or power, having the title to something as property.

Vico's enumeration of "three kinds of authority" (942–46) in Book 4 is part of his mechanical description of a number of characteristics of a nation and of how each of them has a divine, heroic, and human version. Thus Vico delineates three kinds (*tre spezie*) of natures (*nature*), customs (*costumi*), natural law (*diritti naturali*), governments (*governi*), languages (*lingue*), characters (types of writing) (*caratteri*), jurisprudence (*giurisprudenze*), authority (*autorità*), reason (*ragioni*), judgments (*giudizi*), and sects of times (*sètte di tempi*). In the five paragraphs describing the three kinds of authority, there is no mention of a philosophy of authority nor of the new critical art to which it is connected. Vico states: "These three kinds of authority employed by jurisprudence in the course the nations run correspond to three sorts of authority appertaining to senates which succeed one another in the same course" (943). This succession is, Vico claims, from divine governments formed by the founder of the original families from which cities arose, to heroic senates of popular liberty, and finally to the rule of monarchs and their counselors and lawmaking bodies.

What Vico says in Book 4 is not remarkable given his grid of the ideal eternal history of three ages, and if this were all he said about the idea of authority in the *Scienza nuova*, it would scarcely command our attention. Let me return to his claim in his introduction and discussion of method that his philosophy of authority is connected to the idea upon which his science is founded—a new art of criticism.

Vico calls this *nuova arte critica* "metaphysical"—"questa Scienza usa un'arte critica, pur metafisica" (348) and "questa critica metafisica" (350). What is the nature of this new art, this art of metaphysics? Let me attempt to state Vico's case as directly as possible, for it may serve to bring together what has been exposited so far.

A science of the civil world has previously been impossible because two forms of study of this world have not been brought together—philosophy and philology. Philosophy aims at a knowledge of the true (*il vero*) and can understand human beings as they ought to be, but philosophy also has the power to unify and state universals. Philology, which Vico defines as "the doctrine of all things that depend on human choice, as are all histories of the languages, customs and deeds of peoples in war and peace,"

(7) offers a kind of knowledge of the certain (*il certo*). The certain are those things (*le cose*) of the human world that are not done by providence but are established by human choice within the universal structure of the ideal eternal history of nations. Vico's new art of metaphysical criticism is founded by bringing philosophy together with philology so that, as he says, "philosophy undertakes to examine philology" (*qui la filosofia si pone ad esaminare la filologia*) (7). Philology can never unify or show the general truths of the civil world, but it offers to philosophy an account, not of how human beings ought to be, but of how they are in fact. Philosophy, while overcoming its tendency to abstraction by contact with philology, can relate the separately understood things of the human world to a pattern of universal history and a knowledge of the role of providence in this history.

But this new critical art is not simply bringing the study of the universal closer to the study of the particular; something more is required. A master key is required that will let us determine the universal through the particular and vice versa in the civil world, that will lock the universal and particular together in this world the way Galileo was able to lock the universal and the particular together in the world of nature. Galileo founded the modern science of nature by realizing that the structure of natural phenomena could be read by the mind not in terms of the subject-predicate structure of propositions in natural language, but in terms of the "language" of mathematical systems. Numbers offer the mind true analogs to certain natural motions, whereas words and the structure of natural grammars cannot. Thus, as Galileo says in *Il saggiatore*, the book of nature can be read mathematically. In modern physics, the concept or universal can present an actual determination of the particular, whereas Aristotelian physics, with its reliance on the structure of the linguistic proposition, could never formulate a universal that did not abstract from the group rather than express the determinate nature of its members.[5]

The principle that Vico requires for bringing the universally true together with the certain, the specifics of the human world achieved by acts of choice, is the conception of origin. Crucial to his new art is his axiom "Doctrines must take their beginning

from that of the matters which they treat" (314). The error of
the seventeenth-century natural-law theorists was their failure to
ask about the origin of the authority of reason on which they
based their understanding of society. Thus they could give no
account of the philosophical history of the human world to ground
their appeal to the authority of reason.

Philosophy must undertake to examine philology, but it must
do this through an understanding of the origin of the civil world
within which reason, at present, for modern society is a power.
The master key (la chiave maestra), as Vico called it, to the origin
of the human world is that the first gentile peoples "were poets
who spoke in poetic characters" (34). The origin of all things in
the human world is traceable to the human power of fantasia, or
to a power to form truths and things (cose) through imagination,
not reason. This is Vico's doctrine of "imaginative universals"
(universali fantastici).[6]

Vico's new art of criticism traces the origin of the civil world
to fantasia or to what might be termed the "making imagination"
or "imagination that makes." Vico understands fantasia not as a
faculty that creates illusions but as one that makes truths both in
the sense of thoughts and in the sense of making civil things or
institutions. Fantasia does what we usually think of reason as
doing, but it makes its orders not through a power to form abstractions from particulars but through a power to universalize
through the formation of images—imaginative universals.

The formation of the world in images is for Vico a genuine and
first form of human thought. It is through this power of fantasia
that the common sense of humankind is originally formed. Vico,
like Shaftesbury, intends the term common sense—sensus com-
munis, il senso comune—as communal sense, a power distinctive
to the human as a social animal, not as a kind of loose form of
ratiocination used in place of more exact ways of intellectual
ordering. Vico defines common sense in his twelfth axiom: "Common sense [il senso comune] is judgment without reflection, shared
by an entire class, an entire people, an entire nation, or the entire
human race" (142). Common sense is the context through which
human choice is made certain, in which an act of human choice

makes something definite and determines its meaning (141). This conception of common sense as "judgment without reflection" (*giudizio senz'alcuna riflessione*) coupled with the idea that all peoples, all nations, undergo a common pattern of development independently of any contact with each other, Vico claims, provides the basis of his new art of criticism (143–45).

The "old" art of criticism (a term Vico does not use) that occupied philosophers of the civil world or the states before Vico, philosophers such as Grotius, Selden, and Pufendorf, was based on a metaphysics of rational principles. This "old" art is a criticism of the civil world as if it were based on the deliberate pursuit of the rational principles stated by later philosophers. Vico's new art of criticism is built on the realization that the early poets of a nation are not philosophers and that their fables or myths are not noble lies or fantastic ways of stating rational ideas. The fables upon which a nation is based in its origin are "true stories" (403). The new critical art or metaphysics requires a theory of "poetic wisdom" (*sapienza poetica*) that shows the poetic or mythic origins of all human institutions and forms of thought. Social order is not based upon rational contracts or agreements but upon the cohesive powers of fables. The mythic or *fantasia,* which is not itself reason, is the power of "judgment without reflection" that gives form to common sense (*il senso comune*), the original and true basis of social order and the authority through which all social choice is made possible.

I believe that at this point my first question—on the meaning of Vico's idea of a "philosophy of authority"—is answered. At least the outlines of the answer are given, because from this idea one can interpret all of the *Scienza nuova.* My second question involves the authority Vico offers for his science itself. In discussing his "new art of criticism," I have come very close to the answer to this question, and I wish to state the answer here only in brief form.[7]

Vico offers a series of proofs both philosophical and philological for his science (concentrated in the section on "Method," 338–60). But the master proof that he ties to his ideas of the "art of criticism" and the "common sense of the human race" is as follows:

> The decisive sort of proof in our Science is therefore this: that, since these institutions [*cose*] have been established by divine providence, the course of the institutions [*cose*] of the nations had to be, must now be, and will have to be such as our Science demonstrates, even if infinite worlds were born from time to time through eternity, which is certainly not the case.
>
> . . . Indeed, we make bold to affirm that he who meditates this Science narrates to himself this ideal eternal history so far as he himself makes it for himself by that proof "it had, has, and will have to be." . . . O reader, . . . these proofs are of a kind divine and should give thee a divine pleasure, since in God knowledge and creation are one and the same thing. (348–49)

Vico's "decisive" proof, that which *regna in questa Scienza*, is based on a citation of the power attributed in the ancient world (from Hesiod forward) to the Muses—that they have the power to sing of what was, what is, and what is to come. Vico quotes this proof twice in the above passage, saying in the second instance that the proof is for the reader to narrate or make the ideal eternal history for himself by proving "it had, has, and will have to be" (*in quella pruova* "*dovette, deve, dovrà*").

The authority for Vico's science is poetry—that upon which poetry is based, the power of the Muses. The mother of the Muses is Memory, a point Vico emphasizes (699, 819). The Muses are born as a result of Jove lying with Memory on nine nights. They govern the arts of humanity. Jove in Vico's view (a common view in Vico's time) is connected in Latin etymology with *ius* (*Ious, ius*). Jove as embodiment of the divine is the first form of authority and is the first law. The imaginative universal, Jove the thunderer, is the poetic form of law as natural law—the natural law of nations, the *ius gentium, il diritto delle genti*. It is through the response of the first humans to this appearance of Jove as law in nature and their subsequent shaping of their own human nature in terms of it that the common sense, the basis of human society, is formed. Jove, *ius*, is formed by *fantasia* as the true story or fable that begins human society. The master.key to the new critical art is memory, which Vico says is the same as *fantasia* (*la memoria è la stessa che la fantasia*) (819). Vico's decisive proof of his new science of nations is his ability to have access to Jove the thunderer through Memory by practicing the common art of her daughters, the power to have an absolute form of memory that includes the present and future as well as the past. Vico's new art becomes a kind of divination achieved through the power to narrate the providential structure of the civil world by bringing back to life its origin in Jove. This is a new kind of metaphysics that can produce in the reader a divine pleasure that is otherwise experienced only by God, whose power to make and to know are the same.

If I may be allowed a short digression before concluding, I wish to suggest that Vico's new critical art, which is a recasting of the ancient art of the Muses into modern philosophical form, also involves a revival of the art of what in Platonic thought has been called the "noble lie." Vico does not use this term himself, and there is certainly a sense in which Plato does not use this term, although it has become associated with English translations of the third book of the *Republic* (414b) where Plato introduces the allegory of the metals—the tale that those who are fit to rule had gold mixed in their natures by the god who created them, those who are to assist in ruling have silver natures, and those with iron and brass are farmers and craftsmen. Plato introduces this notion with the question of how "might we contrive one of those opportune falsehoods of which we were just now speaking, so as by one noble lie to persuade if possible the rulers themselves, but failing that the rest of the city?" (414b–c, trans. Shorey). As the Plato scholar, F. M. Cornford, points out, the Greek *pseudos* is not properly understood as "lie" or "falsehood" in the modern sense of propaganda but is better represented by the words "fiction" or "fictitious." *Pseudos* covers any statement describing events that never occurred and can be applied to all works of imagination such as myths, fables, and fictitious narratives. I agree with Cornford that the term "noble lie" is a contradiction in terms, if taken from a commonsense perspective or from an ordinary political perspective.[8]

The Muses who inspire poets can sing both true and false songs

and can sing true ones when they wish, as it is reported in Hesiod's *Theogony*. The poets are the makers and the remakers in
language of fictions, Hesiod included. They are the original tellers
of the noble lie. Not being Muses themselves, but only being
inspired by Muses, the poets sing songs that fall between the
purely true and the purely false. Plato, the quarreler with poets,
especially Homer and Hesiod, gives his arguments authority by
telling and retelling the "likely story," the "noble lie," the "fiction"
that persuades his listener or reader of what his dialectical reasonings do not accomplish on their own. The myth or fable in
the hands of the first men who make the original institutions of
nations is a true story. It is a direct formation of perceptions;
myths are made up of judgments without reflection. The myths
of the first men are not, and in principle cannot be, noble lies.
This is because no philosophical meanings are possible in their
first songs.

Vico is a Platonist or neo-Platonist. Plato is one, in fact the
first, of Vico's famous "four authors" whom he describes in the
Autobiography. The center of Vico's *New Science* is the solution to
the ancient quarrel between philosophy and poetry. Vico's science
is based on an identification of poetry and wisdom, of "poetic
wisdom" (*sapienza poetica*), and on his new theory of Homer as
the mind of the Greek people. Vico is firm on the idea that the
ancient poets are not philosophers. The first men are poets who
think in poetic characters and who make the original true stories
or myths. Homer and Hesiod are poets, but they are transitional.
Homer is the end of the heroic age and the beginning of the age
of men in which philosophy will be formed. Homer's fictions,
while true for the heroic mentality and society he describes, are
problematic for the philosophers. The philosophers create the opposition between art and truth, and the poets become the makers
of a mixture of falsehoods and truths about the gods and heroes.
Platonic dialectic persuades not simply by making distinctions but
ultimately through the noble lie and the likely story that, like the
allegory of metals for the founding of commonwealths, hopes to
persuade us of ontological truths in a single act. The Platonic
philosophy takes its authority from a kind of speech that always

falls between the two alternatives of the Muses, between either true or false songs—the noble lie, the fiction, the nonliteral truth.

Considered against this sense of the Platonic philosophy, Vico's philosophy gains its authority by attempting to tell the most likely of likely stories, the truest of fictions, the noblest of lies. Vico's own poetic wisdom, the poetic wisdom of the text of the *New Science*, itself is a series of nonliteral truths that Vico continually insists should be taken literally. The idea of ideal eternal history cannot be verified by any empirical-historical analysis of nations or civilizations, yet Vico insists his three ages constitute the actual course nations run. As is frequently mentioned by his commentators, Vico creates etymologies of words to fit his theories of the development of mentalities and institutions. Vico describes cultures and languages he knows nothing about. But most of all, Vico plays on the very term science itself (*scienza, scienza nuova*), playing on the rising seventeenth-century sciences of nature and their power to explain nature, and on his identification of his science and method with the power of the Muses to foretell the future from the past, thus showing that his science is a type of divine meditation. These oppositions of the rational and the poetic within the form of Vico's science increase his power to persuade us that he has encompassed the oppositions within the civil world and between it and the divine and natural worlds in the same way that the poetic power of myths derives from their encompassing of similar kinds of opposition. Vico, the modern thinker, gives us a new version of how philosophy is poetry and poetry philosophy. His authority for all this is the power of the fabulous, the fiction, the likely story, the single noble lie to persuade. This is of course dangerous business, because nonliteral truth is so close to falsehood and illusion. But, then, it is the only way that the ultimate nature of things can ever be brought into view.

In conclusion, I have attempted to explain the meaning of Vico's claim of having "a philosophy of authority" and to show how this claim is connected to his central claim—to the discovery of a new art of criticism, a new metaphysics. Second, I have attempted to make the idea of authority itself reflexive on Vico's own philosophy and to ask by what authority he holds his science to be true. Vico's "proof" through the Muses takes us where no argument can go, to the truth of the fable that is the basis of our own common sense: Jove the thunderer—and, as Vico states, every nation has its Jove.

Throughout his work, Vico is careful to claim that all of this fits with Christian doctrine. Does it? I think that, assuming there are exceptions so that someone born after the advent of Christianity could be assigned to the place of the virtuous pagans described in Dante's *Divina Commedia*, if we looked, we would find Vico there.

11. Selves Reading, Writing Selves

François Rigolot

Homer's Virgilian Authority
Ronsard's Counterfeit Epic Theory

Between Homer and Virgil, like a demigod, surrounded by spirits, I have my place in their midst.

RONSARD (1560)[1]

It seems unquestionable that Pierre de Ronsard's greatest ambition from youth was to exalt the French language and make it "illustrious." Along with other Pléiade poets like Joachim Du Bellay and Jacques Peletier du Mans, he believed that the best way to accomplish such a task was to write an epic poem in French in the manner of Homer and Virgil.[2] Critics have long debated Ronsard's motivations in writing *La Franciade* (the first four books were published in 1572), his self-proclaimed as well as his unwritten poetics, and his desire to choose Virgil over Homer as a model in spite of his statement to the contrary.[3] From Paul Laumonier to Daniel Ménager and from Paul Lange to Bruce R. Leslie, every Ronsard scholar seems to agree that the principal model for *La Franciade* must have been the *Aeneid*.[4] "The *Franciade* owes more to Virgil than to any other poet," wrote Walter H. Storer in 1923, basing his judgment on a comparative count of figures in the two poems.[5] And Isidore Silver has attributed the French poet's epic failure mainly to his Virgilian prejudice: "It was under the influence of Virgil that Ronsard adopted the great vitiating premise of the *Franciade*: its motivation in dynastic pride."[6]

Ronsard's unqualified admiration for the *Aeneid* is evidenced by many of his own pronouncements. As early as 1572, in the first preface to his heroic poem, he makes passing remarks to the *Iliad* but dwells with much fervor on the Latin epic: "Virgil . . . conceived of this divine *Aeneid* which, we continue to this day to hold with all reverence in our hands."[7] With even greater emphasis, in the posthumous preface of 1587, he lists some twenty-two quotations from the *Aeneid* with laudatory comments and strongly advises his "apprentice reader" to imitate Virgil in the "composition and structure" of future epic poems: "Follow Virgil who is past master of the composition and structure of poems. Consider a moment the sound made by these two lines at the end of the eighth book of the *Aeneid* (ll.689–90). Why don't you try to compose in your own language as many of these as you can."[8]

Various explanations have been proposed for Ronsard's avowed predilection for the Latin model. One of the most convincing ones is that he may have followed Jacques Peletier du Mans's unambiguous recommendation. In his *Art poëtique* of 1555, Peletier had made a comparative study of the *Iliad* and the *Aeneid* and had concluded that Virgil's epic was a far superior poem.[9] Whether Peletier's "idolatry for Virgil" was an "idée fixe" or not[10] (he was himself a translator of the *Odyssey*), Ronsard may have been seduced by his friend's ingenious arguments. The main reason for Virgil's superiority, according to Peletier, was that Virgil imitated all the real beauties he found in Homer while also carefully avoiding Homer's weaknesses: "Virgil imitated whatever he considered admirable in Homer. But he corrected him in several places. And I will list here a number of things which he left aside."[11] For instance, Virgil eliminated Homer's superfluous epithets (Il "a bien sù euiter la superfluité d'Epithetes qui et an Homere") and numerous unwarranted repetitions ("Il s'et gardè des redites qui sont an Homere").[12]

To be sure, according to Peletier, Virgil had an excellent critical mind. He agreed with Horace that occasionally good old Homer fell asleep ("Horace n'a pas dit hors de propos qu' aucunes fois dort le bonhomme Homere")—a reference to the famous line of the *Ars poetica*.[13] Therefore, it was quite natural to expect greater perfection in the *Aeneid* than in the *Iliad*. Peletier was quite clear on this issue. According to him, poeticians had strangely confused Homer's so-called superiority with his temporal seniority. "Homere n'et an rien plus eureus [in no way more felicitous] sinon que pour auuoer précédé an temps."[14] Let us forget for a moment that the *Iliad* came first and let us imagine that the *Aeneid* was the original poem; there is little doubt that we would prefer Virgil's masterpiece over Homer's: "If the *Aeneid* had been composed before the *Iliad*, just think what people would have to say about it."[15]

Another way to produce an aesthetically valid judgment, says Peletier, is to forget about the question of antecedents and base our appreciation solely on a synchronic comparison. After all, does it really matter who wrote first? Homer himself may not have been the "first epic poet" that the poeticians so self-confidently claim him to be. Imitation must be removed from its second-class category; it is not necessarily inferior to invention. We know for sure that Virgil was an imitator; but we can only guess that Homer was an inventor: "Let us say from evidence that Virgil was an imitator and from judgment and opinion that Homer was an inventor."[16]

One of the obvious consequences of Peletier's meliorative theory is that, under appropriate circumstances, Virgil himself can be improved upon, and that it should be the duty of modern poets to take up that extraordinary challenge. Contrary to common prejudice among men of letters, Virgil is not an untouchable model, removed from history to be revered endlessly, like Homer, by future generations. In spite of all his consecrated merits, he did make mistakes (*"fautes poëtiques"*), which his best imitators will be able to correct. Contradiction and lack of credibility, which marred some passages of the *Iliad*, were repeated, sometimes verbatim, in the *Aeneid*: "And yet I find that Virgil fell into a similar error."[17] No work of art, no matter how great, can claim to be flawless.[18] Therefore the golden rule for a future epic poet is to know what should be imitated and what should be left out of the imitation: "Let him know what he should imitate and what he should not."[19] There is an optimistic corollary to this: poets to come will confidently follow Virgil's example; they will imitate him imitating Homer and will write epics that may surpass their classical model in excellence.[20]

Peletier's theory, which is not unique for his time, may very well have appealed to Ronsard by seeming to encourage his limitless ambitions. Nothing could more please the leader of the Pléiade than the idea of an "improved succession" of great classical writers. If the *Aeneid* was indeed better than the *Iliad*, then the *Franciade* had a fair chance to outdo the *Aeneid*. Although Ronsard never refers to it in his various prefaces, Peletier's theory of imitation confirmed, on the poetic plane, Ronsard's dominant political premise: namely, that the French rulers were meant by destiny to be greater than their Roman predecessors. As Jupiter solemnly predicts at the beginning of *La Franciade*:

> From Merove, from conquering peoples,
> Many princes and many great emperors will come;
> They will be elevated in supreme dignity.
> Among them a king, Charles the Ninth,
> (Ninth in name but first in virtue)
> Will be born to see the world conquered
> Under his feet—that world where the sun sets
> And where its rays shine on earth,
> Rising from the seas
> And bringing light to men and gods.[21]

In other words, the French king will achieve what the Roman emperor never managed to complete, except in dreams: he will eventually dominate both the Orient and the Occident, and of his kingdom there will be no end ("Cujus regni non erit finis").[22] Similarly, in the poem that celebrates the king's deeds, Ronsard will surpass his Latin model. With the complicity of the Olympian god of gods, he will be to Virgil what Charles will be to Augustus: an improved version of the greatest preceding exemplar.

Strange as it may seem, Ronsard himself gives us quite another explanation for his almost exclusive interest in the *Aeneid*. In the *Préface sur la Franciade* of 1587, in which he quotes some fifty-two lines from Virgil's epic and paraphrases many others, Ronsard seems to be unduly self-conscious about the weight he gives to the *Aeneid* in his own imitation theory. To deflect possible criticism, he writes: "I am sure that the envious will babble because I quoted Virgil more often than Homer who was his master and his model. But *I did it on purpose*, knowing well that the French have more familiarity with Virgil than with Homer and other Greek authors [italics mine]."[23] Let us not wonder why Ronsard quoted Virgil more often than (or, rather, instead of) Homer. He did it *on purpose* and for purely practical reasons. By concentrating on Virgil's style, he had a better chance to reach his pedagogical goal: namely, to teach his "apprentice reader" ("*Lecteur apprentif*," 331) how to write the best possible imitation of a classical epic.

Let us therefore not be confused about Ronsard's motivations. His admiration for Virgil does not preclude an equal fervor for Homer; it simply means that he was considerate enough of his readers to use examples that could be easily understood. Communication is more important to him than self-indulgent pedantry; or, at least, that is what he would like us to believe. Rhetorically speaking, this argument sells well. Ronsard is eager to proclaim his desire to reach out and identify with the largest number of readers in a common search for national origins. We find here, in his imitation theory, echoes of what Daniel Ménager called his "unanimisme."[24] Yet we know that this desire to reach his audience is mere wishful thinking: *La Franciade* stems from a purely aristocratic vision of art that has nothing to do, despite Ronsard's efforts, with the real aspirations of an actual community of readers and, therefore, is doomed to failure.[25]

The question we now have before us is not which models Ronsard actually did follow in his *Franciade* (he copiously borrowed from Homer, Virgil, Apollonius, and many others); nor is it to what extent "the *Aeneid* furnished him the context and general lines of the story"[26] or even what Ronsard specifically said about each of his possible models. The question is rather *how* he argued his case. In other words, it is a question of intentionality; and this question can only find an answer, it seems, through a close reading of the poet's prefaces and by reference to contemporary theories of imitation.

Ronsard wrote three prefaces for his *Franciade*; they can be found in the 1572, 1573, and the posthumous 1587 editions. In the first preface (1572), he defines his epic poems as "un Roman comme l'*Iliade* et l'*Aeneide*" (5). From the outset, Homer and Virgil are designated as the two chief models he had in mind. Ronsard makes it clear that he wants to emulate their poetics, which is founded—to use Aristotelian language—on verisimilitude ("*vraisemblance*," 5) rather than on truth ("*vérité*," 5): "Yet, whenever possible, I imitated both authors' artificial plots which are based more on verisimilitude than on truth. Following these two great personages, I did as they did."[27]

The same language is used again in the preface of 1587, with perhaps some confusion between the verisimilar and the possible: "Imitating these two luminaries of Poetry, and basing myself and relying on our old Annals, I built my *Franciade* without worrying about whether or not it was true, . . . making use of the possible and not of the true."[28]

Yet this self-conscious effort to present his two classical exemplars on an equal footing becomes somewhat suspicious when confronted with Ronsard's actual practice. In the 1572 preface, for instance, he begins by pointing out Virgil's advantage over himself in dealing with dynastic matters: "If I talk about our kings more at length than Virgil's art allows, you must know, Reader, that Virgil in this respect (as in all others) was luckier than I am: since he lived under Augustus, the second emperor, he had few Kings and Caesars to account for and needed not lengthen much his paper, whereas I carry the burden of sixty-three kings."[29] Hyante's vision of the kings of France in the Underworld (*Franciade*, Book IV) is obviously patterned after Anchises's long lecture on Roman history (*Aeneid*, Book VI). Yet Ronsard's intention is to dramatize the difference between "l'art Virgilien" and "l'art Ronsardien."

The reason for this distinction is given in the next paragraph in which Ronsard shifts emphasis and declares that he has indeed patterned his work on Homer rather than on Virgil: "Besides, I have patterned my work (of which these first four books are samples) rather after Homer's *natural facility* than after Virgil's *careful diligence.*"[30]

In this very important statement, the contrast between Homer's "natural facility" and Virgil's "careful diligence" can be traced back to Quintilian. In Book X of the *Institutio Oratoria,* one reads: "In truth, although we must needs bow before the immortal and superhuman genius of Homer, there is greater diligence and ex-actness in the work of Virgil, just because his task was harder. And perhaps the superior uniformity of Virgil's excellence bal-ances Homer's pre-eminence in his outstanding passages."[31] If this passages is indeed the source of Ronsard's parallel, then there is a considerable difference between the value judgments made by the Latin and the French writers. Quintilian recognized Homer's "immortal and superhuman genius," but, as a dutiful rhetorician, he preferred Virgil's greater "diligence and exactness." "The su-perior uniformity of Virgil's excellence" could "balance Homer's pre-eminence in his outstanding passages."

To be sure, Ronsard parts with Quintilian by deliberately choos-ing genius over work, *natura* over *cura et diligentia.* Obviously this self-proclaimed preference for a naturally inspired poetry (*naïve facilité*) clashes with the textual evidence indicating that he gave much thought to Virgil's ornate style. As we have already seen, the 1587 preface consists mostly of a series of *explications de texte* of the *Aeneid.* Ronsard was never alien to an aesthetics of solid learning and skill. *Ars, studium, doctrina, exercitatio* were key no-tions in the theoretical background of the Pléiade poets. Of course, "le naturel" (natural endowment) was an absolute pre-requisite: poets had to be born poets.[32] Yet, as Grahame Castor has remarked in his study of *Pléiade Poetics,* the neo-Platonic theories of inspiration were so prevalent in the 1550s that Du Bellay felt he should tip the balance again in favor of art and work. In his *Deffence et Illustration de la Langue Françoise,* Ron-sard's friend wrote a whole chapter arguing that "le naturel n'est suffisant à celuy qui en Poesie veult faire oeuvre digne de l'im-mortalité" ("natural endowment is not enough for one who wishes to write poetic works worthy of immortality").[33]

Before suggesting an explanation for Ronsard's preference for Homer's "*naïve facilité,*" let us turn to the second preface of the *Franciade,* that is, to the 1573 "Avertissement au lecteur." In this very short piece of prose, Ronsard talks exclusively about the corrections he decided to make to give a "more perfect" style to his poem: "Following the advice of my most learned friends, I have changed, moved, shortened, lengthened many passages of my *Franciade* to make it more perfect and put it in its final form. And I wish, indeed very dearly, that all our French writers deigned do the same. If they did, we would not see as many aborted works which, for lack of filing and polishing over time, bring only shame to their authors and bad reputation to France."[34]

In this rewritten preface, there is no mention of Homer's divinely inspired poetry. The emphasis is exclusively placed on patient, long-enduring workmanship (*"changer, muer, abreger, alonger"*). *"Cura et diligentia"* have replaced the inborn "immortal and superhuman genius"; the poet is now cast in the role of an *"ouvrier,"* painfully correcting Nature's errors through systematic, practical *exercitatio* ("la lime & parfaicte polissure requise par temps"). Boileau's famous *dictum* will not be very different:

> Twenty times return your work to the loom;
> Polish it all the time, and polish it again;
> Add sometimes, but erase frequently.[35]

There seems to be an insoluble contradiction in imitation theory between the 1572 and 1573–1587 statements. Ronsard would like to have it both ways. On the one hand, true to contemporary attitudes and especially to Peletier's, he welcomes the idea of "improved imitation" and lectures at length on the unequaled value of craftsmanship. The *Aeneid*, then, will be his chief model. On the other hand, he emphatically declares that he has patterned his *Franciade* on the naturalness and spontaneity associated with the *Iliad* rather than the artificiality typified by the *Aeneid*. Even in the last preface, in which Virgil is quoted so copiously, Ronsard fervently clings to his ideal of a "naifve & naturelle poesie": "You will enrich your Poem by using a varied style taken from Nature, without the frenzy of a madman. For, if you are too keen on avoiding or banishing the vernacular and never gaining fame by making grotesque and fanciful monsters, you will imitate Ixion who begot phantoms instead of legitimate and natural children."[36]

It is true that, in his chapter devoted to the epic poem, Du

Bellay had recommended keeping a fair balance between *ars* and *natura*, work and inspiration. The successful poet had to be "gifted with an excellent felicity of nature" as well as "instructed in all good Arts and Sciences."[37] Yet Ronsard's self-proclaimed set of double standards cannot be explained solely in terms of Du Bellay's theoretical compromise. I suggest that the apparent contradiction in the various prefaces to the *Franciade* can be at least partly solved if we can first clear up a problem of semantics. After all, what did Ronsard exactly mean by "imitation"? Do the French verbs *"patroner"* (5), *"suyvre"* (347), *"imiter"* (passim) always mean the same thing when they apply to Homer and Virgil? As we shall see, Ronsard's statements may not be as contradictory as one thinks; they may refer to two different kinds of realities, vaguely subsumed by the term "imitation" but actually corresponding to the distinct classical notions of *mimesis* and *imitatio*. [38]

There is little doubt that for Ronsard, as for Peletier and Du Bellay, Homer stands as the one recognized source of epic inspiration. Disregarding technical superiority, the *Iliad* is anterior to all other imitations, including the *Aeneid*, which it generates. Ronsard says so specifically in the first preface to his poem: "The Trojan War was created by Homer, as several serious authors have firmly established. The stories which came out of it since are all drawn from *the source which is Homer.* . . . The same could be said of Virgil who, having read in Homer that Aeneas did not die in the Trojan War . . . , conceived his divine *Aeneid.*"[39]

There seems to be a definite sense here that Homer stands as the "divine original" as opposed to all his successors, no matter how great, how "divine" they may have been or will be. Yet Ronsard does not simply acknowledge a distance separating his own poem from this timeless, unchanging source, removed from the vicissitudes of history. By introducing a major difference between the *Iliad* and the *Aeneid,* he problematizes the conception of "the classical text" as an undifferentiated font of eternal truth.

In his wide-ranging study of the source *topos* in Renaissance literature, David Quint focused on the debate between alternative methods of reading, allegorical versus historicist, and showed how the Renaissance literary text became an instrument of epistemological criticism.[40] As this reading of Ronsard's theoretical statements seems to suggest, the *Aeneid* cannot make the same claims to transcendent truth as can the *Iliad*. In other words, the awareness of textual historicity is not limited to Renaissance authors with respect to their own texts, but it also extends to some of the greatest classical exemplars.

According to Ronsard, Homer and Virgil are "two luminaries of Poetry" ("deux lumieres de Poësie," 340) and, even more: "two great demigods, each worthy of a temple" ("deux grands Demydieux dignes chascun d'un temple," 354, l.12). Yet, in contrast with the *Iliad*'s timelessness, the *Aeneid* is placed within a specific history, the Augustan Age with its dynamic premise and its emphasis on change over time. This placement is in complete agreement with the French theoreticians of the 1550s who generally considered Virgil a "political" poet. His name was commonly associated with Augustus in the context of Rome's imperialist claims. In his *Art poëtique*, for instance, Peletier exclaimed: "Oh, if only there could be another Augustus, that we might see if there could be another Virgil!"[41] And Du Bellay, in *La Deffence & Illustration*, made a similar comment: "Certainly, if we had a new Maecenas and Augustus, Heaven and earth are not so hostile that they would prevent us from having other Virgils!"[42]

Mostly because of this historical factor, Ronsard probably felt drawn to the Roman epic, which could offer him the guarantee of an illustrious political precedent. Yet, at the same time, France had to establish a direct link with Greek civilization, unmediated by the Latin experience. The foundations of a national mystique could only be built upon the solid rock of an original "primal scene." Since the fall of Troy ("*la guerre Troyenne*") had been the founding myth of the *Aeneid*, it had to play a similar role within the French poem to give credence to its mythical claims. In other words, Ronsard implicitly rejected Virgil's modeling effect. Both Aeneas and Francus had successfully escaped from Troy's inferno, and both had set out to found a "new Troy" ("Pour y fonder une nouvelle Troye" l. 302, p. 43). Therefore, both poets were to be considered equal. They had the same degree of kinship: their common *source* was Homer.

For Ronsard, surprising though it may seem, the ultimate significance of the *Aeneid* and the *Franciade* lies in the same critical gesture: the "allegorical reading" of an all-powerful source of fullness that is identified with Homer's *Urtext*. Once this sameness is accepted, Virgil certainly appears to be an ideal means to transpose into French the best possible rules of structure and composition for an epic poem: "Follow Virgil who is past master of the composition and structure of the poems."[43] This advice holds true even though, at times, Virgil may have lapsed into regrettable mistakes. As we have seen earlier, Peletier followed Horace's identical reproach about Homer. Ronsard's remarks on Virgil's failure to respect the unity of time (in *Aeneid* V, ll.46.-8) may stem from his desire to distance the Latin poet from his Greek source, thereby bringing himself closer to the original locus of transcendent truth.

Ronsard's ambivalent motive was undoubtedly to be both a Homer and a Virgil at the same time; that is, to be able to combine—in spite of his statement to the contrary—a Homeric claim for origins and a Virgilian perfection of style. In fact, this is precisely what he had suggested in his poem *L'Hylas*, published three years before *La Franciade*. In the oft-quoted closing lines, he addressed Jean Passerat, a professor at the Collège Royal, and exposed his imitation theory in a most straightforward way:

> Dear Passerat, I resemble the Bee
> Who goes picking flowers, sometimes bright red,
> Sometimes yellow. Wandering in the fields,
> It flies to the places which are most to its liking
> Mustering many supplies before Winter comes. . . .
> Thus running and leaping through my books,
> I gather, sort and select the finest motif
> Which I colorfully depict in one type of painting
> Or another. Then becoming master painter,
> Without forcing myself, I imitate Nature.[44]

Here Ronsard clearly brings together two types of imitation that profoundly disturbed Renaissance theoreticians. As Grahame Castor remarked, "the poet takes his 'colours' from others, and yet at the same time he claims to be representing Nature."[45] In fact, Ronsard never intends to combine the imitation of model authors and the representation of Nature. On the contrary, he needs to keep the two quite separate, just as in the 1572 preface to *La Franciade* he will make a distinction between "natural facility" and "careful diligence" (5). In *L'Hylas*, Ronsard first says that he needs to imitate the bee's work ("Je resemble à l'Abeille") and gather material from various authors; then, and only then, will he be able to dominate his art (to become "maistre en ma peinture") and to give his own work the seal of originality.

When he writes, "Without forcing myself, I imitate Nature," Ronsard implicitly recognizes within himself the power to reach a god-given, original source of inspiration. It is the equivalent of saying: "I have patterned my work . . . after Homer's natural facility."[46] Therefore, true representation of Nature (*mimesis*) can only be achieved through the conscious and conscientious imitation of previous art (*imitatio*). This idea is no less than the reversal of the normal theoretical order. First comes a necessary rhetorical stage: borrowing arguments, composition, and style, according to the rules of *inventio, dispositio, elocutio*. Then the really creative process can take place, meant to reoriginate the new text and give it an autonomy that somehow makes it participate in a timeless source of truth.

In the opening statement of "Les Argumens . . . de la *Franciade*," Amadis Jamyn, Ronsard's secretary and a poet in his own right, made a similar kind of commentary—again using the classical bee metaphor—on Ronsard's double theory of imitation: "In this laborious work, the *Franciade*, the Author intended to write like the Ancients, and above all like the divine Homer."[47] Divine Homer is thus singled out as the original source of inspiration. Jamyn, who was to achieve the first complete translation of the *Iliad* into French (twenty-four books in 1577), probably had good personal reasons for promoting Homer. Yet he continues his commentary as follows: "Although in this first book he mainly imitated Homer and Virgil, Francus's departure however is imitated from Apollonius of Rhodes."[48] In other words, whereas the general conception of Ronsard's poem is "patterned after Homer," the actual "imitation" of specific episodes can be traced to a variety of classical models (and Homer is one of them). In fact, Apollonius of Rhodes is the primary model for this kind of practical imitation. And Jamyn continues: "He resembles the bee who takes advantage of all flowers to make its honey. This is why, without preferring one Ancient above the others, he considers what is best in each and uses it to enrich (always in a felicitous way) our French language."[49]

We seem to have here another version of Ronsard's "divided aspirations." Whether he expresses it himself or has his secretary come forth as his spokesman, the poet acknowledges his borrowings as being the necessary ingredients of a consciously crafted work of art.[50] At the same time, he strives "to ground his verse in an authorized source and to establish his own individuality as a literary creator."[51]

In their liminary poems in homage to the *Franciade*, Jean Passerat, the addressee of *L'Hylas*, and Amadis Jamyn, the author of "Les Argumens," claimed, both in Latin and French, that Ronsard had moved beyond the quarrel between Homer's and Virgil's supporters (22–23). The point was well taken indeed. Ronsard could afford to welcome both Homer and Virgil into his own epic because they appeared at two very different levels of functionality. Homer was virtually untouchable and served as an allegorical reference to a higher level of truth. Virgil was closer to Ronsard, geographically, linguistically, pedagogically, and politically. The *Aeneid* was so close indeed that one of its lines became an object of parody in the last preface to *La Franciade*: "To what literary heights will French glory soar!"[52] Ronsard exclaimed, alluding to the many great poems that would elevate the glory of France if French writers would write their works in the vernacular. Paradoxically, Ronsard expressed his fervent plea for French greatness in Latin, probably because he wished to position his counterfeit epic in a classical context, between but also beyond Homer and Virgil, thus inviting his "apprentice reader" to reproduce *mimetically* the plenitude regained of lost origins.

David F. Hult

Author/Narrator/Speaker
The Voice of Authority in Chrétien's *Charrete*

Chrétien de Troyes' *Chevalier de la Charrete* (*Knight of the Cart*) is the first fictional text that has come down to us detailing what became the renowned story of the adulterous passion between Lancelot and Arthur's queen, Guenevere. Chrétien does not deal with the grand tapestry of Arthurian history as his contemporaries would have known it through Wace's *Roman de Brut*, nor does his story even approach the narrative complexity of the later Vulgate cycle, to which the Cart episode will be annexed. Rather, Chrétien focuses upon one limited episode in a larger whole, the repercussions of which are neither stated nor alluded to. With respect to its plot, this "romance" has been likened to another courtly genre, the *lai*, which usually limits itself to an isolated episode or to the fictional elaboration of some emblematic object.[1] Briefly, the story goes as follows: In the opening scene, situated, as tradition seems to dictate, at Arthur's court on an important feast day (in this case, the Ascension), Guenevere is abducted through the ruse of an unnamed knight who, we find out somewhat later, is named Meleagant. Son of Bademagu, the benign sovereign of the far-off kingdom of Gorre, Meleagant has taken captive over some period a large number of Arthur's subjects, knights and ladies alike. His aggressions are thus of a personal and political nature. The premier knight of Arthur's court, Gauvain, sets off in pursuit of Guenevere and is soon joined by still another unnamed knight. This knight, not recognized by Gauvain, turns out to be none other than Lancelot. The famous scene that provides the work's title occurs soon after the two knights' departure from court. A dwarf pulling a cart behind his horse offers to provide information as to Guenevere's whereabouts if only the knight will mount the cart. Lancelot hesitates, for in those days this type of cart was used to transport criminals or display them for public vilification—to do so, the narrator informs us, would be tantamount to placing oneself in a position of public disgrace. But spurred on by feelings of love, Lancelot ends up jumping onto the vehicle and is henceforth known as the Knight of the Cart. The association continues for a large portion of the romance, and Lancelot is repeatedly treated with scorn because of it. After a lengthy sequence of adventures, our hero reaches Gorre, nearly defeats Meleagant in single combat, and, having adequately proven himself, is invited to enjoy a night of lovemaking in Guenevere's bedchamber. Lancelot and the queen plan to find Gauvain, who has gotten sidetracked, and return to Arthur's court with all the prisoners, but Lancelot is unexpectedly kidnapped by Meleagant and imprisoned in the castle of his seneschal. After some unspecified amount of time, Meleagant learns that the seneschal's wife has allowed Lancelot a few days' liberty to participate incognito in a grand tournament presided over by Guenevere. Furious, he has a tower built in an isolated stretch of territory to assure himself of the knight's permanent disappearance. To the rescue comes Meleagant's sister, who finds Lancelot, releases him, and sends him back to the court of Arthur where, in the romance's climactic scene, Lancelot defeats and beheads the treacherous Meleagant.

Douglas Kelly's important 1966 study remains the most persuasive attempt to evaluate the romance's structural unity in spite of the long critical tradition which had consistently decried that unity.[2] According to his analysis, the center of the plot revolves around Meleagant's detainment of the prisoners from Arthur's realm; the love of Lancelot and Guenevere, as well as the hatred between Lancelot and Meleagant, are then subplots attaching themselves to the more explicitly political major theme. This analysis of the work's overall structure and organizational principles makes sense, since the romance opens and closes with Meleagant (his arrival at court and his death) while the theme that has struck most readers' fancy, the love story involving Gue-

nevere and Lancelot, is largely left in suspension. I do not intend
here to take issue with Kelly's admirably detailed account of the
work's compositional symmetry, for that is not, to my mind, particularly in question. Having said that, however, I do not believe
that the narrative or thematic structure is the most compelling
critical problem raised by Chrétien's text. I would like instead to
discuss a more basic problem lurking in the background of this
troublesome work—namely, where to situate the frame of interpretation itself.

Our difficulties begin with the end, in the form of a provocative
statement appended to the conclusion of the narrative. Three of
the four manuscripts that contain the concluding narrative portion of the *Charrete* incorporate a curious epilogue that, functioning somewhat as a palinode, suggests a revision of our original
conception of the romance's unity.[3] The epilogue reads as follows:[4]

> Seignor, se j'avant an disoie,
> ce seroit oltre la matire,
> por ce au definer m'atire:
> ci faut li romanz an travers.
> Godefroiz de Leigni, li clers,
> a parfinee LA CHARRETE
> mes nus home blasme ne l'an mete
> se sor Crestïen a ovré,
> car ç'a il fet par le boen gré
> Crestïen, qui le comança:
> tant en a fet des lors an ça
> ou Lanceloz fu anmurez,
> tant con li contes est durez.
> Tant en a fet, n'i vialt plus metre
> ne moins, por le conte mal metre.

(7098–7112)

My lords, if I were to tell more I would be going beyond my matter. Therefore I draw
to a close: The romance ends here. The clerk Godefroy de Leigni has ended the
Charrete. Let no one blame him for completing the work of Chrétien, since he did it
with the approval of Chrétien, who began it. He worked on the story from the point
at which Lancelot was walled into the tower up to this point—as long as the tale lasted.
Just so much of it has he done, not wishing to put in more or less, lest he harm the
story.

The passage incorporates several key terms, the importance of which will shortly become obvious. Godefroi's awareness of something he terms the *matière* and the *conte* (story or tale)—both pointing to a separate existence of the story in some sort of material or ideal form[5]—suggests that Godefroi was following a plan previously laid out or undertaken by Chrétien. Furthermore, Godefroi's claim that he undertook his continuation with the first author's "approval" or "good will" (*boen gré*) accentuates our sense of a unified plan. Yet the fact remains that a break in the text has been brought to our attention. How do we go about locating that break, and how are we to conceptualize the relationship between the two authors? In what way might this authorial change affect our reading of the romance? Although the manuscript transmission of the *Charrete* is decidedly the most corrupt and fragmented of any of Chrétien's romances, even this material fragmentation provides no clues. Of the six principal manuscripts containing the romance, two provide the completed text with the epilogue, one contains all but the prologue and the first few adventures, two break off at different points in the midst of the Noauz tournament near the end, and one follows through to the end from still another point in that same tournament scene.[6] Even if the romance is fragmentary by nature, none of the manuscripts agree upon a specific breaking point, nor do any of the scribes demonstrate an interest in the question. Modern critics have attempted to situate the break alluded to by Godefroi,[7] but unfortunately his reference is to an episode in the plot development—Lancelot's immurement—and not to a specific line, as is, for instance, the case when Jean de Meun informs us of his own continuation of Guillaume de Lorris's *Romance of the Rose*. Only recently has it been suggested through statistical studies that the last section diverges stylistically from the first part of the romance,[8] although this difference has not been felt by most readers.

The questions I ask here are, What status should we grant to the continuator? and How does this additional information contribute to an interpretation of the romance? To answer these questions, I am required to make a slight detour. In recent years, much attention has been paid to prologue material and, in general, to authorial self-expression in the earliest medieval French romances.[9] It has become commonplace to note that, in the mid-twelfth century, the change in literary fashion from the long-popular epic to what would have been considered the "modern" genre of courtly romance was accompanied by a greatly altered vision of authorship and, along with that, new techniques of narrative voicing. I do not wish to address the broad questions raised by the prologues and their rhetorical basis,[10] but I would like to confess a bit of uneasiness with the frequently used expressions "self-consciousness" or "self-awareness" and with, what is to my mind, their dubious application to statements made by medieval authors. The biographical illusion to which these early texts are subject has been criticized by Spitzer, Zumthor and Dragonetti—among others—but I think it bears repeating that authorial self-consciousness in these texts entails neither self-depiction nor self-expression of a personal kind (both of which are largely absent from the corpus), especially when such expression is taken to be an end in itself. I do not mean to say that statements of individual condition are excluded but that they are nearly always a factor in the work's soon-to-be existence. They can take the form of a justification for the act of writing; a statement about where the materials were found and sometimes how; a mention of artistic criteria; or an address to the author's patron. To take one example, Wace's statements about his own poverty evoke the larger question of the economic constraints governing the production of literary and historical works, aspects of patronage, and even the moral virtue known as *largesse*. And for her part, when discussing her work of translation, Marie de France is not trying to tell us that she is trilingual or quadrilingual but is simply providing the authoritative origin for the lais she is about to recount. Authorial naming is not biographical as we use the term; as a literary act, it performs a function within the broader context of literary transmission. By naming himself, the author identifies, justifies, and distinguishes his work from that of others. This is perhaps why such prefatory material often takes the form of oppositions or contrasts (of the sort, "so-and-so is doing that but I am doing this"; "the jongleurs don't know how to tell the story the way I do"; "I alone found the book upon which this story is based"; and so on). It might be added that the fundamental distinction made by modern literary theory between author and narrator is articulated in the separation between the classifying function of the name (usually employed in the third person) and the personal *I* of the narrator, the voice of the text itself. When taken together, the author and the narrator provide a sense of uniqueness within cultural space marked by continuity and adherence to tradition.

The presumed social status of the medieval vernacular author can be used to substantiate the particular qualities of narrative voice I have just outlined. The stereotypical stance of the epic poet was that of a simple, frequently unidentifiable, singer/performer recounting commonly shared political legends to an audience in the know; anonymity and a relative dearth of self-reference are perhaps the natural consequences of a social situation and a communication model both of which imply direct contact between speaker and listener. Be it truth or fiction, romance writers seem always to depict themselves as being apart, as external members invited inside an elite circle in order to share their wit and learning with those who can afford to pay for it. We get a good sense of this precarious situation from Denis Piramus, probably a contemporary of Chrétien, who gives in his prologue to the *Life* of *Saint Edmund* the explanation for his abandonment of courtly literature in favor of hagiography:[11]

> trop ai usee ma vie
> Et en peché e en folie.
> Kant court hanteie of les curteis,
> Si feseie les serventeis,
> Chanceunettes, rimes, saluz
> Entre les drues et les druz.
> Mult me penai de tels vers fere
> Ke assemble les puise treire
> E k'ensemble fussent justez
> Pur acomplir lur volentez.
> Ceo me fist fere l'enemi. . . .

I have greatly used up my life in sin and folly. When I frequented the court with all those courtly folk, I composed *serventeis, chançonetes, saluts d'amour* and various other poems in the company of lovers, both men and women. I gave myself a lot of trouble making up the right type of verses, of such quality that I could pull them together and come up with a harmonious fit, all this in order to fulfill their desires. The devil made me do it.

One gets very much the sense of a servant forced to abandon his own integrity—his very soul—for the sake of commissioned requests. Indeed, the romance writer commonly depicts himself as an in-between character, caught between the library and the court, between the Church and lay society, between a Latin cultural model and the particularities of vernacular expression. But perhaps equally important, the complex communication model created by the additional factor of writing explains the new need for self-justification and authentication, as well as the complexities of narrative voice frequently catalogued under such terms as "irony" and "aesthetic distance."[12]

The self-justification of the *romancier* takes the form of discussions concerning authorial technique, comments on the nature of poetic traditions, and clues to the interpretation of the fiction itself. Such discussions also reflect an increasingly complex expression of authorial pride and, occasionally, even boastfulness, by way of setting the individual work apart from rival poetic creations. Another aspect of such marginal authorial expression is that it serves as a type of guarantor for poetic quality and narrative unity, as well as a point of focus for uncovering factors of intentionality. To be sure, romance authors are forever referring to their sources, usually written and most often in Latin, as a way of substantiating their own poetic authority. But it would be a mistake, because of this rhetorical self-justification, to place into question or to efface the author's own originality or virtuosity. Because this gesture refers backward *only* in order to sacrifice past tradition to present innovation, it is antinostalgic in the most resounding sense. Another of Chrétien's contemporaries, Benoît de Sainte-Maure, after painstakingly describing the transmission of the Trojan War account from the time of the event down to the moment he found it buried away in a library, describes his own activity as translator of the *Roman de Troie* in the following terms:[13]

> . . . Beneeiz de Sainte More
> L'a contrové e fait e dit
> E o sa main les moz escrit,
> Ensi tailliez, ensi curez,
> Ensi asis, ensi posez,
> Que plus ne meins n'i a mestier.

Benoît de Sainte-Maure conceived, composed and recounted the story, and wrote down the words with his own hand, so carved, so polished, so fitted into place and so positioned, that there is need of neither more nor less.

Benoît's sense of his own poetic precision is clear enough, but his studied elaboration of the stonemason metaphor further accentuates the plasticity of the written word, its pliability and materiality—a metaphorical association that will enjoy a great fortune in the speculations of vernacular artists and will carry through to Jean de Meun's elaborate thematics of forging and sculpting in his *Roman de la Rose*. Benoît goes on to suggest that faithfulness to a source and personal innovation are not mutually exclusive but rather coexist in a fluid space of artistic creation:

> Le latin sivrai e la letre,
> nule autre rien n'i voudrai metre,
> S'ensi non com jol truis escrit.
> Ne di mie qu'aucun bon dit
> N'i mete, se faire le sai,
> Mais la matire en ensivrai.
> (*Troie*, ll. 139–44)

I will follow the Latin down to the letter of the original, not wishing to add anything else except as I find it written down. I am not at all saying that I won't add some nice tidbit, if I am capable of it, but I will follow the subject matter [*matire*] of the work.

Chrétien himself shows a great sensitivity to the appropriateness of his own narrative expression, both in relation to his contemporaries and to those who might later spread his works. In the prologue to his first Arthurian romance, *Erec et Enide*, Chrétien contrasts his own version of the story, what he calls the *conte d'aventure*, with that which is, he says, currently being mangled or torn apart by storytellers who run around from court to court. In an even stronger indictment, he notes briefly at the end of *Yvain* that he has told all there is to tell and that if anyone adds something, it will be nothing but a lie (*mensonge*). The problem of textual demarcation is clearly at issue here, with a strong contrast suggested between a sense of appropriate closure and what might be called an "additive aesthetic" endemic to the manuscript circulation and reproduction of fictional works. There is a certain complex interplay in Chrétien's works as a whole between the prior existence of story material or plot—which is undoubtedly what he means by the technical term *matiere*—and the shape of interpretation as determined by a particular author's vision or intention.[14]

Keeping these remarks in mind, let us now turn back to Godefroi's epilogue. If we treat his assertions in a purely historical or biographical context, we are obliged to ask under what circumstances the association or collaboration of the two authors might have taken place. Many hypotheses have been advanced: Godefroi "the clerk" might have been Chrétien's helper or apprentice, a right-hand man under the master's tutelage, to whom a leftover piece of work was handed. Why did Chrétien not finish it himself? Was he bored with the subject matter or, as some have suggested, ultimately disgusted by the theme of adultery imposed upon him? Perhaps Godefroi happened upon Chrétien's unfinished romance independently and proposed a conclusion to which the latter subsequently assented. Maybe the continuator is lying when he tells us that he wrote the final section of the romance with Chrétien's approval. Did they even know each other? How do we begin to sort out lie from truth in such an inscrutable context?

The answer is that we cannot, for we are likely never to know anything more about Godefroi than his name and social status. But this is not the only possibility for sorting out poetic "truth." As per my previous discussion of the medieval author-function, I would suggest that we abandon the dead-end biographical question in favor of an investigation centered upon its inner poetic effect. Instead of "Who is Godefroi?" the question becomes,

"What does it matter?" Rather than attempt to distinguish between "lie" and "truth," we must ask whether these terms have
any place in the margins of a fictional text. As far as its poetic
function is concerned, the epilogue points undeniably to a rift in
the text and, secondly, leaves open a possibility that the unfinished text might have been a part of Chrétien's intention. Thus,
curiously enough, the epilogue can be seen to stand in contradiction with itself, for if one of its expressed purposes is to assert
the work's unity of intention, its very existence bespeaks an opposing disunity. To state the same idea in the psychological terms
typically used to characterize authorial self-expression, Godefroi's
pride as evidenced in the act of naming himself seems to coun-
termand the humility of his expressed relation to Chrétien. Seen
from a rhetorical point of view, Godefroi's epilogue opens up a
space with two possibilities, both disruptive of the unity of intentionality that would be coextensive with the existence of a
single authority. And it is important to see that this disruptive
effect is valid whether we actually believe or discredit the words
of the continuator, for in either case the text remains split in two.
This problem has certain methodological repercussions by virtue
of the fact that our assessment of textual unity and closure is
largely predicated upon our ability to isolate an authorial voice.
Specifically, by admitting a dual authorship without then asking
what is the textual difference introduced by the strategy of authorial naming, we are committing a potential methodological
contradiction. [15] The problem becomes that of attempting to comprehend the romance's dual focus within a single interpretive
frame of the sort that normally depends on a unified model of
authority for its very grounding.

Before addressing the question at hand, we might first investigate the plot for signs of unity or disunity—that is, for evidence
of types of closure that might be involved. From the immurement
of Lancelot to the end of the romance, approximately one thousand lines out of a total seven thousand, one principal action
takes place. Meleagant goes to Arthur's court for the prearranged
rematch with Lancelot and, gloating to his fullest, decries the
absence of Lancelot, which he has secretly insured by means of

his treachery. Once back at his father's court, Meleagant continues to boast of his great valor, and out of nowhere a new character,
the sister of Meleagant, is introduced. For unstated reasons, she
sets out in quest of Lancelot and eventually frees him from the
tower. In a surprising revision of the courtly love theme (expressed
through Lancelot's extravagant adoration of Guenevere), Lancelot
presents his homage to Meleagant's sister as though she were his
beloved. He even grants without restriction his heart and his body,
a symbolic gesture that he had scrupulously resisted making earlier
in the romance in the face of a variety of temptations. Concomitant with what we might call Lancelot's lack of faith, Guenevere
is largely effaced from the romance: Not only does Lancelot not
mention her or even think of her after being placed in the tower,
but even Meleagant's aggressive intentions have turned from a
single-minded desire to possess the queen to a largely self-con-
sumed escalation of boastfulness and rage. The beheading of the
villainous Meleagant proves to be a most spectacular physical
marker of the work's closure—so spectacular that we scarcely
notice or even question the absence of resolution elsewhere in the
plot.

But, to go back a little, when looked at from a literary or
intertextual point of view, Chrétien's immurement of Lancelot
provides a subtle, yet no less convincing, example of poetic closure. Aside from the grandiose metaphor of spatial enclosure provided by the tower construct, the genre of the troubadour love
lyric could very easily have suggested to Chrétien the appropriateness of the pining, solitary lover in the midst of a neverending
love plaint—a theme that is developed ad infinitum in allegorical
literature of the following centuries as the *prison amoureuse*. Had
Chrétien himself not stated in one of the two lyric poems attributed to his hand, "d'amor ne sai nule issue" [I know no exit from
love]?

In addition to this rather crafty show of literary sophistication,
ending the romance with Lancelot's incarceration would also have
freed Chrétien from one or another sticky plot development that
would have taken the romance further afield than he probably
cared to go. The implication of Lancelot's return to court along

with the queen entails an endless sequence of adulterous episodes in the *Tristan* mold, to which legend Chrétien's story is much indebted. Even more drastic, the fall of Arthur's kingdom, which had been associated by the writer Wace with Guenevere's adultery in his well-known translation of Geoffrey of Monmouth's even more widely read *History of the Kings of Britain*, would certainly have come to the mind of Chrétien's readers. There is simply no indication in this or any other of Chrétien's romances (with the possible exception of his last, unfinished one, the *Conte du Graal*) that his frame of reference was anything other than the static epoch associated with the apogee of Arthur's kingship.[16] In other words, I think that the social and political ramifications of the Lancelot/Guenevere affair—ones that were irrevocably encoded in the most famous literary and historical works of the late twelfth century—risked carrying him further than he wished to go with his considerably more modest, episodic romance.

From this point of view, Godefroi's finishing the tale is most convenient, for we are allowed through his agency to partake of a completed adventure tale (one that incorporates the punishment of Meleagant) and, further, Chrétien is cleared of the charge of incoherence or unfaithfulness, since he did not write the end. This resolution is almost too perfect, and it is perhaps at this juncture that we can best understand the devious reasoning behind Chrétien's consent to Godefroi's handiwork, his *boen gré*. The second author's participation allows him to vouchsafe his own subtle, although narratively unacceptable, conclusion, while the other, chivalric, strand of the romance is definitively closed. The otherness of Godefroi's voice, as identified by the epilogue, provides a marvelously pertinent alibi for the unfinished narrative while proposing an acceptable narrative resolution, a "way out." It is possible to suggest, further, that Godefroi's voice and what makes it known to us—the strategically placed and otherwise superfluous, even self-defeating, epilogue—plays a role in, or serves, one important aspect of Chrétien's *plot*. Here I am not thinking so much of his emplotment as of his plotting; for, the role is so well, and so carefully, engineered, that I would advance the possibility that Godefroi is a fiction of Chrétien—a "clerkly" author-figure allowing our devious first author the luxury of two endings, two voices, and thus a highly nuanced, unlocalizable intentionality.[17]

Several narrative factors argue for a uniformity between the two parts of the romance, not the least of which is the frequent adoption by "Godefroi" of the first-person narrative voice and, even more convincing, his exploitation of the very same literary terms that Chrétien had set out in the prologue of the romance, and to which I will turn in a moment. We have already seen Godefroi's reference to the *matiere* and to the tale, the *conte*, in the epilogue, but there is still another passage—the precise moment at which Meleagant's sister is surreptitiously inserted into the plot—wherein the narrator recapitulates in some detail the literary terminology set out at the beginning:

> mes une en i ot avoec eles
> don bien vos dirai ça avant
> (cele estoit suer Meleagant)
> mon pansser et m'antencïon;
> mes n'an vuel feire mancïon,
> car n'afiert pas a ma matire
> que ci androit an doie dire,
> ne je ne la vuel boceier
> ne corronpre ne forceier,
> mes mener boen chemin et droit.
>
> (6242–51)

There was one among them [she was the sister of Meleagant] about whom I shall willingly reveal my thought [*pansser*] and my intention [*antencïon*]; But I do not want to speak of her now, for it is not a part of my story to tell of her at this point; And I do not want to batter it, nor break it apart nor manhandle it, but instead lead it on a proper and straight path.

The placement of this narrative excursus is in itself brilliantly ironic, for it occurs at precisely the moment where the continuator slips the key agent of narrative resolution (heretofore undesignated) into the plot; the narrative reversal is accompanied by a statement of total proprietorship as far as narrative inspiration is concerned (*my* thought and *my* intention . . . *my* subject matter). In view of Chrétien's prudent limitation of his own role in the prologue, stating that he received the subject matter (*matiere*) and meaning (*sens*) from the Countess of Champagne, this claim could be considered rather outrageous on the part of a mere continuator. Furthermore, the narrator's metaphoric handling of the theme of faithfulness to one's subject matter (not wishing to batter, break up, or manhandle it), when we recall the prologue to *Erec et Enide*, which I mentioned previously, should alert us to the possibility of internalized storytelling metaphors being called into service to fill out the romance plot. Here I am not thinking only of the metaphor used in this spot, that of leading the story down the right path, but also that of the stonemason, actualized in the building of Lancelot's tower prison, and that of beheading, which concretizes an Old French expression, *traire a chief* (literally, "to draw to a head," and commonly taken in a figurative sense meaning "to complete or end").

But even with all these parallels, the suggestion of Godefroi's fictionality would not be nearly so compelling could it not itself, as a poetic gesture, be interpreted as the replication on a rather grand scale of a rhetorical strategy exploited by Chrétien in the romance prologue, to which we now turn. It is not my intention to delve into any of the semantic complexities of the prologue to the *Charrete*, which has perhaps received more critical commentary than any other single aspect of Chrétien's *oeuvre*.[18] Suffice it to say that the bulk of critical attention has focused on the nature of Chrétien's dedication to his patroness, Marie de Champagne, and the definition of the many technical terms used therein: *sens, matiere, painne,* and *antancion*. What has received relatively little notice,[19] and yet seems to me to be highly significant, is the manner in which Chrétien voices praise for his lady:

> je l'anprendrai molt volentiers
> come cil qui est suens antiers
> de quan qu'il puet el monde feire
> sanz rien de losange avant treire;
> mes tex s'an poïst antremetre
> qui li volsist losenge metre,
> si deïst, et jel tesmoignasse,
> que ce est la dame qui passe

totes celes qui sont vivanz,
si con li funs passe les vanz
qui vante en mai ou en avril.
Par foi, je ne sui mie cil
qui vuelle losangier sa dame;
dirai je: "Tant com une jame
vaut de pailes et de sardines,
vaut la contesse de reïnes?"
Naie voir; je n'en dirai rien,
s'est il voirs maleoit gré mien.

(3–20)

I shall do so [begin a romance] most willingly, as one who is entirely at her service in anything he can undertake in this world. I say this without any flattery, though another might begin his story with the desire to flatter her. He might say [and I would agree] that she is the lady who surpasses all women who are alive, just as the foehn which blows in May or April surpasses the other winds. Certainly I am not one intent upon flattering his lady; Will I say: "As many pearls and sardonyx as the polished diamond is worth, so many queens is the countess worth"? Indeed not, I will say nothing of the sort, though it be true in spite of me.

Chrétien's strategy of praise, undertaken in a fashion reminiscent of the knight's submission to his lady,[20] is most revealing when he rhetorically attempts to give compliments without really doing so. He initially denies his use of flattery, the implication of the key word group *losange/losangier*—recurring three times in slightly different forms—being that all praise risks being a type of deceit and, therefore, if one really wants to praise someone this praise cannot be verbalized lest it be mistaken for false or insincere flattery. But then he twice voices her praise only to disown his part in it. First he states that some *might* praise her and that he would be in agreement, but that he himself would not be able to perform such an act. The second time, in a highly theatrical move, he actually assumes the voice of another in direct discourse, only to refuse it and yet insist upon his agreement with such a statement, its inherent truth "in spite of himself." The careful line that Chrétien draws here separates the substance or authenticity of praise from the very expression of that praise—which because of its linguistic cover is always at least potentially duplicitous. This careful line also effectively ends up splitting the design attributed to the narrator, who avers the truth of the praise literally against his will (*"maleoit gré mien"*).

The term *gré* is quite important here, not only for uniting prologue and epilogue but also because I think it is the word that comes closest to meaning "intention" in the romance.[21] From the Latin *gratus*, meaning "pleasing" or "agreeable," *gré* can mean "will," "pleasure," or "approval," as we have seen. Two other occurrences of the word, both related to Meleagant's sister, demonstrate further this interesting relationship between "will" and the covert expression thereof.

> An la tor, qui est haute et droite,
> n'avoit eschiele ne degré.
> Por ce croit que c'est fet de gré
> et que Lanceloz est dedanz.
>
> (6450–53)

In the tower, which is tall and straight, there was neither a ladder nor a step. Because of this she [Meleagant's sister] believes that it was done intentionally [*de gré*] and that Lancelot is inside.

> Mes la pucele se desvoie
> tot de gré, por ce qu'an nes voie.
>
> (6643–44)

[The maiden is leading Lancelot along the way.] But the maiden goes off the road on purpose, in order that no one will see them.

In both cases, a direct relationship is established between a duplicitous or hidden maneuver and the fact of its intentionality or purposefulness. In the first case, Meleagant's sister correctly reads the situation, seeing in the absence of any sign of entry a mark of a specific intentionality; in the second, her own will leads her to disguise her trail. If *gré* refers to "will" or "intention," I think it is not coincidental that it is also related to moves of concealment.

To return to the prologue, the problem of flattery leads to a commentary upon the potential contradictions in articulating one's own voice, expressing one's own thoughts. This clever commentary is much to the point in a prologue whose aim seems to be Chrétien's acknowledgment of the Countess's substantial contribution to his own literary creation. And just as Chrétien invents in the prologue a voice allowing him to articulate praise and yet stand at the margins, so I think he conceived of Godefroi de Leigni as a clerkly author-figure, a specular image of himself peering from the outside, who permits him to fuse the political narrative with the exaltation of the love service. Accordingly, he can insert the secret message of love-longing, figured by Lancelot's immurement, within a narrative that must in some way eventually undo it.

This strategy of duplicitous narrative voicing, which we could consider a form of literary counterfeit—abandonment of one's own authority in order to take up another's—can, it seems to me, be related to several episodes in the *Charrete*. The initial linguistic device of the double voice, as articulated in the prologue, is extended to include most forms of perception. What early critics of the work interpreted as sloppy technique—disjointed and incoherent episodes—is more likely the direct result of a studied play with categories of sight and absence, speech and silence, appearance and reality, event and interpretation. And these all take place within the assumed ignorance of the narrator. Quite contrary to the allegorist mentality, Chrétien does not read meaning in or into the world; instead, he regularly posits a disjunction between the materiality of worldly occurrences and what could be considered a mystical, because unknowable, world. The only true messages to be discovered are the unstated, concealed ones that cannot be communicated; this will be the message of the Grail, if message there be.

Accordingly, the *Charrete* abounds in situations that appear one way according to one set of criteria and another way when different interpretive rules are called into play. Among these could be mentioned the cart episode, the bizarre trap conceived by the Amorous Maiden, and the furor surrounding Guenevere's bloody sheets. The narrator takes his place in this mysterious world, rarely divulging the fruits of his foreknowledge or omniscience. Thus he can also deliver his plot of unwanted elements simply by not seeing them or by losing them in his own rhetorical turns. One marvelous example of this is the last "appearance" of Guenevere, which is not an appearance at all, for she is evoked only in her absence. Lancelot has just returned to court for the final combat with Meleagant, and everyone, we are told, goes out to greet him, with one important exception:

> Et la reïne n'i est ele
> a cele joie qu'an demainne?
> Oïl voir, tote premerainne.
> Comant? Dex, ou fust ele donques?
> Ele n'ot mes si grant joie onques
> com or a de sa bien venue
> et ele a lui ne fust venue?
> Si est voir, ele an est si pres,
> qu'a po se tient, molt s'an va pres,
> que li cors le cuer ne sivoit.
> Ou est donc li cuers? Il beisoit
> et conjoïssoit Lancelot.
> Et li cors, por coi se celot?
>
> (6820–32)

And is the queen not there to participate in this joy? Indeed she is, and in the front ranks. How so? Heavens, where else might she be? Never has she experienced greater joy than she feels now at his safe return—so how could she not have come to him? In truth she is so near him that she can hardly restrain—it is all too close—her body from following her heart to him. Where then is her heart? Welcoming and kissing Lancelot. Why then was the body hiding?

The narrator observes the movement of his own plot as though he were an outsider, discovering the queen's absence at the same time as his reader, and without in fact reporting that absence. His question parallels our own: Where *is* the queen? The narrator proceeds to split his voice to present two aspects of the scene, the real physical absence of Guenevere and the inner conflict of the character's likely motivations. But, importantly, during this entire interlude we never *see* Guenevere; we are not even told where she is.[22]

But aside from an astonishing manipulation of narrative perspectivism, however, there is more to be said. The two voices of the narrator suggest two modes of "telling" a scene: through concrete events and through abstract figuration. The question of what "presence" means (physical presence, spiritual presence, presence as motivation) is here brilliantly debated but left ultimately unresolved by a narrator who refuses to dictate the precise terms of the debate. To discuss the queen *in* her absence, *as* an absence, is one way of putting into practice the potentially twisted relationship between words and things. The absent queen is dissolved into the allegorical equivalents of body and heart—clearly, figures for the concrete and immaterial forces at play in the romance.[23] Chrétien's narrative ploy attests to the arbitrariness of a "literal" meaning that can always be turned around rhetorically as a figurative presence. The otherwise banal heart-and-body motif figures not only the disjunction between word and thing, but more importantly, the potential presence of a meaning, a signified, in a space where the corresponding signifier is invisible. And, of course, the fact that this semiotic "twist" occurs within a section of the romance attributable to the continuator—in the absence of authority—suggests that meaning is in perpetual disjunction with expression and, further, that this disjunction is itself the very essence of Chrétien's poetics. In this scene, we are allowed a glimpse of the paradox of representation, only to realize that this apparent contact with authority in expression (through the absent body) is itself staged within the radically inauthentic discourse of Chrétien's doubled narrative voice.

But lest we be tempted to believe that there does exist an essence, a meaning, a desire (on the part of the queen) as is figured by the willful heart, even that assurance is split into duality: the heart, we have seen, is freely kissing Lancelot (6830–31), but it is also tied up by Reason:

> s'ainsi, veant toz, volsist feire
> tot si con li cuers le volsist
> et se reisons ne li tolsist
> ce fol panser et cele rage,
> si veïssent tot son corage
> lors si fust trop granz la folie.

Por ce reisons anferme et lie
son fol cuer, et son fol pansé.
(6840–47)

If, in front of everybody, she decided to do all that her heart wished, and if Reason
did not take away these foolish thoughts and that madness, they would then see her
inner feelings. What a height of folly that would be! Thus Reason has imprisoned and
tied up her foolish heart and thoughts.

The normally unified heart has been split apart (the one kissing
Lancelot and the one tied up) as though, in accordance with the
prologue strategy, any attempt to reach a point of authenticity
metamorphoses into a space of duality, of indecision. Furthermore, this scene explicitly recalls the cart episode at the beginning of the romance,[24] where Love and Reason debate Lancelot's
course of action; but there, Amor, nearly indistinguishable from
the heart, was able to ply Lancelot to his will. Here, in a complete
reversal, Reason ties up the heart in the absence of Love. On the
one hand, the curious absence of the God of Love in the present
scene parallels the absence of Guenevere's body: were Love there,
he would have to be vanquished, and we have seen that Chrétien
does not wish to suggest an end to love. But more importantly,
we should not forget that, as Chrétien said in the earlier scene,
Reason's traditional hideaway, its corporeal referent, is none other
than the mouth: "N'est pas el cuer, mes an la boche, / Reisons"
(370–71) [Reason does not reside in the heart, but in the mouth].
True to its etymology, Chrétien's Reason is also the faculty of
speech (*ratio*), representing a use of words and their logical implications over and against a physical, bodily logic. The disappearance of Guenevere (comparable in this to the "appearance"
of Meleagant's sister) is thus, in another way and as we might
have suspected all along, the triumph of speech and its poetic
outlet, courtly rhetoric; for this speech is also the clever poet's
triumph over the restraints of his *matiere*. And insofar as the
passage is mouthed not by Chrétien but by the second author, as
we have seen, a kind of triumph of semiotic indeterminacy seems
to be assured.

I would now like to come back to some of the issues I have discussed. I have suggested that in many ways the very possibility of evaluating or measuring poetic unity is dependent upon our capacity to perceive an authorial design, what I have perhaps awkwardly referred to as an "intentionality." In the modern world of printed and copyrighted texts, we run into relatively few uncertainties in this domain, but for the medieval period problems abound. We have seen that, in his more theoretical discussions, an author such as Chrétien is well aware of the complexities involved in charting his relationship, as modern author or transmitter of knowledge, to previous tradition and to contemporary audiences. Furthermore, in its material aspects the medieval work maintains a tantalizing uncertainty: it can situate itself within a writerly context while simultaneously making fictional use of that context. After the period of Chrétien, it is not uncommon for narratives to turn themselves inside out, as when Renaut de Beaujeu, in *Le Bel Inconnu*, tells his lady in the closing lines that the romance plot can be altered if she will only give him a fair glance, a *Beau Semblant*. It seems to me that by accepting Godefroi de Leigni exclusively as a historical character—whether we agree or disagree that he fulfilled Chrétien's initial plan—we are stressing his contingency and separation from the first author and thus losing sight of what could be a supremely subtle and very crafty narrative ploy. The copresence of two types of closure, of two endings—and not their opposition—is the very structure of artifice and, according to the model Chrétien provides in his prologue, perhaps the only way to get at authenticity in expression, to balance the weight of poetic *matiere* with the flight of poetic fancy, to achieve the *gré* of the artist. In the present case, however paradoxical it may seem, we are obliged to grant that Chrétien had the last word.

Nancy J. Vickers

Widowed Words
Dante, Petrarch, and the
Metaphors of Mourning

When in the *Vita nuova* Dante presents the first poem to follow his narrative telling of the death of Beatrice, he radically trans-forms the shape of his *libello*. Until her death—the literal inter-ruption of her presence in his world—his volume had moved consistently from prose narration of events, to poetry, to prose division/explication of poetry. Each poem is thus contextualized; it is inscribed within a comfortable cushion, a protective barrier of prose. After Beatrice dies, however, Dante's *materia*, although it remains the same, becomes very different; similarly, his trans-lation from his "book of memory" retains its tripartite organiza-tion but transforms itself through reordering. It commemorates interruption by repeating it; it moves from prose narrative to prose division to poem. Dante explains this structural shift as follows:

E accio che questa canzone paia rimanere più vedova dopo lo suo fine, la dividerò prima che io la scriva; e cotale modo terrò da qui innanzi.[1]

And in order that this *canzone* may seem to remain all the more widowed after it has come to its end, I shall divide it before I write it. And from now on I shall follow this method.

Dante's purpose, then, is to convert all songs and sonnets "*in morte*" into "widows," to underline the loss of the earthly referent for his words of praise, to foreground rupture, emptiness, and vulnerability. Thus the structural gesture of "widowing" is a highly privileged one: for the metaphor "my song is a widow" informs an entire revisionary system of composition. When he

97

concludes the first in his sequence of consciously "widowed words," his *tornada* sends his song to mourn his lady's loss:

> Pietosa mia canzone or va' piangendo
> e ritruova le donne e le donzelle
> a cui le tue sorelle
> erano usate, di portar letizia
> e tu, che se' figliuola di tristizia
> vatten disconsolata a star con elle.
>
> (VN 31.17)

Now go your way in tears my mournful song and find once more the ladies and the maidens to whom your sisters used to bring happiness, and you who are the daughter of sadness, go disconsolate to be with them.

A generation later, Francesco Petrarca significantly, albeit predictably, returns to the notion of words or texts as widows at the end of his first *canzone* after the death of Laura:

> Fuggi 'l sereno e 'l verde
> non t'appressare ove sia riso o canto,
> canzon mia, no, ma pianto,
> non fa per te di star fra gente allegra
> vedova, sconsolata, in veste negra.[2]

Flee the clear sky and greenery, do not approach where there is laughter and singing, my song, no, my lament; it is not fitting for you to be among cheerful people, disconsolate widow in black garments.

There can be no doubt that Petrarch's *tornada* echoes Dante. Its last line identifies this song, too, as a widow, and, in addition, a complex but subtly insistent sequence of reminiscences are taken from the model *tornada* to be inscribed in the copy: "mia canzone" becomes "canzon mia"; "piangendo" becomes "pianto"; a happy/sad rhyme opposition is reworked in "letizia/tristizia," "allegra/negra"; the verb "star" is repeated in "vatten disconsolata a star con elle," "non fa per te di star fra gente allegra"; and the syllables "sconsolata" fill precisely the same metrical space in the same privileged, most widowed, final line, "vatten disconsolata a star con elle," "vedova sconsolata in veste negra." This identification of echoes is no revelation. Indeed, generations of readers have supported the perceivable presence of Dante's subtext in Pe-

trarch's text. Commentators and critics alike call upon us to recognize the Dante in the Petrarch; they take as a given the kinship
of these two widows.[3] The difficulty remains, however, in seeing
the how and the why of it; in defining how the perspective of the
Vita nuova modifies our view of the *Rime sparse*; in understanding
why Petrarch establishes this form of dialogue with Dante.

I would suggest that Petrarch practices here, and by extension
throughout his entire volume, what Claude-Gilbert Dubois has
usefully labeled "imitation différentielle": that is, a form of imitation that inscribes a subtext within a surface text in such oblique
but recognizable ways that it insists simultaneously upon sameness
and difference, upon continuity and discontinuity.[4] Dubois defines
this relationship in ways reminiscent of Harold Bloom—in terms
of a conflict between father and son.[5] Repetition is, at its deepest
level, allied in this interpretation with subversion; and subversion
is an agent of outdoing and overcoming. Petrarch himself, we
recall, proposed an imitative mode that conforms precisely to this
model—without, of course, its post-Freudian gloss. He had urged
the imitation of the classics in an indirect but nonetheless perceivable manner, so that to the reader's eye the imitating text
would resemble the imitated text as a son does his father, "sed
filii ad patrem."[6] In these two parallel *canzoni*—the two *canzoni*
following the death of first Beatrice and then Laura—we can read
the dynamics of such a father/son exchange. It is, moreover, the
metaphor "song is widow" that insists that we acknowledge that
relationship. I will begin, then, by interrogating the metaphor
itself before turning to the paired *tornade*.

Dante introduces the image of the widow in chapter 28,
through a Latin citation that breaks the flow of the *Vita nuova*.
His fiction relates that, having rejected the sonnet form as falling
short of the requirements of his "materia," he is in the process of
writing a *canzone* on the miraculous power Beatrice operates
within him. But the act of writing is interrupted, and interruption
ironically transforms, through abrupt truncation, the would-be
canzone back into a perfectly crafted sonnet. That text is significantly the most "widowed" of the entire volume, for there the
tripartite structure—narration, poem, explication—collapses for

the first and, in an absolute sense, the only time. In the face of an originary, unexpected widowing, the mode of explication applying to every other poetic text in the volume disappears. There is, moreover, no immediate explanation for this striking violation of the framing pattern; we read only "Quomodo sedet sola civitas plena populo / Facta est quasi vidua domina gentium." [How lonely she is now the once crowded city. Widowed is she who was a mistress over nations.] The interrupting citation, notably about widowing, is the opening of the first chapter—thus, *the* opening—of the Lamentations of Jeremiah.

In his works, Dante cites the Lamentations only four times. Three are found in the *Vita nuova,* and the fourth opens his Latin epistle to the Italian cardinals. The first citation in the *Vita nuova* (Chapter 7: "O vos omnes qui transitis per viam," from Lamentations 1.12) appears in Dante's explication of a sonnet he had written in an attempt to seem to be lamenting the absence of the first screen lady from the "sopradetta città." It thus follows the narration about her departure and immediately precedes the narration of another departure, the death of "a young and very beautiful lady who was known in the aforementioned city for her exceeding charm" (*VN* 8: "una donna giovane e di gentile aspetto molto, la quale fue assai graziosa in questa sopra detta cittade"). Both of these events—as the discerning reader, Dante insists through his asides, will know—prefigure the impending death/departure of Beatrice and are so marked by, among other signals, the proleptic citation from the first chapter of Lamentations. All three remaining quotations from Lamentations are of those first lines—again Lamentations 1.1—that, we later discover, announce the death of Beatrice; indeed all three seem, at some level, to refer to one another. The first is that intrusive opening to Chapter 28 which is used to commemorate the lamentable event of June 8, 1290. The second appears two chapters later when the narrator tells us:

After she had departed from this world, the aforementioned city was left as if a widow, stripped of all dignity, and I, still weeping in this barren city, wrote to the princes of the earth describing its condition, taking [*piglando*] my opening words from the prophet Jeremiah where he says: "Quomodo sedet sola civitas." And I mention this quotation now so that everyone will understand why I cited these words earlier: it was to serve as a heading [*come entrata*] for the new material [*la nuova materia*] that follows. (*VN* 30.1)

The "new material," moreover, for which that citation serves as heading ("come entrata") is the "morte nuova" of the "vita nuova": it is the break that redefines a relationship to Beatrice in terms that will persist to the conclusion of the *Commedia*. The speaker then goes on to excuse himself for truncating the citation itself by pointing out that it is in Latin and that he has, of course, promised to write the *Vita nuova* in the newer vernacular.

The third citation from Lamentations is indeed the "entrata" to a Latin letter, Dante's eighth epistle addressed to the Italian cardinals, and this coincidence of the openings of two letters (one described within the fiction of the *Vita nuova* and one extant) each addressed to men in power and each beginning with Lamentations 1.1 is indeed so striking that it has led at least one critic—performing a stunning chronological leap of about twenty years—to equate the two. In Epistle VIII—an epistle, incidentally, known to Petrarch—Dante speaks to those Italians among the cardinals assembled after the death of Clement V at Carpentras. He seeks to provoke a return of the papal see to Rome and therefore extends the tradition figuring the church as the widow of Christ to encompass the widowing of a now twice-widowed Rome (empire and church) through the departure of Christ's vicar on earth. Thus the contexts—*Vita nuova* and "Epistle VIII"—in which Dante cites Lamentations 1.1 relate Florence without Beatrice to Rome without Christ—yet additional witness, as if we needed it, to the Christological marking of the Beatrice experience. Both cities, moreover, point through Jeremiah to a destroyed Jerusalem, to a city capable only in retrospect of acknowledging and lamenting that it was so sinful and corrupt as to have provoked a leveling judgment in the form of a widowing.

It is, in addition, striking that Dante cites only Lamentations 1. Why, for example, does this specific chapter merit three quotations in the *Vita nuova*? Why is no other chapter cited anywhere in Dante's corpus? Where, in other words, does this chapter stand apart from its context? Sapegno's instinct is, I think, correct when he comments that the scriptural "entrata" to *Vita nuova* 28 gives a "liturgical tone" to the text. Indeed, "Quomodo sedet sola civitas" provides more than a liturgical tone; it constitutes a liturgical reference. Chapter 1 Lamentations is the primary lesson read at Matins on Maundy or Holy Thursday; Chapter 2 is read at Matins on Good Friday; and Chapters 3, 4, and 5 on Holy Saturday. Now Beatrice, Dante tells us, died on the evening of June 8, 1290, which, if I calculate correctly, was a Thursday evening. He goes on, of course, to argue that, "secondo l'usanza d'Arabia," that evening was in fact the first hour ("la prima ora," sunset starts a new day) of the ninth day of the month. Hence, what seems to be an end, by Dante's calendrical manipulation, is transformed into a beginning. Likewise, what seems to be the end of the *Vita nuova* will announce the beginning of another text, one that will "say of Beatrice that which has never been said of any other woman," that is, the *Commedia*. *Inferno* 1 continues the Beatrice experience where we leave it in the *Vita nuova*: her death, linked through Jeremiah's widow verse specifically to Maundy Thursday night. This event will in turn lead to the Good Friday of the three beasts, the encounter with Virgil, and the descent into Dis, yet another "città dolente"[7] (*Inf.* 1); for widowed Florence in "Deh peregrini" (*VN* 40.5) proleptically assumes even that label. Lamentations 1.1 thus literally works "come entrata," be it to the Passion and Resurrection, to the re-enacted passion and resurrection that is the liturgy, or to the further re-enactment that is the *Commedia*.

The death of Laura is, of course, also figured in terms of Holy Week experience—specifically, Good Friday experience. Laura died, Petrarch tells us, on April 6, 1348—twenty-one years to the day (indeed, to the hour—"eadem hora prima," the same first hour [remember the "prima ora" of Dante's revised calendar]) from the morning on which the poet initially saw her at the church of St. Clare in Avignon. "Her chaste and most beautiful body," we read inscribed in Petrarch's copy of Virgil, "was placed in the church of the Franciscans on the very day of her death at

Vespers."⁸ Once Beatrice is dead, it should be noted, the *Vita nuova* makes no reference to her body. Dante's evening turned morning here reverberates into a morning turned evening. Laura's death, then, is an event commemorating Petrarch's experience of her, an anniversary of the moment of his *innamoramento*—an event in and of itself cast and then recast (as Thomas Roche, Robert Durling, and Bortolo Martinelli have most recently shown) in Good Friday terms.⁹ In *Rime sparse* 3, April 6, 1327 (the first encounter), had been defined as "the day when the sun's rays turned pale with grief for his maker" (v. 1); on the eleventh anniversary of that event (April 6, 1338) the speaker hoped to lead his wandering thoughts back to a better place, to "remind them that today you [padre del ciel] were on the cross" (*RS* 62.14); and on April 6, 1348—as the very *canzone* here in question testifies—"in un punto n'è scurato il sole" ["in the same instant the sun is darkened for us both" (*RS* 268.17)]. (In Dante's vision poem in *VN* 23, the sun darkened and there was an earthquake.) It would seem that none of these April sixths was indeed a Good Friday any more than June 8 could possibly have been a Maundy Thursday.¹⁰ What is important here, however, is not how historically or biographically exact the poets were in assigning a date to the ladies' deaths, but rather how they chose to figure that date in terms of their own literary imperatives. If Dante uses Jeremiah's "widowed city" to signal a progress, an *entrata* into the *nuova materia* "in morte" that corresponds, in some way, to the *entrata* into Maundy Thursday—and thus into the sacred *triduum* of Thursday, Friday, and Saturday—signaled by the lesson at Matins, can Petrarch then imitate Dante's concept of "widowed words" developed from Jeremiah to signal a radically different, though marked as identical, experience?

Let us return to the conclusions of the two parallel *canzoni* and examine two categories of repetition: (1) the informing metaphor of widowing; and (2) the related lexicon it generates.

1. vedova/vedova: Dante's prospective characterization of his song as widow ("And in order that this canzone may seem all the more a widow [più vedova] after it has come to its end, I shall divide it before I write it . . ."),

and Petrarch's retrospective last-line labeling of his song as "vedova."

2. disconsolata/sconsolata
3. star/star
4. piangendo/pianto
5. mia canzone/canzon mia
6. tristizia, letizia/allegra, negra

Here is the *tornada* from Dante's *canzone* in *Vita Nuova* 31.71:

> Pietosa mia canzone, or va' piangendo
> e ritruova le donne e le donzelle
> a cui le tue sorelle
> erano usate di portar letizia;
> e tu, che se' figliuola di tristizia,
> vatten disconsolata a star con elle.

The *tornada* from *Rime sparse* 268 is as follows:

> Fuggi 'l sereno e 'l verde,
> Non t'appressare ove sia riso o canto,
> Canzon mia, no, ma pianto:
> Non fa per te di star fra gente allegra,
> Vedova, sconsolata, in veste negra.
>
> (vv. 78–82)

This is, it should be noted, the last of three versions of Petrarch's *tornada*, and I would like briefly to work my way back through the two others since they reveal an evolution in Petrarch's echoing of Dante and thus illuminate the meaning of the *tornada* that stands as definitive.[11] The first version bears virtually no resemblance to the final version:

> S'amor vivo è nel mondo
> E ne l'amicho mio al qual tu vai,
> Canzon, tu 'l troverai
> Mezzo dentro in Fiorenza e mezzo fori;
> Altri non è che intenda i miei dolori.

If love is alive in the world and in my friend to whom you are going, Song, you will find him half within Florence and half without; no one else understands my sorrows.

This version contains none of the six reminiscences at issue here—a fact significant in and of itself—but it does still point to the *Vita nuova*. First, it names Dante's unnamed, widowed "sopradetta città," a gesture not repeated elsewhere in the *Rime sparse* except, of course, in that extraordinary first stanza of 166:

> S'i' fussi stato fermo a la spelunca
> là dove Apollo diventò profeta
> Fiorenza avria forse oggi il suo poeta,
> non pur Verona et Mantoa et Arunca.
>
> (vv. 1–4)

If I had stayed in the cave where Apollo became a prophet, Florence would perhaps have her poet today, not just Verona and Mantua and Arunca.

Dante had, of course, opened the canticle in which he names himself *poeta* with his invocation to Apollo.[12] But even more telling, perhaps, is the original *tornada*'s last line—"Altri non è che 'ntenda i miei dolori"—which both echoes and opposes the first line of the first poem after Dante's widowed *canzone*—"Venite a intender i sospiri miei" (*VN* 32.5). Petrarch posits no possible audience but the one friend; Dante's sonnet, written at the instigation of his second friend (the whole volume, he tells us in Chapter 30 goes to his first, Guido Cavalcante), calls upon the community of Love's faithful servants to listen to him.

When we turn to the second revision, we find a version strikingly similar to the final one.

> Bel fonte e fronda verde fuggi,
> e l'aere seren, che *l'aura* sgombra
> Cerca torbido rio, ramo senz' ombra
> Pensa di non uscir tra gente allegra
> Canzon mia lagrimosa in veste negra. [italics mine]

Flee from beautiful springs and green branches and the limpid air that the *breeze* clears; search out murky streams, branches without shade; be careful not to go among happy people, my tearful song in black garments.

Of the six Dante echoes listed above, only two are present here, and they are indeed the two I would qualify as least compelling (the paired rhyme scheme, "allegra /negra" and the "canzon mia/ mia canzone"). It seems, then, that the final *perfezionamento* of the *tornada* entailed a studied, systematic incorporation of Dante's parallel text; the literal, conscious putting on of Dante's widow's weeds. In Petrarch's final recasting of these five lines, he makes virtually no modification in their meaning; and yet, it is here that he adds the repeated verb "star," that he permits the pair "pianto/piangendo," that he places the syllables "sconsolata" on the same beats of the same line as Dante had, and that he writes the unmistakable "widow" into the text. And it is indeed most intriguing that this writing in of Dante is accomplished by a writing out of Laura; for in the final full stanza of *Rime sparse* 268, Love, ostensibly evoking the wishes of the now lost lady, calls upon Petrarch's speaker to "make bright his voice with her name, if her eyes were ever sweet or dear to him" ["anzi la voce al suo nome rischiari, / se gli occhi suoi ti fur dolci nè cari," (vv. 76–77)]. That mission is accomplished only once in this *canzone*, as a logical response to love's command in the poem's only remaining lines, those of the *tornada* (see my italics above). And yet, Laura's name appears only in the penultimate version. Simply put, Dante is highlighted at the expense of erasing the ostensible object of desire; the obsession with Laura clearly yields to an obsession with *lauro*, with the status of the laureate *poeta*.

This penultimate version, in addition, provides a revealing gloss on the first line of the perfected *tornada*—"Fuggi 'l sereno e 'l verde." The sense of this line filled three lines in the previous version: "Bel fonte e fronda verde fuggi / e l'aere seren che l'aura sgombra; / Cerca torbido rio, ramo senz' ombra." The verb "fuggi," of course, remains; but its oppositive, "cerca" disappears. The final song is told what to flee, but no indication is given as to where it is to go. And second, the flight from " 'l verde" is explained through opposition of " 'l verde" to the song's appropriate space, the "ramo senz' ombra"—a branch without a shade, that is, without leaves. Once more then, we return to Good Friday— to the day of contemplation of the leafless, desolate tree of the cross. Leafless trees, moreover, at least within the Latin tradition, are described as "vedove."[13] Indeed, the imperative "fuggi" ultimately controls Petrarch's *tornada*: he tells his song to flee; not to approach ("non t'appressare") and not to stay among (happy) people ("non fa per te di star fra gente allegra"). Petrarch's commands to his song thus stand in specific contrast to Dante's. Dante too follows convention by telling the song to go ("or va piangendo"), but it is to find the ladies who were made happy by his previous songs ("e ritruova le donne e le donzelle") and to stay with them ("vatten disconsolata a star con elle"). Even Petrarch's corresponding verb "cerca," present in the penultimate version, takes as its object not songs or ladies but rather brackish streams and leafless branches.

Petrarch's widow is ultimately a widow in isolation; Dante's, by contrast, is to be inscribed in a community of mourning, in a city that laments. Indeed, at one point Petrarch addresses, albeit briefly, the "donne"—the addressees of Dante's whole song—who had admired the beauty of Laura, if only to ask them to weep for him. Here he tellingly echoes Dante once more. Yet where Dante's text evoked a lady who had left behind the other ladies ("voi, donne, ha lassate"), Petrarch's tells of a lady who left only her poet ("m'a lassato"). This juxtaposition of the contextualized and the isolated carries, I think, broad implications. Dante's "widowed words" are the products of a process set in motion by the death of Beatrice, a process that mirrors the Holy Week movement from death to resurrection, a process that will reach its logical culmination in the *Commedia*. Christ said to his community on Maundy Thursday evening: "Truly, truly, I say to you, you will weep and lament, but the world will rejoice; you will be sorrowful, but your sorrow will turn to joy" (John 16:20). Mourning here is mitigated by the promise of salvation; the immediate audience to that assurance may or may not fully accept or believe it at that moment, but its signs are none the less immanent. Petrarch's "widowed words," on the contrary, situate us in precisely that same space of desperate isolation, suffering, and doubt in which we have been situated since the moment of the *innamoramento*. One need only compare the desolate Good Friday figures of *Rime sparse* 3 with those of *Rime sparse* 268 to appreciate how "in vita" and "in morte" the speaker's experience of his beloved resists change.

Beatrice, we are assured, smiles in heaven at the "true" bliss she will bring to the pilgrim; Laura, the God of Love tells us in that last full stanza of 268, smiles for other reasons:

> è viva colei ch'altrui par morta
> et di sue belle spoglie
> seco sorride et sol di te sospira,
> et sua fama, che spira
> in molte parti ancor per la tua lingua,
> prega che non estingua,
> anzi la voce al suo nome rischiari.

(vv. 70–76)

She is alive who seems dead, and she smiles to herself at her beautiful remains (her body) and sighs only for you; and she begs you not to extinguish her fame, which sounds in many places still by your tongue, but rather to make bright your voice with her name.

Far better, says a Laura splendidly narcissistic even in death, that Petrarch remain earthbound to compose still more exquisite, widowed words. And far more telling when that very same Petrarch systematically writes out her putatively inspired name in order to write in the widowed words of an authoritative poetic master, the words of Dante. In so doing, he articulates the ambivalence of distanced sameness, the self-questioning imposed by experience that does and does not conform to its model. By consciously putting on figurative ornaments so obviously not his own at this most dramatic of narrative moments, by assuming widow's weeds (the only visible mark of widowhood) proper not to him but to his predecessor, Petrarch recasts what seems to be experience as re-enactment, what seems to be expression as repetition.

Marina Scordilis Brownlee

The Counterfeit Muse
Ovid, Boccaccio, Juan de Flores

I

In a characteristically cryptic paradox, Borges remarks that "every writer creates his own precursors."[1] In other words, inter-textuality is inherently counterfeit in that it always involves a two-stage procedure: production of the new text by reinterpretation of the old.

This generative function of the subtext has been profitably recognized in *Decameron* studies: Boccaccio is understood to be recasting pre-existing narratives for new literary as well as meta-literary purposes. This all-important interplay of semantic and syntactic levels—so central to recent advances in *Decameron* criticism[2]—must still be explored in an equally experimental and hermeneutically significant text in the development of Boccaccio's language theory—namely, the *Elegia di madonna Fiammetta*.

In terms of its critical reception, the *Elegia* (dating from 1343–1344), tends to be evoked in two contexts. First, the work is rightly singled out as a notable departure—both formal and se-mantic—from Boccaccio's earlier writings, works in which Fiam-metta served as his muse—the beloved for whom he wrote, whose love he cultivated: the *Filocolo* (1336–1338?), the *Rime* (ca. 1340–1375), the *Teseida* (1339–1341), the *Comedia delle ninfe fiorentine* (1341–1342), and the *Amorosa visione* (1343).[3] In the *Elegia*, the tables are reversed—the lady is rejected. As Thomas Bergin puts it, we can only marvel at the gulf that separates the character of the work from the nature and style of its immediate predecessors in the Boccaccian canon. We have here no allegorical mosaic in Dantean *terza rima*, no seductive nymphs whose rosy flesh and tempting limbs are draped in vestments of ethical symbolism; here is no romanticized would-be classical epic. Instead the scene is contemporary society, calling for our comprehension and compassion, needing no allegorical interpretation."[4]

This assessment is misleading, however; that is, although Boccaccio has left behind the allegorical third-person narrative for the mimetic first-person discourse of a distraught medieval woman, her discourse is, in fact, overwhelmingly mythological—both in its subtextual evocations and in its equally mythological, high-flown rhetorical style. In fact, it is precisely the protrusiveness of myth—its status in the *Elegia*—that has perennially bothered critics, leading them to exaggerate the importance of the text's first-person psychological discourse to the unwarranted exclusion of the mythological discourse. Indeed, the *Elegia* competes in the annals of literary history with the *Vita Nuova*, the *Jehan de Saintré*, and the *Quijote* for recognition as the first modern psychological novel. In addition to echoing the long-standing identification of the *Elegia* as the first modern psychological novel, Vittore Branca further specifies its elegiac classification (because of its subject matter) as deriving from the definition of elegy found in Dante's *De vulgari eloquentia*: "The title itself is Dantean: 'per elegiam stilum intelligimus miserorum'" [elegy is to be understood as having the style of the miserable] (Book 2, Chapter iv, Part 6).[5] Elegy is thus a sad tale about unhappy people.[6] The *Elegia* certainly conforms to this thematic distinction; however, Dante also defines the elegy in terms of diction, and he does so as follows: "si autem elegiace, solum humile oportet nos sumere" (2, iv, 6) [if (the subject is) suitable for the elegiac style, then we should employ only the low (i.e., humble) vernacular]. *Pace* Branca, the style of Boccaccio's *Elegia* is anything but humble.

Robert Hollander voices skepticism concerning Branca's interpretation of the *Elegia* vis-à-vis the *De vulgari* when he remarks that "it seems difficult to believe that [Boccaccio] hoped that his readers would find his sad lady a morally positive creature. Whatever the strength of his desire to create an elegy, to exhibit his talents in still another genre, it seems foolish not to expect him to have been aware of the irrational quality of his heroine's conduct."[7]

In accord with Hollander's thinking and as a logical extension of Boccaccio's pseudo-autobiographical framework, I would argue that it is only the deluded Fiammetta herself who seriously interprets her text as elegy.

It is precisely the disparity between the high-flown (mythological) rhetoric of the text and its novelistic psychological probing of Fiammetta's inner world that perplexes modern readers. Invariably, the positive assessment of the *Elegia's* novelistic dimension is countered by a denigration of the mythological matter that obsesses its eponymous heroine, because the latter seems strangely incongruous in a novel. Unfortunately it tends to be treated evaluatively—as "prolix" and "stilted"—rather than appraised for its poetic function.[8]

As a consequence of the various formal features it exhibits, a critical consensus exists concerning the *Elegia's* initial inspiration in Ovid's *Heroides*. Both texts are pseudo-autobiographies of females written by men, and both contain narrators who are elegiacally love-lorn females. In the case of the Ovidian verse epistles, the legendary women each address themselves to their respective absent lover; whereas Fiammetta's inscribed readers are, significantly, the anonymous "donne innamorate" [enamoured ladies]. Briefly stated, the *Elegia* is considered to be a vast *amplificatio* of the *heroid* genre—a microscopically detailed anatomy of love.[9] Finally, it is recognized that Boccaccio copies into his text lengthy passages from Ovid's epistolary elegies. Despite these very tangible features shared by Ovid and Boccaccio on the formal level, the semantic level—the gallery of Greek and Trojan myths that the *Heroides* supplies to Fiammetta—tends to be systematically minimized.

It is not simply the desire to interpret the *Elegia* as a novel that makes readers reluctant to valorize the integral function of myth to the medieval text, for Boccaccio himself has contributed to this distortion by explicitly stating in his Prologue that we will not find recounted in the *Elegia* "Greek fables embellished with falsehoods" and "Trojan battlefields befouled with blood."[10] It is, however, precisely such remote fables which pervade his text. The distance separating word and deed, what is said from what is done, could not be more blatant. We are meant, I submit, to view this prefatory statement as profoundly paradoxical—a trap for the unsuspecting *literal* reader, as we realize very early in the work when Venus (having just produced a lengthy catalogue of Ovidian tales) remarks to Fiammetta: "Ma perché ci fatichiamo noi in tante parole" (962) [But wherefore do we trouble ourselves with recital of so many examples]?[11]

Clearly, Boccaccio is calling our attention to the unreliability of his initial claim, doing here what he does on so many pages in his *opere*; that is, explicitly enunciating one thing on the semantic level only thereafter blatantly to contradict it on the syntactic level, thereby exposing one of the mechanisms of deception inherent in language. Witness the opening sentence of Day 1 of the *Decameron* where Boccaccio explicitly affirms "the universally compassionate nature of women,"[12] only to undermine thereafter the authority of this judgment in actions and discourses carried out by a myriad of uncompassionate females who populate his encyclopedic text. In so doing, Boccaccio dramatizes the epistemological fissure between enunciation and reference, *signans* and *signatum*, that consumed the attention of philosophers, theologians, and poets in the late Middle Ages.

With this epistemological dichotomy in mind, let us now turn to a consideration of the semantic and syntactic dimensions of the *Elegia* and its Ovidian subtext to arrive at a clearer understanding of the status of myth.

II

Myths—in Ovid and in general—are universal structures: "Myths have a . . . collective existence [, they] unfold their own 'concrete logic' with supreme disregard for the vagaries of individual thought, and reduce any particular consciousness to a mere function of themselves."[13]

The text of the *Heroides* in fact dramatizes this adversarial relationship between the individual and the universal. What we find is a series of individual authors each voicing her own subjective interpretation of the myth to which she pertains. These individualized, hermetic portraits by legendary women of their subjective states each correspond to one exclusive interpretation of one set of existential circumstances.[14] Thus we see Penelope discoursing on her unique form of suffering to Ulysses, as does Phaedra to Hippolytus and Medea to Jason.

By their respective letters we see, first of all, a side of these legendary lovers that differs—in an important sense—from their normal mythical associations. That is, they each initially attained mythic stature for their notable actions: Penelope for resisting would-be suitors during Ulysses' twenty-year absence, Phaedra for her incest, and Medea for her sorcery and infanticide. Here, rather than narrating the *external actions* that made them famous (or infamous), we see them through their *interior monologues*—a totally different dimension of their psychological profiles, viewed for the first time as individual characters and not as mythic abstractions.

In his study of the reading process as an act of construction for the reader, Todorov remarks that "two types of causal construction seem most frequent as Aristotle [has] already noted: [an] event is perceived as the consequence (and/or the cause) either [1] of a character trait or [2] of an impersonal or universal law."[15] Aware of this distinction, Ovid offers us individual psychologies rather than psychological paradigms—the latter being the usual identification of these heroines as universal archetypes: Penelope as an exemplum of uxorial fidelity, Phaedra of incest, and Medea of treachery.

The first type of causal construction—an event perceived as the consequence of a unique character trait—pertains in the Ovidian text to the mode of *signification* as Todorov defines it— direct evocation through speech: "Signified facts are *understood*: all we need is knowledge of the language in which the text is written" (73).

Ovid thus offers us a new dimension of these exemplary women through their direct discourse to their absent lovers, their silent inscribed readers. Moreover, the profound implications of this new discursive framework cannot be overemphasized. The use of direct discourse is highly significant here since it is the only way to eliminate the differences between narrative discourse and the world that it evokes. In this way, each of the narrators has total control over her discourse—a hermeneutic circumstance differing radically from her third-person presentation in the *Metamorphoses* or the *Odyssey* and the resultant spectrum of interpretations to which they are subject.[16]

Of equal importance are the serious implications that Ovid's discursive mode has for the exemplary abstractions that these heroines traditionally embody. As John D. Lyons observes in his important work on theories of exemplarity: "Exemplary narrative [tends to] deny individual, internal values in favor of external, institutional ones."[17] It is, as we shall see, this tension between uniqueness and exemplarity from which Ovid generates the *Heroides*, and from which Fiammetta generates her *Elegia*.

Ovid, in fact, does even more in the *Heroides* than offer an innovative elegy because of its first-person structure; for he juxtaposes the *signified* evocation at the level of each individual letter-writer with the (radically different) *symbolized* evocation that confronts the reader. That is, these unique first-person psychological character studies are each juxtaposed with their third-person (impersonal) mythic (and hence exemplary) associations as a consequence of the *dispositio* of the text. Quoting Todorov again, "*Symbolized* facts are [indirectly] interpreted, [extrapolated by the reader from the text]; and interpretations vary from one subject to another" (73).

Aware of this intersubjective disparity, Ovid structures his text so as to dramatize the epistemological gulf separating the symbolized and signified levels of interpretation, the differences between "objective" event and "subjective" discourse. More precisely, he does so by treating the same event or myth from a number of perspectives. The Trojan matter, for example, is viewed from at least six different perspectives. In so doing, Ovid, in effect, transposes myth into a different dimension. As Howard Jacobsen insightfully observes, "By treating many events or myths more than once in the course of the *Heroides*, Ovid compels us to see that a myth or an event must be understood not as an absolute entity in itself but as the sum of the individual perspectives that bear upon it."[18]

This type of polysemy generated by Ovid in the *Heroides* is, moreover, an inherent function of the epistolary form, as Florence Verducci observes:

> Epistolary fiction imposes upon the reader a kind of vigilant scrutiny very different from the kind of attention exacted by the monologue or soliloquy in the theater: the reader can never be certain whether the authoress is telling the truth as it was, or the truth as she saw it or remembers it, or the truth as she has adjusted it to the rhetorical motive forced upon her by her circumstances. Indeed, sometimes the epistolary revelation will conceal more than it reveals and raise more questions than it answers.[19]

To take one example of this consistently perspectival procedure, let us consider the case of Medea and Hypsipyle (two of Fiammetta's favorite analogues to her own situation), as analyzed by Jacobsen:

> Both Medea and Hypsipyle recount Jason's labors at length. Medea's main interest is in representing herself as a frightened and concerned girl (12.95–104). Thus she describes the task in rather terrifying terms, shows herself an awestruck and scared spectator, and plays down her role in the execution of the great feats. What a difference is Hypsipyle's version of the same events (6.9–14, 32–37)! This is all matter of fact narrative. The emotion, awe, fear, dead colors with which Medea paints the scene are all gone. Moreover, the deeds seem to do themselves; at the least Jason here has no role at all. Hypsipyle, of course, knows how everything has turned out and is unwilling to give Jason any credit. But Medea, too, when her feelings of bitterness and anger become uppermost, sees the feats in the same light: she, not Jason, has accomplished them (109–10, and esp. 165–74). Hypispyle imagines that Medea's powers over animals extend to men also; Medea learns they do not. (355)

As a result, the world of myth in the *Heroides* sheds its identity as universal psychological law, no longer functioning as "reality or a symbolic reflection of reality, but to a large degree as projections or extensions of individual minds" (349).

We thus see that it is essential that these Ovidian epistles be

read in their semantic individuality as well as their syntactic col-
lectivity. Only then can we appreciate Ovid's manipulation of
mythic paradigms to underscore the crucial distinction between
signified and symbolized communication.

It is precisely this Ovidian distinction—arrived at through the
mediation of myth—that, I maintain, is central to interpretation
in Boccaccio's *Elegia*. It is not simply formal affinities which these
two texts share, but—more importantly—hermeneutic assumptions based on a similar perception of the deceptive status of
language per se. The *Elegia* both continues and remotivates Ovid's
meta-linguistic distinction, collapsing the Ovidian character/
reader dichotomy that inhabits two different epistemological
spheres—fusing them into the figure of Fiammetta herself.

III

Structurally speaking, Boccaccio's elegy is divided into nine
chapters, including a prologue. Fiammetta and Panfilo (known
only by these pseudonyms, invented by the couple to protect their
reputations [40]), fall in love and consummate their passion all
in Chapter 1. He abandons her in Chapter 2 and never returns,
the last seven chapters being devoted to Fiammetta's solipsistic
reveries ranging from hope of amorous delectation to suicidal despair. It is important to note, however, that Fiammetta was initially hesitant to consummate her adulterous love, until Venus
appears to her—a commonplace device in medieval erotic literature. What is unanticipated, however, is the argument advanced
by Venus to convince Fiammetta to yield to Panfilo—one that
immediately reflects Fiammetta's intimate identification of herself
with the mythological deities: "Che mattamente fuggi? Se tanti
iddii . . . da questo son vinti, tu d'essere vinta da lui ti ver-
gognerai?" (963) [What dost thou fly? If so many divine Gods
. . . have been conquered by (the God of Love), wilt thou then
think it a shame to be overcome? (38)] In an equally atypical
mode of venereal argumentation (because of its domestic frame
of reference), Venus adds, "Essi medesimi mariti amano le piú
volte avendo moglie: riguarda Giasone, Teseo, il forte Ettore e

Ulisse" (963) [Husbands themselves for the most part love other women, when they have wives of their own, as Jason, for example, Hercules and wise Ulysses (39)].

Both the discourse of Venus here and that of Fiammetta throughout the work are, moreover, legalistic—based explicitly on laws, old and new. Again, if we consider the hermeneutic assumptions of myth, we recall that myth too is, at its core, legalistic to the degree that it exemplifies universal laws of cognition, behavior, and so on.

The "old law" in this case refers to the first age of the world, the Golden Age as expressed in the mode of the *beatus ille*. Fiammetta invokes this familiar "good old days" *topos* as follows:

Oh, felice colui il quale innocente dimora nella solitaria villa, usando l'aperto cielo! . . . Ohimè! niuna è piú libera né senza vizio o migliore che questa, la quale li primi usarono e che colui ancora oggi usa, il quale, abandonate le città, abita nelle selve. Oh felice il mondo, se Giove mai non avesse cacciato Saturno, e ancora l'età aurea durasse sotto caste leggi! Però che tutti alli primi simili viveremmo. (1022, 1023–24)

Oh, how happy is [he] who dwelleth in the solitary village, enjoying only the open air! . . . There is no life [alas] more free, nor more devoid of vice, or better than this: the which our first fathers enjoyed, and with which also he is this day of all others best contented who, abandoning the opulent and vicious Cities inhabiteth the private and peaceable woods. Oh, what a world had it been if Jupiter had never driven Saturn away, and if the Golden Age had continued still under a chaste law, because we might all live like to our primitive parents of the first world (202).

By way of contrast with the putatively old law of the mythological timeframe, Fiammetta introduces the so-called "new laws"—which refer to her unreciprocated love for Panfilo and to her married state in the context of the God of Love, that is, to her self-perceived uniqueness.

In point of fact, both the old laws as well as the new pose serious problems for Fiammetta. While she would like to project the myth of the Golden Age that she alludes to above, the examples of lovers that she offers (drawn almost exclusively from the *Heroides* and *Metamorphoses*) all attest to the untenability—hence fallaciousness—of the old law even for the deities.

It is highly significant that Fiammetta shows herself to be equally contradictory when she alludes to the "new laws." Her first allusion to them underscores once more her deluded perception of herself as unique. Here it is evoked regarding the violence of her infatuation:

Ohimè! che Amore cosí come ora in me usa crudeltà non udita, cosí nel pigliarmi nuova legge dagli altri diversa gli piacque d'usare! Io ho piú volte udito che negli altri i piaceri sono nel principio levissimi, ma poi, a' pensieri nutricati, aumentando le forze loro, si fanno gravi; ma in me cosí non avvenne, anzi con quella medesima forza m'entrarono nel cuore, che essi vi sono poi dimorati, e dimorano. Amore il primo dí di me ebbe interissima possessione. (955)

Alas that love is not only content to use such a strange, and too severe kind of cruelty towards me, but in subduing me to his might, to prescribe *new laws,* clean variant from others. I have oftentimes heard that love in others at his first entrance is but light, but by nourished thoughts augmenting his force is made greater. But so it fared with me: for he entered into my heart with that same force, wherewith he continued ever afterwards, as one who at the very first assault had most entire and free possession of me (17).

The second usage of the "new law" (975) refers to her unrequited love for Panfilo—that he swore an oath of eternal devotion, yet left her seduced and abandoned.

The third usage that Fiammetta ascribes to the "new law" refers to the law of marriage and her status as adulteress. In one breath (very near the end of the eighth chapter), she reviles herself for her infidelity to her loving (and oblivious) husband (1071), reasoning (quite irrationally) that perhaps because of it she is being morally punished by the pagan God of Love (to whom she has always been faithful). Yet in the next breath she rejects this hypothesis, claiming that she is not, by any means, unique in her transgression of the sacred laws of wedlock:

E in questo io non sono prima, né sarò ultima, né sola, anzi quasi tutte quelle del mondo ho in compagnia, e le leggi contro alle quali io ho commesso, sogliono perdonare alla multitudine. (1071)

As I am not the first that hath committed such a friendly fault, so am I not alone, and shall not be the last, but having almost *all* women in the world my companions in this excusable error, I am not so greatly to be condemned for the same (328–29) (emphasis mine).

Fiametta's problem is thus not an ethical but an existential one. More precisely, she cannot admit two things: first, she cannot admit to having been rejected by Panfilo, and second, she is unwilling to have her liaison become public out of the (very unheroic) impulse of *fear.* Feigning religious devotion for public consumption—as a mask for her true narcissism—she explains:

Io, piú peccatrice che altra, dolente per li miei disonesti amori, però che quelli velo sotto oneste parole, sono reputata santa; ma conoscelo Iddio, che, se senza pericolo essere potesse, io con vera voce di me sgannerei ogni ingannata persona, né celerei la cagione che trista mi tiene; ma non si puote. (1027–28)

Myself a greater sinner than any other, and sorrowful for my dishonest loves, yet couching them under the Veil of honest words *am reputed holy*: but the just Gods know that [if I could *without danger of my honor and good name*] with true reports I would make satisfaction to everyone whom in fictions, speeches and gestures I have deluded (212–23) (emphasis mine).

Fiammetta is incapable, in the last analysis, of *action*—of the symbolized event that accorded legitimacy to the signified utterances of the mythological heroines whom she attempts to emulate.

Moreover, it is no accident that Medea is the role model Fiammetta invokes more frequently, by far, than any other, because she functions as a reflection of Fiammetta's own deep-seated inadequacy in the realm of action. It is important to note here that Medea is recalled not in the context of her primary association— the notoriety that resulted from her bloodthirsty revenge—but rather in the context of amorous affect.

Like other readers of the *Heroides,* Fiammetta discerns a number of interpretations of Medea—five, to be precise. Unlike them, however, Fiammetta's views all reflect her own inability to act. We see her transposing Medea into her own inactive (and amorously tormented) identity. She is first presented as healer (because of her medical prowess in rejuvenating her father-in-law, Aeson, to further her own amorous designs [974]); then as abandoned lover (forsaken by Jason [1045]); as "survivor" (because of her subsequent involvement with Egeus [1045]); as seducer of Jason (from Hypsipyle's point of view [1077]); and finally as masochist ("being no less cruel to herself than malicious against her un-grateful lover," namely Jason [1077]).

Because she is afraid, above all, of compromising her public name (that is, her comfortable social status), she keeps her affair secret—spending virtually all her time cloistered in her bedroom, vacillating between the two extremes of hope and despair. She is cut off from society, effectively unable to convince herself for more than a few moments at a time either of being unique or exemplary. Indeed, at the end of her lengthy elegiac confession, she is as unresolved to action as she was at the beginning. *After* her brief and uncharacteristic suicide attempt (Chapter 5), in which she was easily thwarted, she is the same as *before* it—living out a circular progression from hope to despair and back again. This uncharacteristic act, in fact, results from a moment of frenzied hysteria, immediately before which she argues, first, that she should not kill herself for her husband would be greatly saddened (1048), directly thereafter adding that killing herself would fore-close the possibility of being reunited with Panfilo (1048). Im-mediately following her failed attempt, in an even more contra-dictory manner, she is persuaded that: "It is not virtuous to desire death and be afraid of life!" (1053).

This circularity is, moreover, the progression that characterizes lyric, as Sharon Cameron observes in her study of lyric time: "The contradiction between social and personal time is the lyric's gen-erating impulse, for the lyric both rejects the limitation of social and objective time, those structures that drive hard lines between past, present, and future, and must make use of them."[20] It is also significant in this context that no dates are given in the *Elegia* from which we could calculate either the historical timeframe of the work or even the length of the ex-lovers' separation. It is only by occasional references to the seasons of the year (especially springtime—the lyric season par excellence) that we understand the separation to have lasted at least one year.

Fiammetta is thus no Don Quijote or Emma Bovary—each of whom first embrace and then reject the clarity of the world of books, each of whom came to realize the linear (rather than cyclical) trajectory inherent in the novel.

Commenting on the necessarily linear development of the novel, René Girard explains that it "has to take into account both the journey of the character through the domain of desire and at the end of his distancing from it to establish the epistemological privilege of the subject's claim to hold a discourse which is not a discourse *of* desire, but a discourse *about* desire and about the [disenchanting] truth of desire (emphasis mine)."[21] The teleology of Fiammetta's autobiography is quite different. Considering the misfortunes suffered by the gallery of Ovidian heroines whom she recalls as imperfect analogues to her own situation, Fiammetta concludes as follows at the very end of Chapter 9: "se chi porta invidia è piú misero che colui a cui la porta, io sono di tutti li predetti de' loro accidenti, meno miseri che li miei reputandoli, invidiosa" (1077). [If he that beareth envy is more miserable and more wretched than he to whom he doth bear it, then of all the forenamed persons I am the most miserable and unhappy of women. Because I do greatly emulate and not a little envy their *ordinary accidents* (as opposed to her extraordinary fate), accounting them not so grievous nor so full of such misery as mine are (345).] Her final words continue to echo each of the extremes of hope and despair with which the work began:

Di tacere ormai dilibero, faccendovi manifesto non essere altra comparazione dal mio narrare verissimo a quello che io sento, che sia dal fuoco dipinto a quello che veramente arde. Al quale io prego Iddio, che o per li vostri prieghi, o per li miei, sopra quello salutevole acqua mandi, o con trista morte di me, o con lieta tornata di Panfilo. (1077)

There is no more comparison of my shadowed discourse to those substantial dolours which I feel indeed, than there is of painted fire, to that which doth burn indeed: the which I pray all the Gods that either by your meritorious prayers or else by my earnest and effectual orisons, they would with some liquor of comfort extinguish, or with speedy death quite abolish; or else with the joyful return of my Panfilus assuage and moderate the same (347).

Unlike Don Quijote or Emma, Fiammetta is incapable of the linearity required by the novel—unable to mirror in her symbolized actions the substance of her signified utterances, unable to attain the individuality of a novelistic character or the exemplarity of a mythic archetype.[22]

IV

The instability of the word—the configuration of signified and symbolized phenomena that Boccaccio explores in the *Elegia*—is corroborated in reverse by Juan de Flores in Spain in his explicit continuation of the *Elegia* known as *Grimalte y Gradissa*, which dates from the mid-1480s.[23] (This text is perhaps known more widely as a result of Maurice Scève's translation of it, *La déplourable fin de Flamete* (1535), elements of which also figure—in a fragmented way—in his lyric cycle, *Délie*.)[24] As we shall see, Flores distinguishes his text from Boccaccio's by inverting the focus—that is, by focusing on the implications of *action* (rather than speech) in the enunciation/action binome—thus offering his readers as programmatic a rewriting of the *Elegia*'s meta-literary concerns as Boccaccio does of the *Heroides*.

Not one but two couples are at issue in the Spanish text: Boccaccio's Fiammetta and Panfilo (now Fiometa and Pamfilo) and Grimalte and Gradissa—avid readers of the *Elegia*. Gradissa, determined to give Boccaccio's unresolved text a happy ending, instructs her suitor, Grimalte, to reunite the estranged Italian couple. He actually does so, yet his success is very ephemeral, for no sooner have they been reunited than Fiometa is unconditionally rejected by Pamfilo, at which point she dies—presumably of grief.

This characterological configuration is seen by Joseph Gillet as a prefiguration of Cervantine legerdemain in the relationship of the *Quijote*'s second part to its first: "Boccaccio's characters have stepped outside their novel and outside the control of their author to continue their life in a story by another writer, in fact in another century, and the reader is left with a confusing impression of a timeless world inhabited by age-defying, almost permanent characters."[25]

Carrying the Cervantine analogy a bit further, however, I would advise that we remember the words of Sansón Carrasco at the beginning of Part 2 of the *Quijote*—that "second parts are never any good"[26]—a laconic, ironic (consummately Cervantine) way of alerting the reader to the fact that the imaginary universe constructed by a sequel may differ radically from the original text that it continues.

The *Grimalte* replaces the *Elegia*'s first-person subjective structure with a second-person dialogic structure, thus allowing for a simultaneous multiplicity of interpretations of Fiometa's love affair. In spatial terms, there is a movement out of the solipsistic secrecy of Fiometa's chamber to the public arena of the world at large (from Iberia to Asia). There is a very notable absence of mythological discourse in the Spanish continuation, and Fiometa's obsessive claims to uniqueness are systematically countered by the other characters, who assure her that her situation is, in fact, quite prosaically commonplace. We find the pathological, paralytic inaction of Boccaccio's text replaced by a profusion of action in the Spanish continuation. Finally, the *Elegia*'s lyric openendedness is also remotivated in the *Grimalte*, where it achieves novelistic closure.

Briefly stated, the *Grimalte* picks up the narrative thread left hanging in the *Elegia* by following the possibility for closure that Boccaccio suggested (and rejected) in Chapter 5—that Fiometa disguise herself as a religious pilgrim (a socially acceptable pretext to mask her search for Pamfilo).

Flores pseudo-autobiographically identifies himself as both narrator and character in the figure of Grimalte, who has long and faithfully served Gradissa, despite the fact that she remains indifferent to him. One day Grimalte gives her Boccaccio's *Elegia* as a present (presumably because he identifies his unrequited love-suffering with that of the madonna Fiammetta). After reading the book herself, Gradissa, however, arrives at a substantially different reading, concluding that all men are as untrustworthy and perfidious as Pamfilo in the long run. This attitude is what led Barbara Matulka, more than fifty years ago, to describe Gradissa as a "cruel beauty" and feminist who is intent on "inciting women to rebellion against masculine supremacy and faithlessness" (259).

With no intention of acting in accordance with her discourse, Gradissa tells Grimalte that, if he can find and reconcile Fiometa and Pamfilo, she will marry him. As he openly states, however,

Grimalte interprets Gradissa's request simply as an excuse for get-
ting rid of him.[27]

In spite of his correct reading of the situation, he nonetheless
undertakes the mission as literary go-between.[28] (We thus begin
to see the rift between enunciation and action articulated very
early in Flores's text.)[29] Grimalte miraculously manages to sur-
mount insurmountable odds by encountering first Fiometa (on her
worldwide quest for Pamfilo) and then Pamfilo himself. Yet, they
do not, by any means, live "happily ever after."

Pamfilo explicitly spurns Fiometa for several different reasons:
first, because of her extreme egotism—her persistent and annoy-
ing claim to uniqueness ("siempre quisiste en todas cosas so-
brarme, y mostrar mayor amor, y dezir mayores tus quexas" [you
always wanted to outdo me, to show that your love was greater
and your suffering more intense (20)]);[30]—second, because she
has lost her honor and is, therefore, unworthy of love (21); and
third, because he does not want to tarnish her social reputation,
therefore advising her to return to her husband (35)—a blatant
contradiction of his second argument. To Grimalte he adds still
other justifications for his behavior: (1) that no woman can keep
the attention of a man indefinitely (28); (2) that he left to keep
Fiometa from dishonor (29); and (3) (in etymological fidelity to
his name) that a pleasing man should "spread the wealth," as it
were (30).

Fiometa responds to this unconditional rejection by passively
expiring (we assume, since the precise cause of death is never
clarified). Grimalte buries her with great dignity and ceremony
and, to avenge her death, challenges Pamfilo to a duel. Pamfilo,
however, seeing the effects (for him wholly unanticipated) of his
words on Fiometa, chooses instead to condemn himself to a life
of penance in the desert.[31] Thereupon Grimalte returns to Spain,
where he writes to Gradissa explaining Fiometa's death and Pamfilo's vow of eternal penance. Gradissa is so aggrieved by this news
that she swears never to love (63), distrusting men more than
ever and interpreting Pamfilo's penitential oath as nothing more
than a pretext to conceal his cowardice.

Realizing that Gradissa will never love him, Grimalte decides to join Pamfilo to share his life as a recluse. This is easier said than done, however, for only after a twenty-seven year search does Grimalte finally locate Pamfilo in a remote part of Asia. (It is interesting to note that, as a result of this journey, Grimalte incongruously likens himself to Jason in his quest for the Golden Fleece—which is, in an important sense, analogous to Fiometa's equally incongruous identification of herself with Medea through-out the *Elegia*.)[32] When he finds the now savage and barely rec-ognizable Pamfilo (naked, his skin blackened by the sun, walking on all fours), Grimalte learns that he has, in addition, taken a vow of perpetual silence in deference to the memory of Fiometa. Grimalte tries to engage him in speech, but to no avail. Pamfilo refuses to speak even after Grimalte explains that he has come to emulate him, that he too is a forlorn lover who has come to live out his life in the desert.[33] With a considerable degree of per-plexity, critics have noted the incongruity of Grimalte's claim to resemble Pamfilo, since the two are, in an obvious sense, oppo-sites: Pamfilo rejected his lady, whereas it was Grimalte's lady who rejected him. Flores, however, is focusing here not on superficial narrative detail but on his—and Boccaccio's—fundamental theme, namely, linguistic usage.

It is highly significant to the language theory that Flores de-velops in this text that Pamfilo refuses to respond until Grimalte literally gets on all fours and walks like Pamfilo: "fuyme a lo mas spesso de aquell boscaje . . . y las manos puestas por el suelo en la manera en que aquell andava, siguiendo sus pizadas, tom[e]lo por maestro de mi nuevo oficio" [I entered into the deepest part of the woods . . . and, placing my hands on the ground in em-ulation of the way in which he walked, I chose him as the teacher of my new vocation (69)]. Only after Grimalte has guaranteed the truth-status of his *words* by his *action* does Pamfilo break his silence, accepting him at that point as a fellow penitent. In ad-dition, three nights a week they are both subjected to an infernal vision of Fiometa being tortured by ghastly demons who light up the sky with flames that shoot forth from the two linguistically essential sensory organs—their *ears* and *tongues*. After Fiometa has spent the greater part of the night tormented by these devils, she is carried off by them in a cart (71). Grimalte once more swears eternal devotion to Gradissa, at which point he dies, and the work ends there.

No interpretive consensus exists concerning this hellish apparition of Fiometa. It has been viewed alternatively as punishment for her lust, adultery, or, perhaps, suicide—yet none of these ethical concerns figures centrally in the text. Even more disconcerting is the fact that, as Pamela Waley remarks, "in literature, women shown suffering supernatural torments are usually being punished for cruelty towards their lovers" (*Grimalte y Gradissa*, xxxvii).[34] Surely Fiometa cannot be placed in this category.

I would argue, however, that the incongruity is only an apparent one—consistent, in fact, with the rest of the work in terms of the action/enunciation dichotomy that I have outlined. In her infernal existence, Fiometa is, significantly, the victim of an assault on the *ears* and *tongue*, whereby she is denied the power of speech, as Grimalte explains: "ella commenço a llamar mi nombre con proposito de algo dezirme, [pero] . . . por fuerèa sus palabras revocaron" [She would call out my name with the intention of telling me something, (but) the demons who followed her would drown out her words (71)]. Instead of allowing her to speak, they force her to suffer in *actions* the *words* of malediction that she had so deceptively articulated in the *Elegia* (Chapter 5), for example, against Panfilo: "anzi tra li morti spiriti seguitandoti, con quelle ingiurie che di là s'adoperano m'ingegnerò di noiarti . . . vegghiando, orribile mi vedrai, e ne' sonni spaventevole sovente ti desterò nelle tacite notti" (1041) [Pursuing thee amongst the dead ghosts and fiends of Hell . . . I will continually plague and eternally punish thy damned soul for thy condemned and hateful deed . . . thou shalt see me in a most horrible shape, and in thy fearful sleep oftentimes will I awake and affright thee in the uncomfortable silence of the dark night (248–49)]. We see her—finally—being forced to act in accordance with her speech, something that she was incapable of doing "in real life." The action is, moreover, a logical extension of the "quadrupedic alliance" of Pamfilo and Grimalte, underscoring the need for action to guarantee the truth-status of speech so that symbolized event and signified utterance correspond.

Finally, Flores affects closure in such a way that language theory is corroborated by spatial configuration. We have moved from the (inoperative) heavenly realm of mythological deities down to Earth, as it were, with this quadrupedic moment of communication, ultimately—and very appropriately—to the pit of hell. Flores thus continues and completes Boccaccio's metalinguistic act by definitively punishing the *linguistic transgression* of the counterfeit muse.

III. Gender, Genre, Genealogy

Kevin Brownlee

Structures of Authority in Christine de Pizan's *Ditié de Jehanne d'Arc*

On July 31, 1429, Christine de Pizan completed her final work, the *Ditié de Jehanne d'Arc*. Medieval France's greatest woman writer thus ended her long literary career with a celebration of medieval France's greatest woman hero. It is important for the modern reader to understand that the *Ditié was* a celebration, for the poem was written at the moment of Joan's greatest triumph, as a brief recall of its immediate historical context makes clear. Joan's abrupt appearance on the main political stage of the Hundred Years War was a very recent event. She had first presented herself to the beleaguered Charles VII at Chinon on February 23, 1429, claiming a divinely inspired mission to save the French monarchy. During March and April, she was interrogated at Poitiers by a learnèd committee of theologians who authenticated her claims. On May 8 she raised the siege of Orléans, a spectacular military success with great symbolic as well as strategic value. The French cause was saved from what had appeared to be imminent disaster. A series of triumphant advances followed in the Loire valley and in Champagne, culminating in the surrender of Rheims on July 16. On the following day, Joan annointed and crowned Charles king in Rheims cathedral, thus annulling "the deposition illegally pronounced by the Treaty of Troyes [1420] and [restoring] to the Valois the legitimacy which had been questioned for the past nine years."[1] On the morrow of his coronation, Charles received the submission of Laon, and he and Joan entered Soissons together in triumph on July 23. By July 29, the King and the Maid were at Château-Thierry, with Paris as the final objective of their advance. Success seemed imminent; Charles received fresh capitulations from all sides; Joan appeared to be unstoppable. Her extraordinary accomplishments seemed to be quite literally miraculous: a direct intervention by God in contemporary French history. This, then, was Christine's perspective when she composed her poem; these were the historical givens of her understanding of the phenomenon of Joan of Arc.

The question of authority is central to this understanding, both in historical and in literary terms, and it is this question that I propose to explore in the present essay by means of a close reading of the text of the *Ditié*. I will be focusing on three issues: (1) Christine's authority as speaking subject; (2) Joan's authority as historical actant; and (3) the complex relation between these two figures in terms of authority, identity, and authorization.

Before turning to the *Ditié* itself, however, some preliminary remarks are necessary. Christine de Pizan was the first French literary figure explicitly to incorporate her identity as a woman into her identity as an author.[2] Fundamental problems of authority were necessarily involved here as Christine sought to effect an innovative first-person conflation of the learnèd clerk and the self-conscious feminist. To authorize this radically new kind of poetic voice, Christine established an authoritative "alternative" genealogy for herself, an anterior line of authoritative female ancestors, exemplars of superlative achievement in politics, science, scholarship, literature, and religion. It was in the *Livre de la Cité des Dames* of 1405 that this project of feminist self-authorization was most explicitly and most elaborately undertaken. For our reading of the *Ditié de Jehanne d'Arc*, two aspects of the *Cité* are of fundamental importance. First, the taxonomic hierarchy of female exemplarity that Christine establishes in the *Cité* privileges absolutely the figure of the female Christian martyr. While exemplary female warrior figures are systematically valorized, there is no overlap of the component "warrior" with the component "Christian." The heroism of exemplary Christian women is fundamentally passive. Second, Christine's concept of history in the *Cité* consistently links the glorious past to the living present. As E. Jeffrey Richards has pointed out, this is one of the most striking aspects of Christine's transformative rewriting of Boccaccio's *De*

Mulieribus Claris, the primary model text for the *Cité*.[3] Christine consistently collapses Boccaccio's radical gap between present and past. Within the allegorical plot line of the work, Christine the character repeatedly "complements" the examples of illustrious past women, adduced by Reason, Rectitude, and Justice on the basis of clerkly, bookish authority, with equally valid examples drawn from her own experience of contemporary history. Indeed, the figure of "je, Christine" is largely defined by this first-person experience and the kind of authority that it implies.

With these points in mind, let us turn now to the text of the *Ditié de Jehanne d'Arc*.

The *Ditié* is composed of sixty-one stanzas (huitains), and its overall structure is as follows: The first twelve stanzas constitute a Prologue, which establishes the identity of the first-person speaking subject and the status of her literary enterprise. The main body of the poem (stanzas 13–60) is structured around a series of apostrophes, as Christine addresses, in turn, Charles VII, Joan herself, their loyal French troops, the English enemy, and, finally, the French allies of the English. These direct addresses are punctuated by three narrative passages in which Christine recounts the story of Joan of Arc (past, present, and future), and by a series of "glosses" in which she reveals the significance of Joan's achievements. The relationship among these three discursive modes is dialogic: gloss "completes" narrative; narrative authorizes apostrophe; apostrophe confirms and advances narrative.[4] At the same time, Christine's authoritative identity is progressively elaborated by means of her discursive practice and its relationship to history.

The Prologue begins with the words, "Je, Christine,"[5] and the first five stanzas define this *je* in terms of lyric constructs transposed into a historical time that is both private and public. After a long winter, springtime returns: the "bon temps neuf" (v. 19), the "tresbelle / Saison" (vv. 28–29). The poet's grief turns to joy: from "grant dueil en joie nouvelle" (v. 25); and she is moved to song: "Mais or changeray mon langage / De pleur en chant" (vv. 13–14). The lyric "temps yvernage" (v. 9), however, is the real, historical time that has elapsed since May 1418, when the Bur-

gundians captured Paris, forcing both Christine and Charles VII
to flee. For Christine, these eleven years have been years of exile
in a "walled abbey" ("en abbaye close," v. 2); eleven years of
political disappointment and literary silence. The poet's lyric present is the real, historical year 1429. And the cause of her deeply
personal joy is a political event: the triumphant approach of the
newly crowned Charles VII. This event is what moves her to sing
with the stylized intensity and the experiential authority of a lyric
lover.

Her song, however, will be combined with a narrative "explanation" of this event:

> Mais or vueil raconter comment
> Dieu a tout ce fait de sa grace,
> A qui je pri qu'avisement
> Me doint, que rien je n'y trespasse.
> Raconté soit en toute place.
> Car ce est digne de memoire,
> Et escript, à qui que desplace,
> En mainte cronique et hystoire!
>
> (vv. 49–56)

But now I wish to relate how God, to whom I pray for guidance lest I omit anything,
accomplished all this through His grace. May it be told everywhere, for it is worthy of
being remembered, and may it be written down—no matter whom it may displease—
in many a chronicle and history-book!

Christine's first-person lyric voice, then, will also be that of
the chronicler: she is to be clerkly witness to a sequence of historically factual events that constitute a "miracle" (v. 81). Her
authority derives from the truth of history itself, guaranteed, underwritten, by God. And the miracle is the story of Joan:

> Chose est bien digne de memoire
> Que Dieu, par une vierge tendre,
> Ait adès voulu (chose est voire!)
> Sur France si grant grace estendre.
>
> (vv. 85–88)

It is a fact worthy of remembering that God should now have wished (and this is the
truth!) to bestow such blessings on France, through a young virgin.

Christine begins the body of the *Ditié* with an extended direct
address to Charles VII (stanzas 13–19) in which she calls upon
the king to bear witness to the miracle of Joan. It is important
to note that the king is treated as passive subject and the Maid
as active object:

> Et tu, Charles, roy des François,
> . . . or voiz ton renon
> Hault eslevé par la Pucelle,
> Qui a soubzmis soubz ton penon
> Tes ennemis (chose est nouvelle!)
>
> En peu de temps; que l'on cuidoit
> Que ce feust com chose impossible
> Que ton pays, qui se perdoit,
> Reusses jamais. Or est visible—
> Ment tien . . .
> C'est par la Pucelle sensible,
> Dieu mercy, qui y a ouvré!
>
> (vv. 97, 101–109, 111–12)

And you Charles, King of France . . . now see your honor exalted by the Maid who
has laid low your enemies beneath your standard (and this *is* new!) in a short time;
for it was believed quite impossible that you should ever recover your country which
you were on the point of losing. Now it is manifestly yours . . . And all this has been
brought about by the intelligence of the Maid who, God be thanked, has played her
part in this matter! (emphasis mine)

It is only the authorization conferred upon Charles by Joan that
leads Christine to associate him, somewhat tentatively, with
prophecies of a future imperial destiny for a chosen king of France.
This first prophetic moment in the poem is linked to standard
advice on how to be a virtuous ruler. Christine seems to regard
continued divine favor for Charles as conditional, in some sense
dependent upon exemplary royal behavior. The section ends with
an injunction to Charles to thank, serve, and fear God for the
bounty bestowed upon him. As if to provide the king with a
discursive model, Christine's stanza 20 is an inscribed prayer of
praise and thanks addressed directly to God.

It is at this point that Christine turns to consider the significance and the implications of Joan's achievement in detail, in the

longest section of the poem (stanzas 21–36). The opening direct address to Joan explicitly and emphatically affirms her status as God's chosen instrument in France's salvation:

> Et toy, Pucelle beneurée
> . . . Dieu t'a tant honnoré
> Que as la corde desliée
> Qui tenoit France estroit lié . . .
>
> Tu, Jehanne, de bonne heure née,
> Benoist soit cil qui te créa!
> Pucelle de Dieu ordonné,
> En qui le Saint Esprit réa
> Sa grant grace . . .
>
> (vv. 161, 163–65, 169–73)

And you, blessed Maid . . . God honored you so much that you untied the rope which held France so tightly bound . . . You, Joan, born in a propitious hour, blessed be He who created you! Maiden sent from God, into whom the Holy Spirit poured His great grace . . .

In the sequence of six stanzas that follows (23–28), Christine systematically compares Joan to heroic Biblical figures, both male and female, who saved God's chosen people. It is here that the radical newness of Joan's heroic identity is most explicitly linked to her status as woman. Because she is a woman, her achievement is by definition greater than that of her male Biblical models, Moses, Joshua, and Gideon. Joan is thus valorized in terms of the Christian paradox of "low equals high" in the context of divine revelation in human events. At the same time, part of the miracle of Joan is her absolute superiority in military virtue:

> . . . Car tous les preux au long aler
> Qui ont esté, ne s'appareille
> Leur prouesse à ceste qui veille
> A bouter hors noz ennemis.
> Mais ce fait Dieu, qui la conseille,
> En qui cuer plus que d'omme a mis.
>
> (vv. 203–208)

. . . for all the prowess of all the great men of the past cannot be compared to this woman's whose concern is to cast out our enemies. This is God's doing: it is He who guides her and who has given her a heart greater than that of any man.

At the same time, Joan surpasses all previous female exemplars of salvific heroism:

> Hester, Judith et Delbora,
> Qui furent dames de grant pris,
> Par lesqueles Dieu restora
> Son peuple, qui fort estoit pris,
> Et d'autres plusers ay apris
> Qui furent preuses, n'y ot celle,
> Mains miracles en a pourpris.
> Plus a fait par ceste Pucelle.
>
> (vv. 217–24)

I have heard of Esther, Judith and Deborah, who were women of great worth, through whom God delivered His people from oppression, and I have heard of many other women, all full of prowess, through whom He performed many miracles, but He has accomplished more through this Maid.

We have here an implicit figural presentation of Joan of Arc in terms of authoritative Biblical models of active heroism in a politico-religious context. Joan's identity transcends previously operative gender distinctions in this context: she is simultaneously warrior and woman, *"le* champion" who has the "force et povoir" to "ruer jus la gent rebelle" [cast the rebels down] and "celle / Qui donne à France la mamelle / De paix et doulce norriture" [she who nurses France with the sweet milk of peace] (vv. 188, 187, 191, 188–90). She is a kind of conflation of Deborah and Gideon (Judges 4–5 and Judges 6–8). In regard to Christine's earlier models of exemplary female heroic conduct in the *Cité des Dames*, Joan's military prowess combined with her divinely sanctioned mission conflates the Amazon (I.16–19) and the Christian martyr (III.3–11). A radically new category of female heroism is thus established: the bellatrix-crusader (cf. Acre reference v. 379). Further, this category is established not through abstract speculation but historical fact: it is *incarnated* by Joan. According to Christine's concept of history and of feminism, this heroic model represents the ultimate standard, the sole authority. And Joan's literal, historical *success* (in striking contradistinction to the failure of the earlier, exemplary bellatrices Penthesilea and

Camilla, *Cité de Dames* I.19 and I.24)[6] is thus an inherent part both of her identity and of her authorization.

Thus the narrative account of Joan's life to which Christine now turns is simultaneously presented as proof of her divine sanction. The story is told in appropriately Biblical terms, for Joan's life has in effect overwritten contemporary French political history with a Biblical significance:

> Par miracle fut envoiée
> Et divine amonition,
> De l'ange de Dieu convoiée
> Au roy, pour sa provision . . .
>
> O! comment lors bien y paru
> Quant le siege ert devant Orliens,
> Où premier sa force apparu!
> Onc miracle, si com je tiens,
> Ne fut plus cler, car Dieu aux siens
> Aida telement, qu'ennemis
> Ne s'aiderent ne que mors chiens.
> Là furent prins et à mort mis.
>
> (vv. 225–28, 257–64)

She was miraculously sent by divine command and conducted by the angel of the Lord to the King, in order to help him . . . Oh how clear this was at the siege of Orléans where her power was first made manifest! It is my belief that no miracle was ever more evident, for God so came to the help of His people that our enemies were unable to help each other any more than would dead dogs. It was there that they were captured and put to death.

It is in this first sequential narrative of the events of Joan's life in the *Ditié* that Christine first explicitly utilizes the discourse of prophecy to authorize the unfolding present. Significantly, this prophetic authorization is itself part of an episode in Joan's story: her interrogation by the "royal committee" of theologians acting on behalf of King Charles during March and April of 1429.

> Son fait n'est pas illusion,
> Car bien a esté esprouvée
> Par conseil (en conclusion,
> A l'effect la chose est prouvée),

Et bien esté examinée
A, ains que l'on l'ait voulu croire,
Devant clers et sages menée
Pour ensercher se chose voire
Disoit, ainçois qu'il fust notoire
Que Dieu l'eust vers le roy tramise.
Mais on a trouvé en histoire
Qu'à ce faire elle estoit commise;

Car Merlin et Sebile et Bede,[7]
Plus de V cent ans a la virent
En esperit, et pour remede
En France en leurs escripz la mirent,
En leur[s] prophecies en firent,
Disans qu'el pourteroit baniere
Es querres francoises, et dirent
De son fait toute la maniere.

(vv. 229–48)

Her achievement is no illusion for she was carefully put to the test in council (in short, a thing is proved by its effect) and well examined, before people were prepared to believe her; before it became common knowledge that God sent her to the King, she was brought before clerks and wise men so that they could find out if she was telling the truth. But it was found in history-records that she was destined to accomplish her mission; for more than 500 years ago, Merlin, the sibyl and Bede foresaw her coming, entered her in their writings as someone who would put an end to France's troubles, made prophecies about her saying that she would carry the banner in the French wars and describing all that she would achieve.

Three overlapping kinds of authorization are at issue here. First, Joan's achievements are guaranteed by clerkly authority, by writing as authoritative medium, and by historiography as authoritative genre. The clerkly testimony to Joan's life that Christine had called for in stanza 7 is here shown in stanzas 30–31 to have antedated the Maid's birth. Her present deeds have *already* been recorded—in a written history of the future. Second, these prophecies authorize Joan's mission within the inscribed narrative episode of her examination by the council. Her learnèd interrogators are convinced, and are, of course, meant to serve as models for Christine's reader in this respect. At the same time, their belief operates reciprocally to lend authority to the prophecies as such. Third, Christine as writer and the *Ditié* as *écriture* are simultaneously authorized by the articulation and incorporation of these prophecies. Christine's present discursive treatment of the present events of Joan's life is authoritatively "doubled" by these past predictions of the same events. Christine's voice is doubled by the prophetic voices whose authority she is simultaneously invoking and confirming. In this context the figure of the sibyl has a privileged status, for her appearance here is, as it were, overdetermined as a result of her singular importance in Christine's earlier works.

The sibyl's role as an exemplar of authoritative female discourse in Christine's *oeuvre* goes all the way back to the *Epistre d'Othea a Hector* of 1400. The one hundredth (and final) chapter of this work recounts how the Cumean sibyl announced the coming of Christ to the emperor Augustus. What is stressed is that the revelation of the most important event in history to the greatest temporal ruler of antiquity is made by a woman: "que Cesar Augustus, qui prince estoit de tout le monde; apprist a congnoistre Dieu et la creance d'une femme."[8] In the *Livre du chemin de long estude* of 1403, the role of the Cumean sibyl is central, for she functions as Christine's guide on an allegorical journey through earth and heaven. The Dantean model for this journey is explicitly evoked in Christine's text (vv. 1125–52) in such a way as to foreground her substitution of the sibyl for Virgil as guide for the first-person protagonist. This ironic "restoration" of Aeneas's guide involves, however, an important remotivation of the sibyl in Christine's new—and radically feminized—narrative context. It is the sibyl's identity as female authority figure that authorizes her to be the mentor of Christine qua female protagonist. At the same time, the sibyl confirms and valorizes Christine's literary vocation within the context of the *Chemin's* plot line. In the course of their allegorical journey, the sibyl repeatedly identifies Christine as a member of "nostre escole" (e.g., vv. 1588, 6288); and her first speech to her protegée contains the promise that

> . . . ains que vie te decline,
> En ce [l'amour qu'as a science] t'iras tant deduisant

Que ton nom sera reluisant
Apres toy par longue memoire,
Et pour le bien de ton memoire
Que voy abille a concevoir
Je t'aim et vueil faire a savoir
De mes secres une partie,
Ains que de toy soie partie.

(vv. 494–502)[9]

. . . before your life is over you will delightfully pursue your love of learning so far that your name will be remembered long after your death; and because of your excellent memory and your keen conceptual faculty I love you and I want you to know a portion of my secrets.

In the *Livre de la Cité des Dames* (1405), the figure of the sibyl plays an important role in structuring Christine's feminist polemic. At the beginning of Part II of the *Cité*, the allegorical character Rectitude steps forward to help Christine continue building the city by supplying her with "belles reluysans pierres plus precieuses que autres nulles"[10] [beautiful shining stones more precious than any other];[11] that is, with illustrious examples of female achievement. The very first of these exemplars are the sibyls:

Entre les dames de souveraine dignité sont de haultesce les tres reamplies de sapience, saiges sebilles, lesquelles, si que mettent les plus auttentiques aucteurs en leurs institucions, furent dix par nombre . . . Quel plus grant honneur en fait de revelacion fist oncques Dieux a prophete, quel qu'il fust, tant l'amast, qu'il donna et octroya a ces tres nobles dames dont je te parle? Ne mist il en elles saint esperit de prophecie tant, et sy avant, que il ne sembloit mie de ce qu'elle disoient que ce fust pronosticacion du temps a venir, ains sembloit que ce fussent si comme croniques de choses passees et ja avenue[s], tant estoyent clers et entendibles et plains leurs diz et escrips? Et meesmes de l'advenement Jhesu Crist, qui de moult longtemps vint aprés, en parlerent plus clerement et plus avant que ne firent, si qu'il est trouvé, tous les prophettes. Ycestes dames userent touter leur vie en virginité et desprisierent polucion. Sy furent toutes nommees sebilles; et n'est mie a entendre que ce fust leur propre nom, ains est a dire sebille, ainsi que sçavant la pensee de Dieu. Et furent ainsi appellees pour ce qu'elles prophetisierent si merveilleuses choses que il cou/venoit que ce qu'elles disoyent leur venist de la pure penssee de Dieu . . . Et nonobstant que ces sebilles fussent venues et nees des payens, toutes reprouverent la loy d'iceulx et blasmerent aourer plusieurs dieux, disant qu'il n'en estoit fors un seul et que les ydolles estoyent vaines. (pp. 787–89)

Foremost among the ladies of sovereign dignity are the wise sibyls, most filled with wisdom, who, just as the most credible authors note in their manuals, were ten in number . . . What greater honor in revelation did God ever bestow upon any single prophet, regardless of how much God loved him, than He gave and granted to these most noble ladies whom I am describing to you? Did He not place in them such a profound and advanced prophecy that what they said did not seem to be prognostications of the future but rather chronicles of past events which had already taken place, so clear and intelligible were their pronounce- ments and writings? They even spoke more clearly and farther in advance of the coming of Jesus Christ, who came along afterward, than all the prophets did, just as can be seen from their writings. These ladies abhorred pollution and spent their entire lives as virgins. They were all called sibyls, but it should not be taken that this was their own name, for saying "sibyl" means "knowing the thinking of God." Thus they were so called because they prophesied such mar- velous things that what they said must have come to them from the pure thinking of God . . . Even though these sibyls were all born pagans and lived among pagans, they all attacked pagan religion and assailed the pagans for worshipping many gods, declaring that there was only one God and that the idols were useless (pp. 99–101).

Two of the ten sibyls receive more elaborate treatment by Rec- titude: both are explicitly presented as superior to their male coun- terparts, and both are exalted as examples of God's high love for women. Both are also, it should be noted, poets, writing their prophecies in "vers rimés" (p. 793), in "dittiez" (p. 790). Ery- threa's prophecies are more exclusively religious: she foretold the entire story of Christ's life, from the Incarnation to the Crucifix- ion, as well as his coming on the Day of Judgment. The prophecies of Almathea, the Cumean sibyl, are more exclusively political: she foretold, at the time of King Tarquin, the entire future history of Rome. It is this latter achievement that prompts Rectitude to emphasize Almathea's status as a feminist exemplum for Christine the character:

Or prens cy garde, doulce amye, et vois comment Diex donna si grant grace a une seulle femme que elle ot scens de conseiller et adviser non mie seullement un empereur a son vivant mais si comme tous ceulx qui le monde durant estoyent a avenir a Rome et tous les faiz de l'empire. Sy me dy, je t'en pry, ou fu oncques hommes qui ce faist? Et tu, comme folle, te tenoyes naguaires malcomptent d'estre du sexe de telz creatures, penssant que Dieu l'eust si comme en reprobacion. (p. 794)

Now, pay attention here, dear friend, and consider how God bestowed such great favor on a single woman who possessed the insight to counsel and advise not only one emperor during his lifetime but also, as it were, all those who were to come in Rome as long as the world lasts, as well as comment upon all the affairs of the empire. Tell me then, please, where was there ever a man who did this? A short while ago, like a fool, you considered yourself unlucky to be a member of the sex of such creatures, thinking that God held this sex in reprobation (p. 104).

In Christine's earlier works, then, the sibyl's function as authoritative female figure of religious and political prophecy is deeply linked to Christine's sense of her literary vocation, and of her identity as a woman in this context. There is thus an added significance to the sibyl's role in the *Ditié* as one of the prophets of the coming of Joan of Arc, for the figure of the sibyl, embodying authoritative female discourse—poetry and prophecy—underwrites the figure of Christine as she speaks in the *Ditié*. A powerful female configuration—or, better, genealogy—of authority is thus suggested at the very midpoint of the poem, for the inscription of the names of Joan's three prophets occurs in the first line of the *Ditié*'s central stanza (number 31).[12]

What follows is the poem's most explicit and emphatic celebration of Joan's female identity (correctly understood as a mark of divine favor) in words that recall Rectitude's feminist explanation of the sibyl to Christine in the *Cité*:

> Hee! quel honneur au femenin
> Sexe! Que Dieu l'ayme il appert,
> Quant tout ce grant peuple chenin,
> Par qui tout le regne ert desert,
> Par femme est sours et recouvert,
> Ce que C mille hommes [fait] n'eussent,
> Et les traictres mis à desert!
> A peine devant ne le creussent.
>
> (vv. 265–72)

Oh! What honor for the female sex! It is perfectly obvious that God has special regard for it when all these wretched people who destroyed the whole Kingdom—now recovered and made safe by a woman, something that 100,000 *men* could not have done— and the traitors [have been] exterminated. Before the event they would scarcely have believed this possible. (emphasis mine)

The implications of this extraordinary *fact*, God's public inscription of female preeminence in the book of contemporary history, are of course directly applicable to Christine, even as she writes. The authority of her poetic voice is strengthened by virtue of her shared female identity with her heroic subject.

Her apostrophes to the French and English troops (in stanzas 37–38 and 39–40, respectively) are thus commands, positively and negatively marked, which simultaneously presuppose and confirm her position as authoritative speaker vis-à-vis her addressees. In terms of discourse analysis, Christine incorporates into her very identity as speaking subject the appropriateness condition of the illocutionary act of commanding.[13] Further, this authority now allows her to speak from the privileged position of a prophet. Old Testament and *chanson de geste* elements are combined in the context of contemporary history as crusade.

Christine thus addresses the French troops as follows:

> Et vous, gens d'armes esprouvez,
> Qui faites l'execution,
> Et bons et loyaulx vous prouvez . . .
>
> Soiés constans, car je vous jure
> Qu'en aurés gloire ou ciel et los!
> Car qui se combat pour droiture
> Paradis gaigne, dire l'os.
>
> (vv. 289–91, 301–304)

And you trusty men-at-arms who carry out the task and prove yourselves to be good and loyal . . . Be constant, for this, I swear to you, will win you glory and praise in heaven. For whoever fights for justice wins a place in Paradise—this I do venture to say.

To the English, on the other hand, Christine says:

> Si rabaissez, Anglois, voz cornes
> Car jamais n'aurez beau gibier!
> En France ne menez voz sornes! . . .

Vous irés ailleurs tabourer,
Se ne voulez assavourer
La mort . . .

   (vv. 305–307, 316–18)

And so, you English, draw in your horns for you will never capture any good game!
Don't attempt any foolish enterprise in France! . . . Go and beat your drums elsewhere,
unless you want to taste death . . .

Christine's identity as prophet only becomes fully realized,
however, when she speaks of the future achievements of Joan of
Arc in stanzas 41–45. A universal significance is revealed for
Joan's mission as God's chosen vessel. Not only will she defini-
tively defeat the English (stanza 41), but she will reform the
Church and reconquer the Holy Land, where she will establish
Charles as emperor (stanzas 42–43):[14]

En Christianté et l'Eglise
Sera par elle mis concorde.
Les mescreans dont on devise,
Et les herites de vie orde
Destruira, car ainsi l'acorde
Prophecie, qui l'a predit . . .

Des Sarradins fera essart,
En conquerant la Saintte Terre.
Là menra Charles, que Dieu gard!
Ains qu'il muire, fera tel erre.
Cilz est cil qui la doit conquerre.
Là doit-elle finer sa vie,
Et l'un et l'autre gloire acquerre.
Là sera la chose assovye.

   (vv. 329–34, 337–44)

She will restore harmony in Christendom and the Church. She will destroy the un-
believers people talk about, and the heretics and their vile ways, for this is the substance of a prophecy that has been made . . . She will destroy the Saracens by
conquering the Holy Land. She will lead Charles there, whom God preserve! Before
he dies he will make such a journey. He is the one who is to conquer it. It is there
that she is to end her days and that both of them are to win glory. It is there that the
whole enterprise will be brought to completion.

By this point in the *Ditié*, Christine has become a new, Christian sibyl with regard to Joan. She speaks with the voice of an authoritative—and authentic—female prophet. In the unfolding both of Christine's text and of Joan's life, a kind of continuity is involved here: the sibyl had predicted Joan's arrival and accomplishments up to the historical and textual present; Christine "takes over," in her own voice, for the narrative of Joan's future. Past, present, and future converge in Christine's feminist reading of Joan's historico-political significance; God's active agent is a woman:

> Donc desur tous les preux passez,
> Ceste doit porter la couronne,
> Car ses faiz ja monstrent assez
> Que plus prouesse Dieu lui donne
> Qu'à tous ceulz de qui l'on raisonne.
> Et n'a pas encor tout parfait!
> Si croy que Dieu ça jus l'adonne,
> Afin que paix soit par son fait.
>
> (vv. 345–52)

Therefore, in preference to all the brave men of times past, this woman must wear the crown, for her deeds show clearly enough that God bestows more courage upon her than upon all those men about whom people speak. And she has not yet accomplished her whole mission! I believe that God bestows her here below so that peace may be brought about through her deeds.

Christine's discourse as woman prophet figure, as new sibyl, is authorized by Joan's appearance in history as a new kind of woman hero: a divinely sanctioned military leader with a mission that is at once religious and political.

In the final section of the *Ditié* (stanzas 46–60), it becomes clear that Christine's discursive act is also a political act, an attempt to influence the course of events in which Joan is involved,[15] for Christine's apostrophes to the French allies of the English are designed to effect an extra-textual transformation, to change these present enemies into the loyal French subjects they all potentially are—to effect, in other words, a (politico-religious) conversion. Her direct address to "vous, rebelles rouppieux . . . gent aveugle" (vv. 361, 369) [you base rebels . . . you blind people] is intended to convince them of Joan's divine backing. Once again, it is the simple, historical narrative of Joan's miraculous past deeds that is presented as proof of her status as God's chosen one:

> N'a el le roy mené au sacre,
> Que tousjours tenoit par la main?
> Plus grant chose oncques devant Acre
> Ne fu faite . . .
>
> A tresgrant triumphe et puissance
> Fu Charles couronné à Rains.
> L'an mil CCCC, sans doubtance,
> [Et XXIX, tout] sauf et sains,
> Ou gens d'armes et barons mains,
> Droit ou XVIIe jour
> De juillet. [Pou plus ou pou mains,]
> Par là fu V jours à sejour,
>
> Avecques lui la Pucellette.
>
> (vv. 377–80, 385–93)

Has she not led the King with her own hand to his coronation? No greater deed was performed at Acre . . . It was exactly on the 17th day of July 1429 that Charles was, without any doubt, safely crowned at Rheims, amidst great triumph and splendor and surrounded by many men-at-arms and barons; and he stayed there for approximately five days, with the little Maid.

At this point, the historical present and the textual present merge, for the triumphant advance of Charles and Joan through the French countryside (narrated in stanzas 50–52) is taking place as Christine is writing. The emphasis is on Joan's invincibility— not as desired result but as imminent historical reality:

> En retournant par son paîs,
> Cité ne chastel ne villete
> Ne remaint . . .
> . . . N'y a si forte
> Resistance qui à l'assault
> De la Pucelle ne soit morte.
>
> (vv. 406–408)

As they return through his country, neither city nor castle nor small town can hold
out against them . . . No Matter how strong the resistance offered, it collapses beneath
the Maid's assault.

The cumulative effect of Christine's rhetorical strategy here is
very powerful, and she uses it to focus on the immediate object
of the French military advance: the city of Paris. The key question
at the time of writing is: Will Paris resist the royal army under
Joan and Charles? Christine's fundamentally polemical purpose
at this crucial point in her text is to convince Paris to yield. To
this end, she threatens, warns, and advises, exploiting the authority established thus far in the *Ditié* both for her own voice
and for the figure of Joan:

> Ne sçay se Paris se tendra
> (Car encoures n'y sont-ilz mie),
> Ne se la Pucelle attendra,
> Mais s'il en fait son ennemie,
> Je me doubt que dure escremie
> Lui rende, si qu'ailleurs a fait.
> S'ilz resistent heure ne demie,
> Mal ira, je croy, de son fait,
>
> Car ens entrera, qui qu'en groigne!
> —La Pucelle lui a promis . . .
>
> O paris tresmal conseillié!
> Folz habitans sans confiance!
> Ayme[s]-tu mieulz estre essillié
> Qu'à ton prince faire accordance?
> Certes, ta grant contrariance
> Te destruira, se ne t'avises!
> Trop mieulx te feust par suppliance
> Requerir mercy . . .
>
> (vv. 417–26, 433–40)

I don't know if Paris will hold out (for they have not reached there yet) or if it will
resist the Maid. But if it decides to see her as an enemy, I fear that she will subject it
to a fierce attack, as she has done elsewhere. If they offer resistance for an hour, or
even half an hour, I believe that things will go badly for them, for [the King] will enter
Paris, no matter who may grumble about it!—The Maid has given her word that he
will . . . Oh Paris, how could you be so ill-advised? Foolish inhabitants, you are lacking

in trust! Do you prefer to be laid waste, Paris, rather than make peace with your prince? If you are not careful your great opposition will destroy you. It would be far better for you if you were to humbly beg for mercy.

In the final apostrophe of the *Ditié*, Christine elaborates, in a strategically inclusive way, the target audience of her poem's polemical intent. Her focus widens from the specific and immediate political objective (the surrender of Paris) to the global context— the reestablishment of the French kingdom under its legitimate sovereign:

> Et vous, toutes villes rebelles,
> Et gens qui avez regnié
> Vostre seigneur, et ceulx et celles
> Qui pour autre l'avez nié,
> Or soit après aplanîé
> par doulceur, requerant pardon!
> Car se vous este[s] manié
> A force, à tart vendrez au don.
>
> (vv. 449–56)

And as for you, all you rebel towns, all of you who have renounced your lord, all of you men and women who have transferred your allegiance to another, may everything now be peacefully settled, with your beseeching his pardon! For if force is used against you, the gift [of his forgiveness] will come too late.

Just as it is Joan who guarantees the threat of Charles's use of force, so it is also Joan who guarantees the offer of royal pardon:

> [Charles] est si debonnaire
> Qu'à chascun il veult pardonner!
> Et la Pucelle lui fait faire,
> Qui ensuit Dieu.
>
> (vv. 465–68)

[Charles] is so magnanimous that he wishes to pardon each and everyone. And it is the Maid, the faithful servant of God, who makes him do this.

In her final exhortation, Christine articulates the transformation that the militant strategy of the *Ditié* as a linguistic act is meant to effect in its audience:

. . . Or ordonner
Vueillez voz cueurs et vous donner
Comme *loyaulx François* à lui!
(vv. 468–70; emphasis mine)

Now as *loyal Frenchmen* submit your hearts and yourselves to [your king].

The inscribed prayer with which Christine closes is part of this militant strategy, relying for its effect on the extraordinary authority the *Ditié* has conferred upon her:

Si pry Dieu qu'Il mecte en courage
A vous tous qu'ainsy le faciez,
Afin que le cruel orage
De ces guerres soit effaciez,
Et que vostre vie passiez
En paix, soubz vostre chief greigneur,
Si que jamais ne l'offensiez
Et que vers vous soit bon seigneur. Amen.
(vv. 473–81)

And I pray to God that He will prevail upon you to act in this way, so that the cruel storm of these wars may be erased from memory and that you may live your lives in peace, always loyal to your supreme ruler, so that you may never offend him and that he may be a good overlord to you. Amen.

This prayer as speech act, contextualized and given full meaning by the poetico-political context of the poem as a whole, is Christine's final tribute to Joan. As such, the prayer and the *Ditié* that contains it must be seen as an act of *collaboration* between Christine, the woman poet, and Joan, the woman hero, for the poem that celebrates Joan's career in history is also meant to advance that career, to function, in a real sense, as part of that career, to help fulfill Joan's mission. Christine's *Ditié* thus becomes part of the very historical process to which she is authoritatively bearing witness. At the same time, Joan of Arc qua historical fact authorizes, validates, not only the literary enterprise of the *Ditié*, but Christine's entire previous literary career, her very identity as female *auctor*, her self-created *je, Christine*.

William J. Kennedy

Petrarchan Textuality
Commentaries and Gender Revisions

Petrarch's texts and the earliest commentaries on them straddle a fault line between the Middle Ages and the Renaissance. To question either Petrarch's authority or the authority of subsequent interpretations and imitations is to evoke a scandal of authority in both Middle Ages and the Renaissance. Conflicting interpretations of Petrarch's fundamentally unstable texts by several Renaissance commentators lay bare this scandal. Among poets they generate an agonistic rivalry to imitate the *Rime sparse* in different ways, drawing from the model implications and applications that expose it in a new light. In the commentators' wake, poets may aim to create a deliberately unstable text like Petrarch's that will lend itself to extended understandings from many different angles, an iridescent text whose meanings take on distinctive shades and tones with each new performance. When its meanings concern issues of gender and gendering, they may breach Petrarch's authority in important ways. A woman poet like Louise Labé necessarily revises the genderings of Petrarchan textuality when she addresses her beloved. A male poet like Shakespeare revises it no less palpably when he addresses a male audience. In both cases, gender revisions augment the commentaries that call into question Petrarch's already self-divided authority.

Neither the Middle Ages nor the Renaissance recoiled from challenging authority, but the ways they did so differed. If a medieval interpreter disagreed with current readings of a canonical text, he or she would unapologetically substitute a new reading. The principle was additive rather than disputative; each new commentator juxtaposed his or her commentary against existing ones.

Thus when Bernardus Sylvestris (ca. 1136) finds Fulgentius's commentary on the *Aeneid* sketchy or incomplete, he posits his own moral equivalents for the epic's actions. When John of Salisbury (1115–1180) feels that Bernardus missed the forest for the trees, he surveys the text anew to recount what he finds. When Arnolphe of Orléans (fl. 1175) sees Ovid's *Metamorphoses* as a compendium of science and history, he writes about it in those terms and also clears the ground for successors like Giovanni del Virgilio (fl. 1322–1323) and Petrus Berchorius (ca. 1340) to discover yet more science and history in it. The basis for this accommodation is Augustinian hermeneutics, which asserts that as long as readers understand the text in the light of a central illumination, their readings are legitimate. "Whoever finds a lesson there useful to the building of charity, even though he has not said what the author may be shown to have intended in that place, has not been deceived, nor is he lying in any way."[1] This principle of accommodated allegory reaches its zenith with the author of the *Ovide moralisé*, who construes the canonized original text as an allegory of the life of the Church, the deeds of its saints, and the action of grace. The author picks no quarrel with earlier interpretations; to the contrary, he agrees with them, adds to them, and complements their work.

This kind of agreement crumbles in the Renaissance. The authority of both the text and the interpreter becomes controversialized and ironized. The hermeneutic strategies of Renaissance commentary entail suppositional argument, reasoned disagreement, and a spirited defense of contested explanations. They examine, challenge, assert, juxtapose evidence with contrary evidence, question every assertion, and debate both sides of every proposition. One can speculate about the reasons for this controversialized hermeneutics. Print technology might be partly responsible.[2] The increased production of books and commentaries on them make available a bewildering variety of interpretations, all sanctioned with the authority of print. Expanding in geometrical progression, they in turn invite refutation, argumentation, and confirmation in yet more editions. Then, too, editors print discordant commentaries side by side and so motivate successive readers to take a critical stand, argue a position, and generate yet more controversy. Also responsible is the climate of controversy inherent in Renaissance rhetorical practice itself. Such practice views as an ideal the rhetor's talent to argue both sides of any proposition *in utramque partem,* whether in dialogue with oneself or with others.

Even if these commentaries imply norms of reading that govern the reception of Renaissance poetry, they must still confront the authority of Petrarch's precursor texts. The commentators challenge that authority with their interpretations, while successor poets challenge it with their imitations. The earliest commentators, Antonio da Tempo (late fourteenth century, first printed in 1471) and Francesco Filelfo (early fifteenth century, first printed 1476), attempt to identify figures, allusions, and mythic and historical references. Alessandro Vellutello (1525) not only situates each of Petrarch's poems within a specific dramatic context, but he also rearranges their sequence to tell a better story and to make the moral and sometimes ironic order more apparent. Sebastiano Fausto da Longiano (1532) and Antonio Bruccioli (1548) interpret the dramatic situations from a problematic moral and sometimes political perspective. Giovanni Andrea Gesualdo, the author of the lengthiest commentary (1533), integrates a general stylistic appreciation with pointed ethical interpretation. Bernardino Daniello da Lucca (1541) calls attention to elocutionary devices and figures of speech that distinguish Petrarch's diction, while Ludovico Castelvetro (1545?, published 1582) clarifies many subtle details of style and interpretation.[3]

The commentators, of course, are male, and they contend with each other in the agonistic context of rhetorical debate, a phenomenon of the schools that educate some males to compete with other males. Through such competition they establish competence. The effects on creative imitations of Petrarch by later poets who read Petrarch's text through these commentaries are considerable. In this essay, I will examine these effects on one of Petrarch's sonnets that develops a musical *topos,* "Io canterei d'Amor

si novamente" (sonnet 131); I will also look at the Italian commentaries on this sonnet and review its distant imitations by
Louise Labé in France and William Shakespeare in England.

In "Io canterei d'Amor si novamente," Petrarch's speaker characterizes his beloved less as a particular woman than as an abstract
figure of all women, and less as his partner in an amatory relationship than as the female audience of his poetry, the recipient
of his male poetic skill.

> Io canterei d'Amor si novamente
> ch' al duro fianco il dì mille sospiri
> trarrei per forza, et mille alti desiri
> raccenderei ne la gelata mente;
> e 'l bel viso vedrei cangiar sovente,
> et bagnar gli occhi, et più pietosi giri
> far, come suol chi degli altrui martiri
> et del suo error quando non val si pente;
> et le rose vermiglie infra la neve
> mover da l'ora, et discovrir l'avorio
> che fa di marmo chi da presso 'l guarda,
> e tutto quel per che nel viver breve
> non rincresco a me stesso, anzi mi glorio
> d'esser servato a la stagion più tarda.[4]

I would sing of Love in so rare a way that from her cruel side I would draw by
force a thousand sighs in a day, and a thousand high desires I would kindle in
her frozen mind; and I would see her lovely face change expression frequently,
and her eyes become wet and make more merciful turnings, as one does who
repents, when it is too late, of another's suffering and of his own error; and I
would see the scarlet roses moved by the breeze amid the snow, and the ivory
uncovered that turns to marble whoever looks on it from close by; and all for
the sake of which I am not a burden to myself in this short life, but rather glory
in keeping for a later season.

Right from the beginning the speaker's voice betrays an obsession with professional competence more than with private affection. The emphatic last word in the first line, the adverb
novamente, seals this emphasis. It describes the manner of the
speaker's performance. He would sing so freshly, so creatively, that
externally he would draw *mille sospiri* from his beloved's *duro*

fianco, and internally he would enkindle *mille desiri* in her *gelata mente*. These effects impute to the beloved a string of ethical qualities conventionally associated with female character. Their attributes betray immoderate, unbalanced drives that push at moral extremes. The suppleness of her *sospiro* contrasts with the hardness of her *duro fianco*; the warmth of her *desiri* contrasts with the ice of her *gelata mente*. Their impact on the speaker disturbs his own place in a male-centered hierarchy, reducing his status among other males. The poem enacts the speaker's attempt to displace this influence, and it provides him with an important weapon, the *forza* of his own poetry.

As a sign of its efficacy, this *forza* would show on the beloved's *bel viso* a fluttering of roses amidst snow, exposing ivory that could turn onlookers to marble. In the first tercet, these metaphors equivocate the speaker's poetic competence more than they affirm it. They wrench verbal signifiers away from concrete signifieds, and they upset both syntax and logic. For example, if we leave aside the aural pun that links *L'ora* to *Laura*, we can see that *de l'ora* can refer either to the speaker's sighs, or to Laura's, or to both. If it refers to the speaker's sighs, the roses amid snow signify a pink blush that his sighs bring to the beloved's white cheeks. If it refers to her sighs, the roses signify her lips quivering with sighs. The aural pun complicates this ambivalence, at once associating the speaker's sighs with hers and suggesting a loss of his identity in hers.

The metaphoric ambivalence of *avorio* as a metonymy for the beloved's white teeth echoes this possible loss and suggests a reason for the speaker's act of aggression. On the one hand, the open lips that reveal Laura's teeth create a hollow to entrap the speaker. On the other, they display a cutting edge to unman him. Laura's teeth evoke the power of a woman over men: "et discovrir l'avorio / che fa di marmo chi da presso 'l guarda" [and the ivory uncovered that turns to marble whoever looks on it from close by]. They paralyze the onlooker, turning him to marble, annihilating his control over himself and others. They limit freedom, prevent movement, block flight.

From yet another perspective, however, Laura's teeth acquire the contrary significance. Earlier in the poem, the speaker validated his image of female nature by invoking a quasi-theological diction. The second quatrain figures a kind of sacramental action. The speaker would see the beloved's face change (*cangiar*) with outward signs of a new grace; her eyes bathe (*bagnar*) in purgative, cleansing tears; her obduracy undergo a conversion to pity (*più pietosi giri far*). She would recognize her lover as a victim of *martiri* and herself as a begetter of *error*. The moral character of this language sanctions the speaker's image of the woman as a threat to him, but it also suggests his own threat to himself and his need for grace. Though in *Rime sparse* 131 the speaker himself does not know it, Laura *in morte* will become a source of redemptive strength for him.

The conclusion of the *Rime sparse* destabilizes the entire sequence by shifting the associations of Laura's teeth from claustration and castration to redemption and salvation. The metonymic *avorio* as a sign for Laura's teeth returns in canzone 325 of Laura *in morte*, but there it acquires a wholly new meaning. Laura now regenerates the speaker: "d'avorio uscio, et fenestre di zaffiro / onde 'l primo sospiro / mi giunse al cor et giugnerà l'estremo" (325.17–19) [the entrance of ivory and the windows of sapphire whence the first sigh reached my heart and the last shall reach it]. Like those saints whom St. Augustine cites from the *Canticle of Canticles* in *De doctrina christiana* 2.6, her teeth adumbrate "the teeth of the Church cutting off men from their errors and transferring them to her body after their hardness has been softened as if by being bitten and chewed" (p. 37). If we return to *Rime sparse* 131 after reading this canzone, we will perceive Laura's *avorio* as a shifting, unstable figure. Fully polysemous, it lends itself to diverse understandings on different, even contrary and antithetical horizons.

Petrarch's complex gendering of Laura, then, contributes to the poem's productive instability. It pits one poetic meaning against another in multiple, adversarial, even mutually irreconcilable ways. For the reader it generates self-cancelling but also self-expanding and self-fulfilling possibilities for interpretation. The commentaries in early printed editions of the *Rime sparse* reflect these possibilities, and they suggest readings that accommodate such instability to the rhetorical norms of Renaissance debate. These norms disposed Petrarch's commentators to approach the poetry in startling new ways, to contend with each other in explaining the deeper significance of words, phrases, clauses, echoes, allusions, and whole poems. By recognizing alternative possibilities of meaning, by allowing contradictions, by arguing with each other for favored interpretations, the commentators expand the horizons for understanding Petrarch's textuality. Their work clearly influences the production and revision of new poetry based on the Petrarchan model, and successor poets gain in power as their inspiration passes through the crucible of printed commentaries on Petrarch's poetry.

The earliest commentators on the *Rime sparse* emphasize the text's instability, and some of them thematize it. Filelfo, for example, represents the speaker of sonnet 131 as a victim of unstable passions caused by the love of a woman. Heterosexual relationships prove threatening. They deprive the male of autonomy, upset his balance, dislodge him from his place in the hierarchy of gender, make him as changeable as the woman he loves, "demonstrando le contrarie passioni de gli amanti" (LXIIII^r) [demonstrating the contrary passions of lovers]. Expanding Filelfo's commentary a few years later, Antonio da Tempo emphasizes the speaker's attempt to reassert his masculine dominion. His chief means is song, with its capacity to move the beloved's obdurate heart: "per le rose vermiglie intende il poeta il cor purpureo de M. Laura" (LXIIII^r) [by the scarlet roses the poet refers to Laura's crimson heart]. The speaker proves his moral character through his song's rhetorical effect on others.

The author of the most influential sixteenth-century commentary, Alessandro Vellutello, explicitly identifies the speaker's sexual power with rhetorical efficacy. In the beloved's response, Vellutello demarcates "tutti quelli effetti che ne seguirebbero" (63^r) [all those effects that would follow from it]. Rhetoric will awaken in the beloved a sexual response: "Quando adunque M. Laura intesa per questa tale, havesse la sua parte del caldo, seguita in dire quello che ne seguirebbe, cio è che Amore si desterebbe

in lei" (63ʳ) [when through it Laura then reached such an understanding, she would have shared in his feelings, for as a consequence Love would awaken in her]. For Vellutello, then, rhetoric
becomes a mode of aggression, a phallic instrument to control
others. The speaker masks its nakedness with the colors of figure,
colores figurae, a psycho-sexual gesture that Vellutello insinuates
when he refers to *Rime sparse* 125.1–3: "Se 'l pensier che mi
strugge / com' è pungente et saldo / così vestisse d'un color con-
forme" [If the care that torments me, as it is sharp and dense, so
were clothed in an appropriate rhetorical figure]. If his expression
wears suitable rhetorical colors, then his song will have a potent
effect on the beloved.

If Vellutello discovers sexual power in the speaker's rhetoric,
Sebastiano Fausto da Longiano discovers female mystery in the
beloved's response. When he glosses *novamente* as *stranamente*
(47ʳ), Fausto implies that the speaker's rhetoric is efficacious because of its strangeness, its violation of convention, its defiance
of expectations. When he glosses *avorio* as the beloved's teeth,
however, he refers to Laura's beneficent effect on the speaker who
contemplates her *in morte* in *Rime sparse* 325.17–19: "hor nel
parlar e nel ridere si mostrano li denti; altrove dice chi non sa
come dolce parla, e dolce ride, non si meraviglia com'amor la
faccia sopra lui si forte" (47ʳ) [teeth become visible in speaking
and smiling; elsewhere he says that whoever does not know how
sweetly she speaks and smiles, will wonder how Love gives her
such power over him]. Here Fausto asserts a dialectic between the
sexes that counters Vellutello's impression of male dominance.
The beloved's feminine qualities emerge not as a weakness but as
a strength; they render her flexible and adaptable, not so much
subject to male power as complementary to it. The sexes come
together not in war but in dynamic reciprocity.

These commentaries, then, suggest something important about
the academic climate and literary economy of the Renaissance.
They locate Petrarch's poetry in a world of aggressive rhetorical
action and controversialize it with opposing interpretations. Like
Vellutello, some commentators assert male power over the female
object; like Fausto, others assert the power of the female object

over the male subject; and, as we shall see later with Gesualdo and Daniello, still others assert the force of male competition among other males. The commentaries of Vellutello and Fausto directly suggest a conflict associated with gender, and they clear the ground for poetic imitations that challenge Petrarch's view of gender. This challenge acquires a special significance when a female poet like Louise Labé counterfeits the structure of Petrarchan gender by addressing a male beloved, and when a male poet like Shakespeare upsets the balance altogether by addressing a male counterpart. In both cases, the successor poets rework Petrarch's unstable and controversialized implications about gender.

Like Petrarch's speaker, Louise Labé's speaker is separated from her beloved. For both poets, separation gives way to a yearning that generates poetry. For the male poet, reunion with the beloved allows him immediately to begin importuning her with words. Even if their affair is adulterous, society allows him to try to bend her will, and it even expects him to make the first move. The more she resists, the more he persists. For the female poet, however, reunion with the beloved poses only a new threat. Custom forbids her to make not only the first move, but any move at all. Culturally conditioned to passivity, she must displace any aggression that she might feel in herself. In "Lut compagnon de ma calamité," she displaces it on to her lute, companion of her distress. The lute becomes an object of her aggression, while it performs yet another role. As an instrument of her artistic expression, the lute figures those artistic conventions that she manipulates as a poet. Upon them, therefore, the speaker projects her own anxieties as both lover and artist.

Composing her poetry in mid-sixteenth-century Lyon, the crossroads of French and Italian culture, Louise Labé came to Petrarch's model through the commentaries affixed to every printed edition since 1475. The publication of her *oeuvre* in 1555 situates it wholly within that interpretive tradition, and the debate about gender in her texts echoes the tradition. Labé's own social position gave her access to that debate and encouraged her to enter it directly. As a member of bourgeois competitive society, Labé knew how to value competence. Not only could she compete with Petrarch in the latter's own poetic modality, but just as Petrarch could thematize his own professional competence, so too could she.

To validate her own authenticity, Labé formalizes her poetry with a series of intricate internal and external rhymes, assonances, and consonances. Carefully woven strands of oral-aural harmony and dissonance echo her own emotions as they waver from release to constraint, from pleasure to sorrow, and back again.

> Lut compagnon de ma calamité,
> De mes soupirs témoin irreprochable,
> De mes ennuis controlleur veritable,
> Tu as souvent avec moy lamenté:
> Et tant le pleur piteus t'a molesté,
> Que commençant quelque son delectable,
> Tu le rendois tout soudein lamentable,
> Feignant le ton que plein avoit chanté.
> Et si te veus efforcer au contraire,
> Tu te destens & si me contreins taire:
> Mais me voyant tendrement soupirer,
> Donnant faveur à ma tant triste pleinte:
> En mes ennuis me plaire suis contreinte,
> Et d'un dous mal douce fin esperer.[5]

Lute, companion of my distress, irrefutable witness of my sighs, faithful recorder of my sorrows, you have often lamented with me; and my pitiful tear has so much moved you that, after beginning some delightful strain, you suddenly make it sorrowful, muting the note which it had sung full and clear. And if I try to force you to the contrary, your strings grow slack and so you oblige me to be silent; but when you see me tenderly sighing and approve my sad grieving, I am obliged to take pleasure in my sorrows, and to hope for a sweet outcome of a sweet pain.

The sonnet's first quatrain evokes the speaker's own sense of place in this verbal network. She characterizes her lute first as a companion (*compagnon*), implying parity between herself and it, and then as *temoin*, implying distance and difference. As companion the lute shares in her self-reflection. As witness or on-looker it tests that self-reflection and allows her to see herself as others see her. In line 3 she attributes to the lute yet another function that heightens the contrast between parity and difference. As a metonymic figure for her poetic skill, the lute is *controlleur* of her emotions in the literal sixteenth-century sense of "recorder."[6] The lute records the speaker's emotions. But the lute is also *controlleur* in a more aggressive sense. It can control her emotions, leading her to express not so much what she thinks or feels as what the conventions of her art expect her to think or feel. When those conventions reflect a male sensibility, as Petrarchan ones do, they can betray her very sense of purpose, her own intention as a female poet to express a woman's point of view about love.

This poem records the speaker's effort to define her role in relation to such conventions. In dramatic terms, she seeks to evade the female role that Petrarchism forces upon her. At the same time, she knows that rejecting it can expose her to confusion and diffusion. To overcome that threat Labé needs to increase her self-esteem, and she can do so by proving her own competence as a poet. She therefore begins the second quatrain with a strong assertion of the poetic competence that struck Petrarch's commentators in "Io canterei si novamente." Here the speaker imagines a control over the lute that guides it oxymoronically from *delectable* to *lamentable*, muting the tones that she had first selected. The irony is that even its new tones echo conventions defined by Petrarch's commentaries. The lute pursues a Petrarchan modality at the very moment when it expresses the speaker's own emotion.

The conjunctive misuse of *et* that opens the sestet underscores this problem. The word initiates a contrast that properly implies "but" rather than "and." The lute that echoed the speaker in the second quatrain now resists her. So much has the lute absorbed her sorrow that, even when she wishes it to respond with a happy strain, it slackens. The ambiguity of *controlleur* turns full circle. Formerly a recorder of her emotions, the lute now becomes the controller of them. Its artistic conventions shape the pattern of her sentiment. When the speaker tries to force its compliance, it refuses. She has become thrall to her own poetic instrument.

As an emblem of the speaker's relation to her art, the lute now takes on the characteristics of the male beloved. Seeking to dominate the speaker, the lute engages her in a struggle for control. The sestet's syntactic drift mirrors an indeterminate outcome. Its control shifts from the speaker as perplexed subject of line 9 ("Et si te veus efforcer") to the lute that emerges in the next line ("Tu te destens"), and finally back to the speaker who reasserts herself as subject of the final clause: "En mes ennuis me plaire suis contreinte." At the problematic center of this construction, a pair of ambiguous participles in lines 11 and 12 upsets the balance: "Mais me voyant tendrement soupirer, / Donnant faveur à ma tant triste pleinte." Their position is awkward. Syntactically they refer back to the masculine gendered lute (*voyant, donnant*), but logically they reach forward to the feminine speaker. Grammar confounds logic with a blurring similar to the blurring of Petrarch's sighs with Laura's in *Rime sparse* 131. The lute's identity seems to cross with the speaker's. This blurring is significant. The speaker's own loss of self in the conventions of her art poses a threat that she must overcome, just as Petrarch's speaker had to overcome the loss of himself in the beloved.

Labé's speaker resolves the threat by reasserting herself as subject of the poem's final clause. Here she takes her cue from the lute itself. In line 9 the lute constrains her to silence. In line 13 she accedes to pleasure in sorrow. When she does, she reconciles the oxymoronic contradictions of pleasure and sorrow, *plaire* and *plaint*, linking those words through alliteration and assonance and binding them with internal rhyme to *contraire* (9) and *taire* (10). This binding heals the speaker's fear of the lute's incantatory power over her; it confirms her power over the instrument. The action ratifies the lute's otherness, but it also establishes the speaker's separateness. If the lute is autonomous, so too is the speaker. At the same time, the rhetorical binding implies that the speaker does not exist in splendid isolation. The channels of transference permit a flow both ways, and the act of healing allows for acts of reciprocity. The speaker recognizes that she can take from convention as much as she gives.

The reemergence of "I" as subject in the final lines substantiates the speaker's discovery that responsiveness to herself need not be opposed to responsiveness to others, that one can experience a relationship with another only by differentiating oneself from the other, just as one can know oneself as separate only by acknowledging one's connection with others. This discovery affects the speaker's sense of her role as lover, certainly, but just as certainly it affects her role as poet. It implies a series of complex interactions with the norms of poetic convention that establish her own artistic identity. It implies, too, Labé's poetic response to social claims about a woman's place in a male hierarchy. It implies, finally, an authoritative reinscription of her own voice in a new poetic register. She fully authorizes her own poetic persona.

The instability of Petrarch's own view of gender in the *Rime sparse* encourages this new authorization. The early commentaries on "Io canterei d'Amor si novamente" by Vellutello and Fausto associated rhetorical skill with sexual power, and they would certainly challenge a woman poet like Louise Labé to respond artistically to them. Other commentaries by Gesualdo, Bruccioli, and Daniello associated the rhetorical situation of Petrarch's poem with an arena of male competition, and they might challenge male poets to respond by addressing other males in the Petrarchan mode. Shakespeare's sonnets to a young man provide a case in point. The commentaries did not necessarily influence Shakespeare's choice of topic or audience, but they certainly did illuminate for him the sharp sense of contention in Petrarch's model.

Gesualdo, author of the lengthiest commentary, initiates the discussion of male competition. For him, the poem's dramatic situation provides a key to the speaker's character and rhetoric. The conditional mood of the verbs *canterei* and *vorrei* stimulates Gesualdo's interest. The mood implies a protasis stated in earlier dialogue. In one possible interpretation, the speaker has been separated from the beloved, whether by exile or official business, and he is now lamenting her absence to a friend. Gesualdo imagines that his friend has asked, "What would you do if she were present?" and to that question he replies with the conditional "I would . . .": "Risponde ad un suo amico, il quale dimandato havea, s'egli far potesse cantando quello ch'egli qui dimostra, che far potrebbe" (CLXXXVII[r]) [He replies to his friend, who has asked whether by singing he could do what here he proves he could do]. Gesualdo's imagined context is significant. The friend with whom the speaker converses is male, and his mode of discourse is a boast. The speaker brags that his song can change the beloved. Laura becomes a compliant object upon whom the speaker projects his own wish-fulfillment. The poem's real competitor is the male interlocutor who motivates the boast. Laura, merely the pawn in this contest, serves only to define male aggression.

Among Gesualdo's successors, Sansovino, Bruccioli, and Daniello also emphasize the poem's rhetorical situation. Like Gesualdo, they imagine the speaker in a dramatic dialogue with a male friend, boasting about what he would do if Laura were present. Bruccioli explicitly refers to the male interlocutor: "Appare, che alcuno gli havesse domandato quello che facesse se fusse apresso à M. Laura" (102ʳ) [It seems that someone had asked him what he would do if he were with Laura]. Daniello also recounts the rhetorical situation: "Risponde il poeta ad alcuno, che dimandato gli havea, Quello ch'esso farebbe se appresso à M. Laura si ritrovasse" (83ʳ) [The poet replies to someone who has asked what he would do if he were with Laura]. Daniello notes the elocutionary aim of the boast when he glosses *novamente*: the poet wishes to speak "si eccellentemente, & altamente" (83ʳ) [with such excellence and nobility]. Rhetoric establishes the speaker's power, asserts his control over the audience, and allays his anxieties about being caught in the instability of the female world. It also expresses the speaker's wish to be alone at the top, his craving for distinction in the field of his art, his fear that the competition will get too close.

Comparable subtexts animate Shakespeare's sonnet sequence to the young man. Sonnet 8 provides a good example. Like Petrarch's "Io canterei d'Amor si novamente" and Labé's "Lut compagnon de ma calamité," it develops a musical *topos*:

> Music to hear, why hear'st thou music sadly?
> Sweets with sweets war not, joy delights in joy.
> Why lov'st thou that which thou receiv'st not gladly,

Or else receiv'st with pleasure thine annoy?
If the true concord of well-tunèd sounds,
By unions married, do offend thine ear,
They do but sweetly chide thee, who confounds
In singleness the parts that thou shouldst bear.
Mark how one string, sweet husband to another,
Strikes each in each by mutual ordering;
Resembling sire, and child, and happy mother,
Who all in one, one pleasing note do sing;
Whose speechless song, being many, seeming one,
Sings this to thee: "Thou single wilt prove none."

One way to understand the audience of this sonnet is to con-
strue it as a dialogue whose first three words are metonymic address. The speaker attributes to his partner's voice the quality of
music itself: "You whose voice is music to hear." The metonymy
in turn generates a form of Petrarchan oxymoron that questions
the audience's sweet delight in sad music: "Music to hear, why
hear'st thou music sadly?" (1). In line 2 the speaker challenges
this antithesis: one emotion or state of mind ought not generate
its opposite in response. "Sweets with sweets war not, joy delights
in joy" (2). Lines 3 and 4 ask the audience why it enjoys harsh
music, taking pleasure in annoyance. With skepticism in his
voice, the speaker exposes the proposition's apparent contradiction as a form of logical paradox. He casts in question any text
that elicits from its audience such contradictory responses. Foremost among them might be those Petrarchan sonnets whose oxy-
morons embody the very principle of contradiction that he finds
so problematic.

Other aspects of that speaker's skepticism emerge in the second
quatrain. There his chiding evokes a sexism that finds male celibacy incomprehensible and implies scorn towards female celibacy.
The speaker, however, does not chide in direct address. Instead,
he frames a logical statement in an if/then conditional clause. Its
protasis fixes the musical figure of married sounds as an emblem
of marriage: "If the true concord . . ." The apodosis reminds the
audience of his reluctance to marry. Its construction, however,
violates grammatical parallelism. The shift from a single subject

\

(*concord*) in the protasis to a plural subject (*they*, referring to *sounds*) in the apodosis upsets the balance. Its movement towards the plural suggests a gathering of forces against the audience, while the collapse of its parallelism enacts a version of Petrarchan antithesis that juxtaposes the many against the one. Its statement begins with an oxymoronic containment of opposites implied in the word *concord*: if the speaker urges the audience not to remain one, he nonetheless urges it to become one in marriage with another. Oxymoron blurs into paradox. One should not remain one, but should become one with another by virtue of being two.

With this paradox, the speaker's voice reveals its own instability. It is a voice somewhat less than confident and assured. It grasps irony, articulates its elusiveness, sustains its varied levels of complexity, integrates them in a full rich statement; yet it also allows these levels to retain a life of their own that one can distinguish, analyze, and comprehend on different horizons of understanding. It is a voice that has acquired this skill through dialogue with itself and others. With its perverse will to manipulate language to its own ends, it is a male voice, trained as young male voices were trained in Shakespeare's day in the school of debate.

Its audience, or, as will become clear, its opponent, is also male. We of course know that the audience is male from the context of Shakespeare's earlier sonnets, but the sestet of this sonnet plays on his maleness in its mode of address. It opens with a strong imperative on line 9, where the speaker as adversary commands his listener to attend to yet another aspect of his musical analogy. Logical argument becomes a form of combat as the speaker directs its weapons against his silent partner, thrusting and parrying until the young man concedes. He sharpens its point upon the word *husband*, where he again reproaches his audience for refusing to become a husband. With a flourish, the speaker aims at the entire Petrarchan tradition whose audience is conventionally female. Shakespeare's decision to rework the genre with one male as speaker and another as audience forces now a new revision of gender.

In the poem's final couplet, the speaker curiously refrains from directly addressing his male audience in dialogue. Instead, he exacts an address from the song implied in his analogy: "Whose speechless song, being many, seeming one, / Sings this to thee: "Thou single will prove none" (13–14). The strategy is odd, as though the speaker had judged the song's admonition on the one hand too simple, too direct, too pat for him to express, and, on the other, too disturbing, too controversial, too unsettling for his male audience to accept from him. By attributing it to the song, the speaker preserves his own distance while yet conveying the burden of his admonition. Yet how reticent is the speaker? The warning is clearly his, a fact that the printing of the 1609 text points to by omitting quotation marks from the song's citation, and it harbors a good deal of mocking word play that echoes his own voice. Earlier the speaker had teased his audience with a pun on *parts* in line 8. Metaphorically, that word refers to a musician's playing of parts in a polyphonic composition, but it also insinuates a slang term for the organs of procreation that celibacy confounds with disuse. A similar undercutting of the speaker's elevated tone occurs in the last line. There, after two uses of *sing* and one of *song* in lines 12–14, their echo in *single* mocks the audience as one excluded from the music of human life. More egregiously, after three uses of *one* in lines 12–13, the word *none* mocks the audience in a double way. It affirms that unless he marries and fathers children, he will amount to nothing when he dies without issue. It also makes an execrable pun on the homophonic *nun*, implying that the audience's celibacy relegates him to the cloister of a nunnery. The pun mocks the audience first by feminizing him and then by consigning him to a sheltered life, but it also upsets the balance of gender that the poem had worked so hard to achieve.

Why does Shakespeare conclude by upsetting this balance, feminizing the audience, and denigrating women and the religious life? Is the poem after all just a mockery of the Petrarchan tradition, a palinode in the manner of "My mistress' eyes are nothing like the sun?" I think not. The equivocal, highly ambiguous ending reinforces the subtextual power of dialogue at the poem's center. The speaker has engaged in the kind of rhetorical exchange that Petrarch's commentators imagine in the *Rime sparse*, but he is yet too cautious, too wary, too wise to take the results for granted. Here and elsewhere in the sonnets, he has experienced the slipperiness of language, and he knows the consequences of its instability. No Petrarchan text, and certainly not any of Shakespeare's Petrarchan texts, is a stable entity, a substance of absolute and idealized monumentality. Its textuality is transitory and provisional, subject to endless dramatic revisions; it is not a finished product, an achieved system of signs, but a contested model whose ironies and ambiguities confirm its vitality.

Shakespeare's gender revisions sharpen these proclivities of Petrarchan textuality already explicated in the Renaissance commentaries on the *Rime sparse* and reworked in Louise Labé's version of the Petrarchan sonnet. Shakespeare's address to the young man exploits the rhetorical strategies noted by commentators like Gesualdo and Daniello, who construed Petrarch's sonnets as textual dialogues, debates staged in an aggressively competitive world of rhetorical action. In quite a different way, Louise Labé's address to her male beloved exploits rhetorical strategies noted by commentators like Vellutello and Sebastiano Fausto, who construed Petrarch's sonnets as narratives about sexual power, moral representations of a desire both threatened and enriched by the absence of the other. Both imitative reworkings of the Petrarchan sonnet develop potentials that commentators keenly perceived. In so doing, they reveal an authority implicit in the *Rime sparse* all along.

Walter Stephens

Saint Paul Among the Amazons
Gender and Authority in *Gerusalemme liberata*

Nowhere more thoroughly than with Tasso's *Gerusalemme lib-erata* has hagiography of the author been confused with interpre-tation of the text. For biographers, painters, dramatists, and poets of the eighteenth and nineteenth centuries, Tasso was "a proto-type of the Romantic poet, loving passionately but hopelessly and beyond his station, the victim of political oppression, maintaining his dignity and essential nobility of heart through intense and prolonged suffering, the hypersensitive creative artist at odds with society, wandering restlessly from court to court or chained in a lunatic's cell."[1] The "hopeless unavowed loves" of the *Liberata* helped propagate the legend of Tasso's love affair with Eleonora d'Este, sister of his patron Duke Alfonso of Ferrara. As early as the seventeenth century, Alfonso's jealousy for his sister's honor was regularly advanced as the "true reason" for Tasso's impris-onment in the Hospital of Sant'Anna.[2] Critical and theoretical developments from New Criticism to Deconstructionism have thoroughly discredited such attempts to interpret Tasso's biogra-phy with the "evidence" of his text, and psychoanalytic criticism has transformed the task.[3]

The reverse impulse, however, that of interpreting the poem with the aid of biography, has persisted among *Tassiani*. The wealth of Tasso's autobiographical and theoretical writings, which are among the most abundant left by any writer of the Renais-sance, provides a natural temptation to discover "Tasso's true de-sign" and its fulfillment in the poem. And given the prominence of women in the *Liberata*, Armida or Erminia often replaces Eleanora as object of Tasso's affections. Thus Marilyn Migiel recently laments that critics should "stop assuming that the text necessarily tells the story Tasso claims he wants it to tell" about the individual characters, especially women, whose fates are usually left so tantalizingly unresolved by the plot. Migiel attacks this "faith in the triumph of a unified point of view," warning rightly that "Tasso's theoretical stamp of approval is no guarantee of the legitimacy of a reading."[4] Migiel herself seeks the points where desire threatens loss of control over the narrative, yet her overall conclusions are rather conventionally deconstructive: the slippages of *Gerusalemme liberata* turn out to be about what and where one would expect and produce about the same cautionary allegory about the limits of language that one would expect from any text.

Sergio Zatti, on whose work Migiel depends heavily, sees the slippage in even starker terms than she does. His meticulous psychoanalytic and deconstructive reading describes the *Liberata* as "a precarious and unstable balance" of opposing forces, and he concludes that Tasso's poem is "probably the first manifest example in Italian literature of a conscious identification (although repudiated at the level of ideology) with the forces of evil, the first great example of solidarity with the 'pagan enemy.' "[5] Zatti quite elegantly encapsulates and explains the history of reader uneasiness with *Gerusalemme liberata* when he asserts that pagan romance multiplicity (*multiforme*) ultimately subverts or suppresses Christian, epic uniformity in the poem.

But Migiel's reading is more than just a continuation of Zatti's and is filled with insights, especially about the heroine Erminia, that stimulate rethinking. She is particularly cogent in attacking readings that seek to discover a "happy ending" for the story of Tancredi and Erminia.[6] Another quite recent interpretation of the *Liberata* attempts to counter such "happy endings" by recourse to a feminist narratology. In her examination of the *Liberata*'s ideology of gender, Maggie Günsberg criticizes other such studies for failing to observe a distinction between "the feminine" as "an ideologically-determined set of narrative constructs," and the "female character," which, as "some sort of indivisible narrative block, . . . suggests a unity corresponding to a 'real person,' and thereby ignores the literariness of the text." By avoiding character,

Günsberg hopes to unmask "the rather more significant and less overt levels" that either reinforce or subvert "the dominant ideology at work in a specific complex of power-relations" overtly described by the text.[7]

However, it is doubtful that her conclusions about the poem add significantly to our appreciation of its workings as a text or of its ideological situation with regard to gender. Her typology of idealized and aberrant sets of masculine and feminine attributes does not move far beyond what critics have long observed about "characters" in this and other heroic poems: passivity and stasis are "ideal feminine" but "aberrant masculine," heroic achievement is "ideal masculine" but "aberrant feminine," and so on (9). And, despite sallies of psychoanalytic acumen in her inquiry, her conclusions are depressingly predictable: gender relations in the poem, like relations of social class, are for her governed absolutely by a process of "ideological reinforcement" between overt and covert levels of the text.

There is an extremely curious literalism in Günsberg's analysis, for she accepts the words of any male character at face value as expressions of the "deeper ideology" of the text. This practice not only betrays her effort to transcend the concept of character; it also reveals the unspoken axiom of her approach—that the assertive woman is always a scapegoat (in a cliché pre-Girardian sense).

The feminine attributes of Gildippe, a minor [Christian] character in the GL, are rather different from those of Clorinda. Ideal beauty and youth are not mentioned, and the threat of her sexuality is circumscribed by marriage to Odoardo. However, her rejection of traditional feminine pursuits in favour of ideal achievements on the battlefield becomes an issue at her death, when the [pagan] male warrior Solimano slays her after the following reprimand: "Meglio per te s'avessi il fuso e l'ago, / Ch'in tua difesa aver la spada e 'l vago" ["You'd defend yourself better with spindle and needle than with your sword and lover"] (20.95). Solimano is here accusing her of wrongful appropriation of the phallus/ sword; at the same time he negates the couple's marital relationship by describing them as "la putta e 'l drudo" ["the whore and her paramour"] and Odoardo as "vago." (They are, interestingly, referred to elsewhere in the poem not only as "sposi," but also as "amanti," in the same phrase [1.56; 3.40; 7.67].) In the GL, then, the deaths of Clorinda and Gildippe, both as warriors and as women, put an end to what amounts to a transgression of the social norm; there is no room for androgyny in this poem. (21–22)

Although, like Zatti, she postulates the text's "sympathy with the devil" (in this case the pagan Solimano), Günsberg is essentially arguing for another version of that "triumph of the unified point of view" that Migiel deplores. Rather than "Tasso," it is now "the text" that works obsessively and perhaps unconsciously to produce a "unified point of view," in this case a twentieth-century formulation of gender ideology that transcends considerations of religious doctrine or cultural history. The Text assumes the role of sexual oppressor once accorded to Alfonso, while women have inherited the role of victim formerly assigned to Tasso the Author.

Günsberg purposes to rely in part on the examination of plot inconsistencies, junctures "which show that the attention of the text is centred on an area of opposition other than that expressed by the progression of the plot" (33). Here again the Text has been personified and substituted for Tasso the Author and has taken over those functions, "attention" and desire, once reserved for him. In fact, all but one of her examples of plot inconsistencies come from *Orlando furioso* rather than from Tasso (33–34). This is perhaps just as well, for her concept of inconsistencies specific to *plot* is vague: in her examples the inconsistency is often ethical, whereas from the point of view of plot, they can form moments of inappropriate consistency. Pursuit of this analysis in the *Liberata* might soon have forced her to agree with critics who find contradictions between the overt and covert ideologies of the poem.[8]

Zatti, the most careful and radical exponent of ideological inconsistency in the *Liberata*, and Günsberg, the describer of extreme ideological consistency, both assert that the poem's representations of women prevent any substantive differentiation among them. Günsberg invites us to see Clorinda and Gildippe as victims of an oppressive male principle that makes no distinction between Christian and pagan, while Zatti sees even the physical descriptions of Armida and Sofronia as having the same potential for indiscriminacy. He maintains that the identifiability of Armida and Sofronia as agents of opposing ideologies ("pagan" and "Christian" respectively) is continually menaced by the fact that physical descriptions of them share the same identifying stylemes (*stilemi identificatori*) of a Petrarchan and/or Mariological character.[9]

Their critical approaches are to a degree mirror-reversed images of each other. Günsberg asserts that inconsistencies in plot (actually, in ethics) reveal hidden ideological consistency. Zatti argues more cogently for an ideological inconsistency determined in part by excessive lexical and stylistic consistency. Together, their analyses demonstrate the necessity of reading the *Liberata* intertextually, something neither they nor Migiel do to any significant extent. Tasso's poem is so intensively structured around *imitatio* of other texts that to ignore this aspect is never to proceed beyond plot. What Günsberg calls plot inconsistencies invite an intertextual reading precisely because they occur so often in conjunction with apparently inappropriate lexical consistencies of the sort Zatti discerns. For deconstructionists, the most significant form of the latter are intratextual, but historically, critics' attention has centered on what can be provisionally described as "too obvious echoes" of other texts.

"Too obvious echoes" help conceptualize why readers continue to read the *Liberata*'s representations of women in the way that Migiel deplores. By highlighting converging levels of inconsistency, they reveal the strategies whereby the poem seduces the reader into ignoring the constraints of plot and into projecting those happy endings that it never explicitly sanctions. The critic's irrepressible habit of personifying the text is actually helpful here, for nodes of ethical and lexical inconsistency emerge quite clearly as signs of what might indeed be called the "desires" of the text. They point to areas of repression, conclusions toward which the narrative—sometimes the plot itself—was being drawn almost irresistibly but which were never allowed explicit fulfillment. For whatever reason, these moments of closure were censored out at the explicit levels of the text.

What sort of echo is "too obvious"? Here Tasso himself is of little help. Writing to Scipione Gonzaga on 15 April 1575, Tasso brings his friend and favorite critic/censor up to date on changes he has effected in the poem, including the wording of a verse: "Il verso 'Per tempo al suo dolor, tardi all'aiuto,' era troppo rubato dalla *Canace*" [The verse "In time for his own pain, too late to aid his friend" was too (obviously) stolen from (Sperone Speroni's) *Canace*].[10] Tasso accuses himself of plagiarism, of copying a verse too literally, but without mentioning whether the "theft" was conscious or unconscious. Speroni's verses read: "*Tardi* a l'altrui soccorso / *giungi*, signor, ma a la tua pena a *tempo*" (emphasis mine).[11] Since the lexical coincidences are so few, it appears likely that the nature of Tasso's worry was rhetorical as well, that is, the chiastic opposition *late:to aid/to suffer:on time.*

Yet this "theft" is significantly less obvious than numbers of others that have remained in the text. On occasion, the *Liberata* repeats entire verses practically verbatim from texts more likely to be known—often by heart—than Speroni's tragedy, even in Tasso's own time. In canto four, a description of Armida wiping the tears from her eyes repeats an entire verse from Petrarch, without alterations. The previous verse in Tasso's text differs from another Petrarchan original only because it changes the grammatical person to fit the new context.

> Tasso: ch'innamorò di *sue* bellezze il cielo,
> asciugandosi gli occhi co 'l bel velo.

> Petrarch: che 'l ciel di *tue* bellezze innamorasti
>
> . . . .
>
> asciugandosi gli occhi col bel velo.[12]

The most famous and glaring example is found in Armida's expression of submission to Rinaldo in canto twenty. The echo of the Blessed Virgin's response to the angel Gabriel is absolutely unmistakable:

> "Ecco l'ancilla tua: d'essa a tuo senno
> dispon," gli disse "e le fia legge il cenno."
> (GL 20.136.7–8)

Dixit autem Maria: "Ecce ancilla Domini, fiat mihi secundum verbum tuum." (Luke 1.38)

Furthermore, Armida's response is inconsistent with Tasso's own vocabulary: the Latinizing form *ancilla*, which does not occur elsewhere in the text, unnecessarily reinforces the echo of the Gospel. Why, then, should Tasso have been disturbed by a minor "theft" from Speroni but not by such truly massive lexical repetitions, which could not escape his or anyone else's notice? Clearly, it is useless to pursue the question any further in a biographical register; or rather, it is well to keep in mind the obliquity and indirection characteristic of Tasso's correspondence, the unreliability of his pronouncements about his intentions and commitments.

There are still other problems with the closure of the *Liberata* that should disturb anyone interested either in its treatment of women or in its degree of ideological consistency. The Mariological "echo" in Armida's conversion has always seemed to highlight its more fundamental problems. As a character, Armida is inconsistent: her sudden conversion cannot be explained in psychological or mimetic terms.[13] Günsberg's attempt to circumvent character, seeing Armida as "recuperated in overt narrative terms of religious conversion accompanied by a drop in social status ('ancilla')" (16), is even less satisfactory, since it ignores this most obvious of "too obvious echoes." There is a further ethical inconsistency that appears to subvert the Christian "message" of the poem. Why should the vain and willful Armida be salvaged at the cost of Gildippe, who is both a Christian and a faithful wife? Even worse, the last incident before the fighting ceases in Jerusalem is Goffredo's decision to spare Altamoro (20.140.3–143.3), who is not only male and pagan but also an adulterer, at least in intent: he has been Armida's staunchest pagan "champion" (19.69ff.; 20.69ff.). Why should the text redeem Armida's pagan *soupirant*—who shows no sign of intent to convert—and kill the Christian Gildippe? Perhaps, after all, the text is punishing Gildippe's transgression of gender stereotypes. Aside from slaying numbers of other males, she has exchanged violent blows with this same Altamoro; the narrator referred to her as an "Amazon" and spoke of the "offenses" (*ingiurie*) and shame (*onta*) her powerful blow caused Altamoro (20.41–42).

But more interesting readings, which also make more sense in textual and ideological terms, are possible. The three incidents in canto twenty have one important consistency: they covertly partake of a discourse that betrays both a nostalgic idealization of marriage and deep anxieties about the human body. These two concerns are in turn linked at an intertextual level.

I cannot deal adequately here with all three incidents of canto twenty. For the moment, it will have to suffice to note that Altamoro is not important *in himself* for what I am calling the "desires" of the text. His salvation is imperative because three cantos earlier his wife was introduced through a precise echo of Andromache's attempt to prevent Hector's departure for battle. In canto twenty, Goffredo acts as a reformed Achilles: whereas Achilles long refused to return his foe's corpse to his father for ransom, Goffredo immediately vows to return his prisoner alive and gratis to his wife. These changes, and the fact that Altamoro's nameless wife was portrayed only through her words and a reference to her "chaste bed," evoke Andromache's threnody over the corpse of her husband: "You left *for your parents* mourning and sorrow beyond words, *but for me passing all others* is left the bitterness and the pain, for you did not die in bed, and stretch your arms to me, and tell me some last intimate word that I could remember always, all the nights and days of my weeping for you."[14]

It is pointless to object that Goffredo is the "Agamemnon" of the poem rather than its Achilles, or that he spares Altamoro out of Christian charity: these are surface conventions. Clearly, the "desire" of the text looks beyond Altamoro to his wife. In himself, as character, he merits no extraordinary grace, having earned no sympathy; and from the standpoint of epic tradition, his death would be more logical than deliverance. But the text spares him, against both morality and the epic tradition. The "desire" of the text, however, reinforces its overt ideology, though in a way diametrically opposed to what Günsberg imagines: while the *Iliad* takes most of three books to move from Hector's death to the burning of his corpse and the construction of his tomb, the *Liberata* ends two stanzas after the surrender of Altamoro, with the *empty* tomb of the resurrected Christ. The refusal to

take Altamoro/Hector from his "Andromache" is a private, domestic, and secular substitute for Christ's victory over death, the
best that the text can offer to non-Christians.

The covert association of marriage and the body created by the
simultaneous, significant absences of Altamoro's wife and Christ's
body might be called meta-thematic. With this somewhat clumsy
expression, I mean only to designate the process whereby a thematic connection that appears overtly in one or more other texts
recurs covertly in the *Liberata* with obsessive frequency, especially
at points where overt thematic corroboration is missing.

Despite her obscurity, or rather because of it, Gildippe is, like
Altamoro's wife, one of the most important women of the poem,
since its meta-thematic treatment of her marriage and her body
miniaturizes and explicates its treatment of other women who
receive more attention in the plot and overt thematics. In particular, the narrative *entrelacement* of Gildippe's and Armida's
fates in canto twenty corresponds to an intertextual process that
contrasts them at the meta-thematic level.

Given her obscurity during the rest of the poem, Gildippe's
brief moment of heroic action is so inconsistent that it should long
ago have provoked a closer look. Her rare appearances before
canto twenty are not distinguished by memorable action but rather
by a recurring, unchanging tag-verse that invites us to neglect
her: "Gildippe ed Odorardo, amanti e sposi" [lovers and spouses
(1.56.6; 3.40.7; 7.67.8)]. As Günsberg points out, Gildippe is
faceless and unspecific, and married as well; thus her erotic appeal
is minimal. But despite what Günsberg attempts to imply, Gildippe is not an object of scorn: there is no semantic or textual
basis for accepting the narrator's term *amanti* as ideologically
equivalent to Solimano's pejorative epithets. A better assessment
of Gildippe's status for the narrator and the "desires" of the text
might begin from the description of her given by another woman,
Erminia. As Migiel remarks of Erminia, "Desire makes of her a
remarkably perceptive observer and an accomplished narrator."[15]

In canto three, Erminia and King Aladino observe the Christian army from a high tower on the walls of Jerusalem, and she
points out the principal Christian warriors to him.[16] Of the En-

glishwoman and her husband, Erminia says: "E son que' duo che van sì giunti in uno, / e c' han bianco il vestir, bianco ogni fregio, / Gildippe ed Odoardo, amanti e sposi, / in valor d'arme e in lealtà famosi" [And those two who go so joined in one, whose dress is all white with white ornamentation, are Gildippe and Odoardo, lovers and spouses, famous in arms and loyalty (3.40.5–8)]. Erminia's description of the two warriors appears to be essentially allegorical, expressing their emotional and legal unity in physical terms as "two in one." Since we already know that Erminia is in love with Tancredi, and since she later masquerades unsuccessfully as a *guerriera* like Gildippe and Clorinda in order to meet him, it is not too reckless to see Gildippe and Odoardo as her ideal of marriage.[17]

The narrator shares Erminia's ideal, but he expresses it even more strongly. When he first introduces Gildippe and Odoardo, he portrays their unity as not "metaphorical" but substantial: "Colpo che ad un sol noccia unqua non scende, / ma indiviso è il dolor d'ogni ferita; / e spesso è l'un ferito, e l'altro langue, / e versa l'alma quel, se questa il sangue" [No blow can wound only one of them, for the pain of every wound is indivisible; often one weakens because the other is wounded, and he pours out his soul if she bleeds (1.57.5–8)]. Their unity is so physiological that pain is not "shared," but indivisible; nor do they share a common fate in any hackneyed figurative sense, because they are inseparable, almost literally "attached" to each other: "[Gildippe] va sempre affissa al caro fianco, e pende / da un fato solo l'una e l'altra vita" [Gildippe is ever affixed to the side of her husband, and one and the other life hangs from a single fate (1.57.3–4)].

The physicality of their union is almost grotesquely brought out by such expressions of inseparability, which threaten to make Gildippe and her husband into some sort of composite monster. Looking back over Erminia's and the narrator's descriptions, one is reminded of certain Dantean infernal figures, especially of Bertran de Born: "Ed eran due in uno, e uno in due."[18] The "monstrous" quality of Gildippe and Odoardo's unity is even acknowledged overtly by the narrator as he prepares to recount their death, although he presents them positively as "noble prodigies of virtue

and love" ["ben nati *mostri* / di virtute e d'amor" (20.94.5–6)].
It is perhaps worth pointing out that the narrator refers to his
own intentions as he prepares to describe their death: Solimano
fell like a lightning bolt onto the field of battle, he says, killing
"over a hundred" Christians, but the narrator has chosen to commemorate only these two (20.93). Given such a confession, it
would seem that there is at least an ostensible reason why the
couple enacts an ideal of marital unity with such thoroughness
that descriptions of them threaten to blur the boundary between
metaphor and literality.

But the reason is not immediately apparent. As the battle begins, Gildippe is actually alone, having outdistanced her husband
and everyone else in the charge of the Christian cavalry. Only
one other time has she appeared in the poem without Odoardo:
in canto nine, she also outperformed many male warriors (9.71).
At that time, she narrowly missed a duel with Clorinda, and the
narrator foretold both their deaths. Gildippe has not been mentioned since this earlier moment of separation, solitary prowess,
and near-confrontation with the pagan "double" who shares her
fate.

As lone *feritor cristiano* in the vanguard of the final battle,
Gildippe uses her "virile right hand" to transfix, lop, and divide
the bodies of her adversaries, creating the same sort of "miserable
monsters" (worthy of the Dantean circle of Bertran) that Clorinda
created earlier when they almost met.[19] But her moment of solitude is broken as Odoardo catches up to her, and their physical
unity contrasts with the bodies Gildippe has divided. Their final
moments, especially their death at the hand of Solimano, are the
ultimate enactment of Erminia and the narrator's ideal: there they
appear "due in uno, e uno in due" more grotesquely than ever.

> Ma lo sposo fedel, che di lei teme,
> corre in soccorso a la diletta moglie.
> Così congiunta, la concorde coppia
> ne la fida union le forze addoppia.
>
> Arte di schermo nova e non più udita
> a i magnanimi amanti usar vedresti:
> oblia di sé la guardia, e l'altrui vita

difende intentamente e quella e questi.
Ribatte i colpi la guerriera ardita
che vengono al suo caro aspri e molesti;
egli a l'arme a lei dritte oppon lo scudo,
v'opporria, s'uopo fosse, il capo ignudo.
　　Propria l'altrui defesa, e propria face
l'uno e l'altro di lor l'altrui vendetta.

. . . .

　　Tal fean de' Persi strage, e via maggiore
la fea de' Franchi il re di Sarmacante. . . .
　　　　　　(20.35.5–37.2; 38.1–2)

But her faithful spouse, who fears for her safety, runs in aid to his beloved wife. Thus joined together, the concordant couple redoubles its powers in faithful union.

Now you would see these magnanimous lovers use a new and unheard-of art of fencing: each of them forgets to keep up their own guard, and instead concentrates on defending the life of the other. The fearless warrior-woman beats back the harsh and harmful blows that come to her dear one; he opposes his shield to the weapons directed at her; were it necessary, he'd shield her with his bare head.

Each makes the other's defense their own; each takes vengeance for the other. . . .

Thus did they massacre the Persians; but Altamoro slaughtered an even greater number of Franks. . . .

This passage is remarkable for several reasons: first, because the enacted ideal of marriage as union is so exquisitely choreographed that the two spouses appear to become *literally* "due in uno, e uno in due." Their absolute unity is given expression in a "new art of fencing," where there is no distinction between offensive and defensive maneuvers.

In addition, as the last two verses quoted indicate, it is at this moment that they first encounter Altamoro. Gildippe's blow, which breaks and scatters the diadem on Altamoro's helmet, is answered by one of his that almost knocks her from the saddle. Yet although Odoardo has not been mentioned as part of the "duel" with Altamoro, he is still beside Gildippe. Thus he is able to catch his wife and hold her in the saddle: "cadea, ma 'l suo fedel la tenne in sella" (20.43.4). Odoardo will later repeat this action in the fatal combat with Solimano; significantly, he and his wife disappear until that moment. In the later duel it is again Gildippe who strikes the foe, and as Solimano stabs her mortally in reply, Odoardo supports her once more, while attempting to attack Solimano. It is this dispersion—or, to quote the narrator—"division" of Odoardo's attention and labors that dooms him as well, for in this moment Solimano lops off the arm with which he has supported his wife and maintained their unity.

> Ma voler e poter che si divida
> bastar non può contra il pagan sì forte
> tal che non sostien lei, nè l'omicida
> de la dolce alma sua conduce a morte.
> Anzi avien che 'l Soldano a lui recida
> il braccio, appoggio a la fedel consorte,
> onde cader lasciolla, ed egli presse
> le membra a lei con le sue membra stesse.
>
> (20.98)

But will and power divided against itself cannot long endure against the mighty pagan, so that Odoardo neither supports her adequately, nor deals death to the murderer of his sweet soul. Instead, Solimano chops off his arm, the support of his faithful consort, so that he let her fall, and falling, he crushed her members with the members of his own body.

Their grotesque death finally begins to reval the "meta-theme" that has underwritten their marriage all along. The rhyme *morte/consorte* recalls their introduction in canto one, where the narrator declared the meaning of his contention that a single fate united the couple: "o ne la guerra anco *consorti*, / non sarete disgiunti ancor che *morti*" [O you who are partners in war as well, you will not be divided even when dead (1.56.7–8)].

The rhyme helps explain Erminia's and the narrator's predilection for "literalizing" the verb *giungere* and its compounds when describing the English warrior-couple. In one of his most famous and most "autobiographical" prose writings, Tasso defines the word *consorte* as a one-word explanation of the ideal "conjunction" in marriage.

. . . di marito . . . altro nome forse più efficace è . . . consorte, conciò sia cosa ch'il marito e la moglie debbon esser consorti d'una medesima fortuna e tutti i beni e tutti i mali della vita debbono fra loro esser communi in quel modo che l'anima accomuna i suoi beni e le sue operazioni co 'l corpo e che 'l corpo con l'anima suole accomunarle: e sì come, quando alcuna parte del corpo

ci duole, l'animo non può esser lieto e alla mestizia dell' animo suol seguitar
l'infermità del corpo, così il marito dee dolersi co' dolori della moglie e la moglie
con quei del marito. E la medesima comunanza dee essere in tutti gli affetti e
in tutti gli offici e in tutte l'operazioni: e tanto è simile la *congiunzione* che 'l
marito ha con la moglie a quella che 'l corpo ha con l'anima, che non senza
ragione così il nome di consorte al marito e alla moglie s'attribuisce, com'a
l'anima è stato attribuito; conciosia cosa che, dell'anima ragionando, disse il
Petrarca: "L'errante mia consorte," ad imitazion forse di Dante, che nella canzona
della nobiltà aveva detto che l'anima si sposava al corpo. . . .[20]

[A more fitting name for the husband is] consort, for husband and wife should
be sharers of the same fortune, and all the good things and all the evils in their
lives should be held in common, just as the soul shares all its good and its
activities with the body and the body likewise shares with the soul. As the soul
cannot be joyful when some part of the body suffers, and as infirmity of the
body usually follows upon affliction of the soul, so a husband ought to suffer
along with the sufferings of his wife and the wife with those of her husband,
and in the same way they ought to share all of their affections, their duties, and
their activities. So similar is the [conjunction] of a husband and his wife to that
of the body and the soul that the name consort [is] attributed not without reason
to [husband and wife, just as it has been attributed to the soul, for] Petrarch
speaks of the soul as "my wandering consort." In this he may have been imitating
Dante, who says in his poem on nobility that the soul is married to the
body. . . .[21]

We notice, in fact, that as Odoardo moves to support his *fedel
consorte* in her death throes, she is also referred to as his "sweet
soul," *la dolce alma sua* (20.98.6, 4).

But there is an important difference between the two texts:
whereas the dialogue describes the soul/body "consortium" as an
apt simile for marriage, here it is enacted. And attention is focused less on the brief mention of Gildippe as "soul" than on a
paradoxical continuation of their bodily unity. At the moment
when Odoardo's arm has been literally divided from the other
members of his body, he becomes most fully unified with Gildippe, pressing his *membra* to hers. At this point, and for the
only time, a simile is introduced to describe their relation. But
the *topos* of the elm and the vine, a traditional figure of marriage,
is turned inside-out to describe their *death*.[22] When they are felled

by the axe, elm and vine become most fully "one," as the elm unwillingly crushes its "wife" and "companion."

> Come olmo a cui la pampinosa pianta
> cupida s'aviticchi e si marite,
> se ferro il tronca o turbine lo schianta
> trae seco a terra la compagna vite,
> ed egli stesso il verde onde s'ammanta
> le sfronda e pesta l'uve sue gradite,
> par che se 'n dolga, e più che 'l proprio fato
> di lei gl'incresca che gli more a lato;
> così cade egli, e sol di lei gli duole
> che 'l Cielo eterna sua compagna fece.
>
> (20.99.1–100.2)

Like an elm to whom the leafy vine attaches and marries herself eagerly with her tendrils, if the iron cuts him down or whirling wind uproots him, so that he drags his companion vine to earth with him, and strips away the greenery in which she mantles herself, and crushes her pleasant grapes, he seems to complain, and more than for his own fate to grieve for her, who dies alongside him; so he [Odorado] falls, and is pained only for her, whom Heaven long ago made his eternal companion.

Gildippe and Odoardo "consummate" their marriage when, most literally, the marriage becomes that "two in one monster" of mixed members that the couple has enacted all along. In another grotesque reversal of traditional *topoi*, they die a real death that is a literalization of the *petite mort* of sexual union (100.2–7), and their souls fly heavenward "joined" (*congiunte* 100.8). But the narrator asserts that Heaven made them "eternal companions" long before their death (*fece* 100.2), so that their united souls merely continue their bodily unity.

Throughout the poem, and most fully at their death, Gildippe and Odorado have enacted—without the narrator or anyone else ever explicitly saying so—the ideal of marriage as enunciated by Saint Paul. Quoting verbatim from the Hebrew legend of Eve's formation from the rib of Adam (Genesis 2.24), Paul foreshadows Erminia's description of the English spouses when he says that marriage makes "one flesh" of husband and wife, replacing the fleshly bond of child to parent: "Propter hoc relinquit homo pa-trem et matrem suam et adhaerebit uxori suae, et erunt *duo in carne una*" [For this reason a man shall leave his father and mother and shall be joined (adhere) to his wife, and (they shall be *two in one flesh*") (emphasis mine)].[23] Paul does not mean this "metaphorically." He understands the union of marriage so literally that it is the basis for his injunction against fornication. No one, he says, may have relations with a prostitute, for the sexual act is the means whereby two bodies become one:

> An nescitis quoniam qui adhaeret meretrici, *unum corpus* efficitur? Erunt enim (inquit) *duo in carne una.* . . . Fugite fornicationem. Omne peccatum, quodcumque fecerit homo, extra corpus est: qui autem fornicatur, in corpus suum peccat.

> Do you not know that he who joins himself [adheres] to a prostitute [is made] *one body* with her? For, as it is written, "[They shall be *two in*] *one flesh.*" . . . Shun [fornication]. Every other sin which a man commits is outside the body; but the immoral man sins against his own body (1 Corinthians 6.16, 18; emphasis mine).

Paul's ideal of marriage is also found, and in especially literalizing form, in another famous Scriptural text, Christ's injunction against divorce. To the Pharisees who ask him if divorce is ever permissible, Christ quotes the same verse (Genesis 2.24) later used by Paul, and explains it: "Propter hoc dimittet homo patrem, et matrem, et adhaerebit uxori suae, et erunt duo in carne una. Itaque iam *non sunt duo, sed una caro.* Quod ergo Deus *coniunxit,* homo non separet." [For this reason a man shall leave . . . So they are *no long two but one flesh.* What therefore God has *joined together,* let not man put asunder. (Matthew 19.5–6; emphasis added).] Gildippe and Odoardo, "quei *duo sì giunti in uno,*" whom Heaven made eternal companions, thus enact this ideal with extreme precision. Ironically, the two compatriots of Henry VIII enact the Counter-Reformation's reaffirmation of the eternity of the marriage bond.

John Robinson has demonstrated that, contrary to what one would gather from the history of exegesis, it is inaccurate and misleading to interpret Paul's discourse on the body as metaphoric.[24] It is not necessary to read Robinson's own sophisticated exegesis to grasp such a point, however; it is enough to mind the

language of the interlocking passages of Genesis, Matthew, Ephesians, and 1 Corinthians, as Christian readers or church-goers
could have done in Tasso's time. Paul's use of language shows
plainly enough that "metaphor" is an inappropriate description of
his discourse on the body. Besides, it is ultimately not important
whether Tasso or his audience would have thought Paul had spoken literally or metaphorically; the point is that Gildippe and
Odoardo enact and thus literalize an echo that could otherwise
have remained metaphoric in the discourse of Erminia and the
narrator.

Their enactment of Pauline marriage is an important meta-
theme for the *Liberata*. For one thing, it defines the way in which
the poem attempts to turn Christian misogyny, of which Paul was
essentially the founder, into a kind of feminism. But Paul was not
simply and purely a misogynist; there are actually two currents of
feeling about women in Paul's ethical and ecclesiological writings
that touch on the theme of the body. One current is surprisingly
egalitarian. Gildippe and Odoardo act out, among other things,
Paul's dictum that neither spouse has power over his or her own
body; rather, they hold power reciprocally, over each other.

. . . propter fornicationem autem unusquisque suam uxorem habeat, et una-
quaeque suum virum habeat. Uxori vir debitum reddat: similiter autem et uxor
viro. Mulier sui corporis potestatem non habet, sed vir. Similiter autem et vir
sui corporis potestatem non habet, sed mulier.

. . . because of the temptation to [fornication], each man should have his own
wife and each woman her own husband. The husband should give to his wife
her conjugal rights, and likewise the wife to her husband. For the wife does not
rule over her own body, but the husband does; likewise the husband does not
rule over his own body, but the wife does (1 Corinthians 7.2–4).

In this, Paul is more egalitarian than the patriarch of Tasso's own
dialogue, who declares in a blaze of contradiction that sexual
infidelity is acceptable in men but not in women, because women
are by nature just as libidinous as men.[25] But there is another,
more pervasive current in Paul's discourse on the body, which
moderns—and, I suspect, Tasso—have found oppressively misogynist. This is the corollary that posits a strict homology between

the relation of women to their husbands, and the relation of the Church to Christ. In the first passage against adultery quoted above, Paul explains that all believers' bodies are "members" of the Body of Christ, which is vivified by the Holy Spirit. Here is Paul's more famous use of "body-language," the so-called Mystical Body, the notion that Christians collectively form the Body of Christ. It is noteworthy that Christ's relation to the Church as Body is not that of "soul," a role that would more likely correspond to the one Paul assigns to the Holy Spirit. Rather, since Christ shares the bond of flesh with humanity through the Incarnation and through the Eucharist, he is the Head of the Church as Body. Since Christ and the Church are "one flesh," like man and wife, the Church is also called the Bride of Christ. But the analogy cuts both ways: since human brides are "one flesh" with their husbands, they are also "bodies" who must be ruled by a male "head" as Christ governs the Church.[26]

Paul's analogy of the Head as governor of the Body is the foundation for all his ethics and politics. On the one hand, it undergirds his attempt to unify early Christians into a homogeneous, orthodox "body" of believers, his attempt to "incorporate" the Church. At the individual level, body imagery informs Paul's "sexual politics" or ethics of domestic life. In both cases, Paul's literalizing interpretation of the head/body relation excludes women from any form or level of power. Writing to Timothy, Paul declares that women must not be allowed to teach or otherwise hold authority in congregations of Christians. Ironically, this injunction comes from exactly the same source as his egalitarian declaration that, as "one flesh," husband and wife hold reciprocal power over each other. Women may not hold authority, he says, because Adam was formed before Eve, and Eve was formed from the body of Adam. Thus, being weaker, she allowed herself to be seduced into sin (foreshadowing Milton, Paul insists that Adam was not deceived). Adam's ontological superiority derives from his temporal and material anteriority to Eve, and the "proper" relation of husband and wife is nothing more than a continuation in history of Eve's status as literal body of Adam.[27]

Paul's pronouncements on the role of the wife in marriage, which depend on this myth, make extensive use of the hierarch-

ical image of the Head and the Body to stress the "fact" of wom-
ens' continuing ontological inferiority, their need to be guided by
their husbands. "Wives must be subject to their husbands," he
says, using a word (*subditae*) whose primary meaning is political.[28]
This is because there is a *strict* analogy, as far as Paul is concerned,
between the microcosmic relation of husband and wife and the
macrocosmic relation of Christ and the Church:

Mulieres viris suis subditae sint, sicut Domino: quoniam vir caput est mulieris:
sicut Christus caput est Ecclesiae: ipse, salvator corporis eius. Sed sicut Ecclesia
subiecta est Christo, ita et mulieres viris suis in omnibus.

Wives, be subject to your husbands, as to the Lord. For the husband is the head
of the wife as Christ is the head of the church, his body, and is himself its
Savior. As the church is subject to Christ, so let wives also be subject in
everything to their husbands (Ephesians 5.22–24).

There is, in fact, a kind of corporeal "chain of being," wherein
each superior being is Head to an inferior: "Volo autem vos scire
quod omnis viri caput, Christus est: caput autem mulieris, vir:
caput vero Christi, Deus" [I want you to understand that the head
of every man is Christ, the head of a woman is her husband, and
the head of Christ is God (1 Corinthians 11.3)]. Thus women
must veil their hair when praying, to demonstrate their ritual
acceptance of subjection to men within the hierarchy of relations:

Vir quidem non debet velare caput suum: quoniam imago et gloria Dei est,
mulier autem gloria viri est. Non enim vir ex muliere est, sed mulier ex viro.
Etenim non est creatus vir propter mulierem, sed mulier propter virum. Ideo
debet mulier potestatem habere supra caput propter angelos.

For a man ought not to cover his head, since he is the image and glory of God;
but woman is the glory of man. For man was not made from woman, but woman
from man. Neither was man created for woman, but woman for man. That is
why a woman ought to have a veil on her head because of the angels.

Milton later paraphrased this declaration rather shockingly in his
depiction of Adam and Eve before the fall: "He for God only, she
for God in him."[29]

And yet, even within this most doctrinaire of statements, Paul
cannot resign himself to subjecting women to men absolutely and
without qualification, for he adds, "Verumtamen neque vir sine

muliere: neque mulier sine viro in Domino. Nam sicut mulier de viro, ita et vir per mulierem: omnia autem ex Deo." [Nevertheless, in the Lord woman is not independent of man nor man of woman; for as woman was made from man, so man is now born of woman. And all things are from God (1 Corinthians 11.8ff., esp. 11–13).] Even at his most doctrinaire moments, Paul attempts to compensate for the subordination of women by urging husbands to be "benign despots," and by explaining why they should be so: "Mulieres, subditae estote viris, sicut opportet, in Domino. Viri, diligite uxores vestras, et nolite amari esse ad illas." [Wives, be subject to your husbands, as is fitting in the Lord. Husbands, love your wives, and do not be harsh with them (Colossians 3.18–19).] Men must love their wives precisely because women are "inferior," in the way that Christ loves the Church *because* it is inferior and subject to him.

Viri diligite uxores vestrae, sicut et Christus dilexit Ecclesiam, et seipsum tradidit pro ea. . . . Ita et viri debent diligere uxores suas ut corpora sua. Qui suam uxorem diligit, seipsum diligit. Nemo enim unquam carnem suam odio habuit: sed nutrit et fovit eam, sicut et Christus Ecclesiam: quia membra sumus corporis eius, de carne eius et de ossibus eius.

Husbands, love your wives, as Christ loved the church and gave himself up for her. . . . Even so husbands should love their wives as their own bodies. He who loves his wife loves himself. For no man ever hates his own flesh, but loves it and cherishes it, as Christ does the church, because we are members of his body, [parts of his flesh and of his bones] (Ephesians 5.25, 28–30).

Paul stresses that the two relations are exactly congruent by alluding to Adam's speech on why husband and wife are literally two in one flesh: "Dixitque Adam: Hoc nunc, os ex ossibus meis, et caro de carne mea" [And Adam said: "This now is bone of my bones, and flesh of my flesh" (Genesis 2.23)].

Paul's ambivalence reflects the ideological incompatibility between two needs: a desire to reaffirm the subjection of women in Old Testament society, and a wish not to betray either his own assertions that Christ's message is universal or Christ's personal empathy with marginalized and powerless "subjects," including women and children. But the strongest contributor to Paul's ambivalence is probably the organization of all his social thinking according to analogies with the body. This is especially true for his ontology of gender. His dependence upon the myth of Adam's rib gives him what appear to be perfectly compatible reasons for both women's subjection and the equality men owe them in marriage. Since husband and wife become "one flesh," they hold authority over each other's sexual lives. But since women originated in a piece of Adam's body rather than through direct creation, they are clearly the "flesh" or Body of men, and the fact that Eve listened to the snake and fell first must be proof of her and her daughters' need for male domination.

Both at the level of individual ethics and at that of ecclesiastical organization or politics, Paul's reliance on the image of the Body and the Head is an attempt to provide a substantial, non-metaphoric rationale for unity and peace, rather than dissent and discord. He admonishes the Ephesians to be "eager to maintain the unity of the Spirit in the bond of peace. There is one body and one Spirit, just as you were called to the one hope that belongs to your call, one lord, one faith, one baptism, one God and Father of us all, who is above all and through all and in all [of us]" (Ephesians 4.3–6). The ultimate aim of his hierarchical organization is stasis, but for the sake of peace, rather than as an end in itself. We are now so accustomed to the rationalizations of power that we may be disinclined to discern real compassion for anyone in Paul's usage of body analogies to enforce organization. But Paul's residual compassion for women and his ambivalence about the relation of man to woman is reflected in the uncomfortable "feminism" of Tasso's poem. Although on the surface its attempts to "redeem" women often appear indistinguishable from misogyny, at a level underneath plot, traced by inconsistencies and "too obvious echoes," there runs a vein of empathy that defines "redemption" as salvation from misery and solitude. Such is the case for Gildippe as well as for the wife of Altamoro.

Although Gildippe is "two in one" with Odoardo and "affixed to his side" in a way that recalls Eve, she has two moments of glory without him. In addition, the narrator apostrophizes her directly as she dashes into battle, telling her that "heaven conceded such glory to the hand of a woman."[30] Furthermore, we saw that she was called the "sweet soul" of her husband. This could be nothing more than a moment of sentimentality, but in light of Gildippe's other qualities, it seems like another "redemptive" gesture. In the same dialogue where we found his egalitarian definition of *consorte*, the patriarch who is "Tasso's" interlocutor discusses the body/soul analogy and stresses that the *husband* must be seen as the "soul" who governs his wife, the "body." Gildippe is therefore in direct contradiction to Tasso's own overt portrayal of a patriarchal ontology.[31]

Yet, even in the dialogue, it is rather unclear precisely to what degree the wife must be subservient to the husband. On the one hand, "no difference in rank (*nobiltà*) is as great as the difference in nature between men and women. As a result of that natural difference, women are born to be men's subjects (*soggette*)" (*Dialoghi* 1.93; *Tasso's Dialogues* 83). On the other hand, " 'The virtue of a woman . . . is to know how to obey a man *not as a servant obeys a lord or the body the soul* but in a civil manner (*civilmente*), as the citizens of a well-ordered city obey the laws and the magistrates, or as the passions of the soul—for the soul's faculties are arranged (*ordinate*) like the ranks (*ordini*) of citizens in a city— usually obey reason.' "[32] Aside from remotivating Paul's analogy between domestic and political relations, Tasso's patriarch also distinguishes between males and females, as Paul had done (1 Corinthians 11.14–15), on the basis of hair. But his treatment is both more extreme, since it attempts to make hair-length a question of biology rather than custom, and less severe, since it tapers off into a simile that uses this "natural" difference as an index of women's essential happiness.

"One must not act too harshly toward [*acerbamente offender*] the feminine spirit, which by nature longs to adorn the body. Among the animals, nature has sought to adorn the males more than the females. . . . With respect to human beings, however, we see that nature has paid more attention to the beauty of women than of men. Woman's flesh is softer and ordinarily more attractive to the eye, and their faces are not encumbered by beards. . . . Hair is a very great natural ornament, but it never grows as long or as soft or as fine on men as on women.

Women rejoice in their long hair as the trees rejoice in their leaves. . . ." (*Dia-loghi* 1.95–96; *Tasso's Dialogues* 87–89)

Altogether, the words of the patriarch appear to constitute a stern palinode to the kind of Pauline egalitarianism embodied by Gildippe and Odoardo. But even here there are moments of ambivalence.

This ambivalence, and its Pauline subtext, can be seen more clearly in the contrasting fates of Gildippe and Armida in canto twenty of the *Liberata*. It should by now be clear that Gildippe's death with her husband is far less a punishment for infractions of gender-role norms than a sublimation of their previous relation, a kind of second and higher marriage in which their souls achieve the kind of "literal" unity their bodies had known in life. The epic subtext for the narrator's final apostrophe to Gildippe and Odoardo reveals that their simultaneous death is a way of recuperating or redeeming Vergil's Nisus and Euryalus, and similar passionate friends in epic.[33]

But there is more to Gildippe's significance than this. It should be noted that Gildippe and her husband die at a moment that is numerologically significant, stanza 100. In isolation, this detail means little, but it is not isolated. To begin with, there are only five other cantos that have 100 or more stanzas, and in each of those, stanza 100 appears to be reserved for a significant event; indeed all stanzas 100 appear to be intimately related. Four of them regard the triangular relation of Clorinda, Tancredi, and Erminia. In canto six, Erminia, disguised in the armor of Clorinda, announces her intention to await Tancredi outside the Christian camp. In canto seven, a devil disguised as Clorinda incites a pagan to break the truce during which Raimondo has taken the place of Tancredi, who has wandered off in search of this ersatz "Clorinda." In canto nineteen, Erminia confesses to Tancredi's servant Vafrino that, although "tante volte *liberata* e serva," she has never ceased loving Tancredi. In canto twelve, the news of Clorinda's death at the hand of Tancredi reaches Jerusalem, and the text ironically echoes Clorinda's own words to make a lie of her assertion that "the bewildered city" would not suffer from her death since she was "only a woman."[34]

What all these cantos have in common is their reference to marriage through the symbolism of the number 100 as plenitude. I shall have to discuss elsewhere the text's creation of allusive marriages for Tancredi, Clorinda, and Erminia.[35] Stanza 100 of canto eighteen, however, which has no direct relevance to these personages, is related meta-thematically to its counterpart in canto twenty. In canto 18.100, Goffredo plants the Christian battleflag on the ramparts of Jerusalem, after having been inspired with a vision of the conjunction of the heavenly and earthly Jerusalems (18.92–96). A symmetry between the two stanzas 100 is established by the plot, for the death of Gildippe and Odoardo follows immediately upon a second planting of the Christian insignia, this time on the last pagan stronghold of Jerusalem. Thus there appears to be a link between Gildippe and Odoardo's transition from bodily to spiritual marriage and the unification of earthly and heavenly Jerusalems. The link is easier to see if we recall that canto one, as beginning of the poem, and canto twenty as its end are both characterized by other apparently numerological stanzas, placed at the beginning of canto one and the very end of canto twenty.

Canto one begins like a hexameron: six years of combat in the Holy Land are ending for the Christian army, as the narrator tells us in *stanza* six. In stanza seven, God the Father looks down over all creation at once; what he sees will cause him to decide that the time has come to perfect the army by organizing it under one "Head." In stanza thirty-three, Goffredo is elected captain, at the behest of Peter the Hermit, who has declared "fate un corpo sol de' membri amici, / fate un capo che gli altri indrizzi e frene" [make a single body of the friendly members, with a head that guides and curbs the others (1.31.5–6)]. Furthermore, the angel Gabriel has undergone an "imitation" of the Incarnation by putting on a fictive body visible to humans in order to announce to Goffredo that he will be elected (1.13–17). This combination of overt references to Paul's discourse of the Body with numerological references to the creation of the world, the Incarnation, and the completion of Christ's life in the body, creates a covert double to the official allegory of the poem.[36] Goffredo's explanation (1.23) of why the organization is necessary—so that pilgrims may fulfill their vows to adore the tomb from which Christ was resurrected in the body—recurs, right down to its rhyme in *devoto/voto,* in stanza 144 of canto twenty, the last of the poem. Now we have seen the importance of the "perfect" number 100 in stanza numbers (and Dante ended the *Divine Comedy* at canto 100). Why then should the *Liberata* end at stanza 144?

In light of the combination of numerological and corporeal allusions with enactments of Incarnation, incorporation, and marriage, this ending can only be significant as an eschatological allusion evoking the 144,000 souls to be saved at the end of time. These 144,000 souls, whom Saint John calls virgins, were traditionally thought of as the "brides" of Christ, in accordance with Paul's thematics of marriage to Christ at both collective and individual levels. In the context of the liberation of Jerusalem, this allusion is all the more probable since the Apocalypse ends with a vision wherein Saint John sees "the Holy City, New Jerusalem, coming down out of Heaven from God, made ready like a bride adorned for her husband" ["sanctam civitatem Ierusalem novam descendentem de caelo a Deo, paratam, sicut sponsam ornatam viro suo"].[37] As witness to the Incarnation and the Resurrection, Christ's empty tomb at the end of Tasso's marriage canto also recalls to mind the voice that accompanied John's vision, proclaiming the definitive reunification of humanity with God, when "he will dwell with them, and they shall be his people . . . and death shall be no more, neither shall there be mourning nor crying nor pain any more . . . ," ending the human anguish epitomized by the building of the tomb at the end of the *Iliad.*[38] Thus, the numerological and other correspondences of canto twenty with cantos one and eighteen suggest that, as consummation of their marriage, the death of Gildippe and Odoardo is a miniature and prefiguration of the "happy end" promised to humankind, a unification taking place in the body and through the Church as Bride and Body of Christ, at the end of time.

I have just referred to canto twenty as a marriage canto. But I have not yet discussed Armida. The importance of marriage and the body to canto twenty, however, should have suggested a way of regarding her repetition of the Blessed Virgin's response to the Incarnation. In fact, as if the "too obvious echo" of Scripture were not enough, the text reinforces it by repeating the same *senno/cenno* rhyme used in the Incarnational stanza thirty-three of canto one to describe the election of Goffredo. Goffredo's powers over the army as described by this rhyme are exactly congruent with the powers Armida gives Rinaldo over herself;[39] that is, Armida's words allusively declare her the "body" of Rinaldo, in covert response to his overt proposal of matrimony (20.134.6–135.8). This is a symmetrical reversal, in Pauline terms, of their sinful relation as described in her garden: "L'uno di servitù, l'altra d'impero / si gloria, ella in se stessa, ed egli in lei" [one glories in servitude, the other in empire, she in herself and he in her (16.21.1–2)]. This passage enacted in reverse Paul's dictum that woman was created for (*propter*) man, not vice-versa, and until 'her conversion, Armida reversed the relation that should make her the *subdita* of Rinaldo. *Impero/imperio* (*imperium*), the military and political term for the power to command, is thus used to characterize both Goffredo at his election (1.33.6) and Armida in her garden. Her repetition of Goffredo's *senno/cenno* rhyme "returns" this power to Rinaldo. Given the explicit carnality of their former relation in the garden, and the Pauline discourse of corporeality and incorporation they enact in canto twenty, it is obvious that the words of Armida and Rinaldo are an agreement on marriage, and the logical conclusion of their relation as "one flesh." "It is obvious," and yet a Migiel or a Zatti could with perfect reasonableness object that the text does not sanction such a reading.

But the *senno/cenno* rhyme adds still another covert dimension to Armida's conversion, since it indicates a change in her mode of imitating the Blessed Virgin, an imitation that the text has suggested through "echoes" or *imitatio* ever since she was introduced. This rhyme, which occurs only once in Petrarch's published lyrics, is highly characteristic of Dante. It is the rhyme of ideal authority by the very nature of the words that compose it—*wisdom* and the *gesture* of command that requires no speech to be understood and obeyed. Most visibly, it occurs in the *Divine*

Comedy at moments of reunion with authoritative figures.[40] In the Garden of Eden, Virgilio declares to Dante that his will is now rectified and that Beatrice will soon arrive; in the Heaven of Mars, Dante converses with the soul of his paternal great-great-grandfather Cacciaguida, a Crusader who discourses on justice and the simplicity of the past. Both contexts combine nostalgic restitution with a discourse on justice, and both are set in a garden (Dante's meeting with Cacciaguida tropes that of Aeneas with Anchises in the Elysian fields).

Armida's "echo" of Mary's words in a Dantean rhyme of authority thus reinforces the contrast between her present behavior and her reversal of Paul's dictum about female subordination in the garden of canto sixteen. Not only is the power she gives Rinaldo over herself congruent with Goffredo's power over the army, but her precise quotation of Scripture substitutes Rinaldo (*tu*) for Mary's *Dominus*. This move is congruent with Paul's dictum that wives must be subject to their husbands "as to the Lord" to avoid repeating Eve's archetypal sin. The movement from the "Edenic" canto sixteen to canto twenty thus plays upon the traditional view of the Blessed Virgin as the woman who reversed and redeemed the sin of Eve (Eva-Ave) through her humility. Dante, who places a prayer to Mary in the final canto of *Paradiso*, says that she was both the humblest and the most exalted of humans ("umile e alta più che crëatura"[33.2]). In the final *canzone* of the *Canzoniere*, Petrarch refers to her as one who always answered well ("colei che ben sempre rispose") and who turned Eve's weeping to joy ("che 'l pianto d'Eva in allegrezza torni" [366.7, 36]). The Latin tradition of scriptural commentary also identified Mary with the Spouse of the Song of Songs, who was a closed garden (*hortus conclusus*), making her the ideal figure both of the Church as Spouse of Christ and of womanly virtue.[41] Thus Armida's answer reinforces in a number of ways Paul's dictum that husbands must be "lords" over their wives as Christ is over his.

But Armida's conversion is still likely to appear startlingly abrupt. This is because dependence on traditional mimetic notions of "character" and plot (even by deconstructionists) obstructs a view of the purely textual, nonmimetic mechanisms by which her conversion takes place. Those mechanisms, "too obvious echoes," are strong forms of *imitatio* that produce a kind of supplement to the plot. They occur not only in canto twenty but also, and especially, in canto four, where Armida was first introduced. Since this introduction, she has most often been presented as a Petrarchan *donna* (etymologically a *domina*), who dominates her admirers as the sun "governs" the snow in Petrarch's canzone 127.[42] In fact, at the point when the text "stole" two entire verses from Petrarch, it was describing Armida's first and greatest triumph as *donna-sole*, the moment at which it became clear that she would have her way with the Christian army despite the opposition of its *capitano* or Head. Having first compared her to a number of other "heavenly bodies" when she appeared in the Christian camp, the text finally settled on the sun as the closest approximation of the splendor of her beauty, and then described her in conventional Petrarchan terms (4.28–30). But her real triumph came when Goffredo "surrendered" ("Cedo . . . e vinto sono") to his subordinates' desire to espouse Armida's fraudulent cause (4.82.5). In the next moment, as she learned the news of her victory, she "became"—incarnated—the sun through the rhetorical figure of catachresis or implicit metaphor. "Serenò allora i nubilosi rai / Armida, e sì ridente apparve fuore / ch'innamorò di sue bellezze il cielo / asciugandosi gli occhi col bel velo" [Then the clouds withdrew leaving Armida's rays serene, and she shone forth so laughingly that she enamored the sky of her loveliness, drying her eyes with her lovely veil (4.84.5–8)].

The origin of these verses is meant to be apparent, and to shock, but for a reason. Verse seven comes from the final prayer-*canzone* to the Virgin, while verse eight describes the moment in Petrarch's other most famous *canzone* at which Laura's lover imagines her returning to the landscape where he once espied her bathing and discovering his lifeless body: "Oh the pity! seeing me already dust amid the stones, Love [perhaps] will inspire her to sigh so sweetly that she will win mercy for me and force Heaven, drying her eyes with her lovely veil."[43] Both Petrarch's poems are about incarnation, but one depicts Laura as a secular,

even pagan version of Mary, through allusions to Actaeon's metamorphosis, to Diana, and to Danaë. The lover remembers Laura
as a kind of composite Mary-Danaë, noting that she sat "humble
in such a glory, already covered with the loving cloud" of falling
blossoms ("umile in tanta gloria, / coverta già de l'amoroso
nembo" [Petrarch 126.44–45; Durling 246]). Throughout canto
four, Armida has been described in terms that were appropriate
to both Laura and the Virgin. But perhaps the best other example
is the very moment of her introduction, where references to her
"grey-haired wisdom" and "masculine heart beneath blond hair"
closely echoed Petrarch's sonnet 213, in which he praised Laura
with *topoi* appropriate to encomia of Mary: "Gratie ch'a pochi il
ciel largo destina: / rara vertù, non già d'umana gente, / sotto
biondi capei canuta mente, e 'n umil donna alta beltà divina"
[Graces that generous Heaven allots to few, virtues rare beyond
the custom of men, beneath blond hair the wisdom of gray age,
and in a humble lady high divine beauty].[44]

All these "too obvious echoes" have portrayed Armida as a
counterfeit Blessed Virgin, a new, sinister Laura conscious of and
willing to manipulate the pseudo-religious sexual fantasies that
men spin about her, as the Christian soldiers do so intensely in
cantos four and five. Indeed, Petrarch's sonnet 213, the echo of
which introduces Armida, provides an intertextual "prophecy" of
her counterfeit Mariological power over men; after having enumerated Laura's charms, it concludes, "by these magicians was I
transformed" ("da questi magi transformato fui"). Armida's "magic,"
her manipulation of erotic desire through "metamorphoses," is a
fraudulent version of the Incarnation that only Mary could effect
through *charitas*. Armida's art literalizes the Medusan power of
Laura's "lovely eyes that turn hearts to stone, powerful enough to
brighten the abyss and night and to take souls from their bodies
and give them to others," especially when she causes the metamorphosis of her captive knights.[45] These are the eyes that the
reformed "Petrarch" repudiates in his final palinode to the Virgin.
Complaining that "Medusa and my error have made me a stone,"
he begs her to "turn those beautiful eyes that sorrowing saw the
pitiless wounds in your dear Son's sweet limbs, to my perilous

state" (Petrarch 366.111, 22–25; Durling 576). Like both the *Divine Comedy* and Petrarch's *Canzoniere*, *Gerusalemme liberata* ends by turning its attention and "desire" from a *donna* to the supreme *Domina*. In order to recuperate Armida, the text strips her of pseudo-Mariological powers (another way of saying that it restores Rinaldo's autonomy) and leaves her only the humility of the *ancilla*, through which Mary was exalted.[46]

I will not dwell in detail on the intense *imitatio* through which this change is effected, except to note that, just before her conversion, Armida's successive defeats in Petrarchan enactments as *donna, maga,* and *guerriera* are crowned by her defeat as *donna-sole*. When Rinaldo seizes Armida, preventing her from killing herself on a literalized Petrarchan arrow of love (20.123–128.7), his act is expressed through the ironic recall of a verse in Petrarch's apotheosis of Laura: "le fe' d'un braccio al bel fianco colonna."[47] The rest of her defeat is effected through Rinaldo's protestations of love and his tears—the medium of her own sunny triumph in canto four. He glosses her Petrarchan veil, the other vehicle of her triumph as *donna-sole*, as pagan ignorance, hoping that it will be rent by the rays (*raggi*) of divine illumination. Finally, he becomes an anti-Petrarchan *dominus* or *donno-sole*, and the rhetorical intensity of his transformation into a "sun" melts the last icy vestiges of Armida's Petrarchan identity: "sì come *suol* nevosa falda / dov'arda il *sole* o tepid'aura spiri, / così l'ira che 'n lei parea sì *salda* / *solvesi* e restan *sol* gli altri desiri" [just like a bank of snow where the sun shines or warm air blows, so her wrath that seemed so firm dissolves leaving only the other desires].[48] It is here that Armida gives her "too obvious echo" of the Virgin's response to the Incarnation, the act by which Mary's humility made her paradoxically "alta più che crëatura." Given the fact that Armida's transgressiveness has been consistently expressed in terms of Pauline body-discourse, it is clear that her *imitatio* of the Virgin's words signals an ideal subordination that embraces both Christianity and a specifically Pauline wifely virtue by pointing to the ideal of Christian womanhood. In so doing, Armida ends her rivalry with Christ, her status as object of idolatrous desire, which has been expressed through her sunniness, for Christ is "the Sun of justice, who makes the world bright though it is full of dark thick errors."[49]

In the fates of Gildippe and Armida, the "desire" of canto twenty strains to reconcile two contradictory ways of attaining harmony between the sexes. Gildippe and Odoardo die together, and their corporeal marriage is sublimated into spirit, while hinting at the eventual cosmic reconciliation of flesh and spirit. Neither is left to mourn the other, and they enact that aspect of Paul's thought that attempts to concede equality of rights in marriage. Armida enacts a movement from Petrarchan domination to Marian humility, along with Paul's dictum that, through the literal union of the flesh, "duo in carne una," the unbelieving spouse will be saved by a believer. However harsh the recuperation of Armida may seem to a post-Pauline society, the poem saves her from what she has feared all along: absolute humiliation, defeat, and slavery (see 20.131–33). To this extent, both Gildippe and Armida resemble Altamoro's wife, since the text saves them from experiences of Andromache: widowing and slavery.

At the same time—and this is what has marred her mimetic appeal to readers—Armida's movement from *domina* to *ancilla* has been accomplished almost exclusively through intertextual recall and the enactment of the Pauline "meta-theme." It would require a separate essay to investigate why Armida's marriage is never effected "onstage," or even sanctioned overtly (a problem complicated by the analogous case of Erminia). But it can be safely concluded that two of the most obscure women of the *Liberata* are important in inverse proportion to their prominence, because their proximity to Armida implicates her in a thoroughgoing, even obsessive discourse to which wives are important, both as analogy and as ethical ideal. In varying ways, Gildippe and Altamoro's "Andromache" demonstrate the importance of intertextual recall and "meta-thematic" enactment to the *Liberata*'s discourses on authority in two apparently unrelated fields—gender relations and poetics.

The enactments of canto twenty do not necessarily prove the adequacy of Tasso's theorizing about the symbolism of the human body for the organization of his poem, or even for the overt theme of organizing the army.[50] But they do show that, as an emblem of triumph over isolation and loss, the human body obsessed Tasso at a level that found differing expressions in both his literary theory and his poetic praxis. The point is not that Tasso's theoretical works and declared intentions for the poem are "fulfilled" by it, but rather that his pronouncements and the overt themes of the poem only partially address its deepest concerns. Tasso's theory is not an "adequate" description of his praxis, and he is not a reliable guide to the workings of his text—except in that his pronouncements are an overt discussion, oblique and noncommittal as was his habit, of the covert "desires" of the text.

iv. Empowering

James F. Burke

Counterfeit and the Curse of Mediacy in the *Libro de buen amor* and the *Conde Lucanor*

Modern ideas of intertextuality, forgery, and counterfeit are largely the product of a long development that followed the invention of the printing press at the end of the fifteenth century. The Augustinian world view, which dominated the thinking of medieval Christian Europe for a thousand years, and the manuscript culture that conveyed that world view had, in fact, implied a concept diametrically opposed to our modern notions.[1] The medieval idea was that the truth about the world and what it is, about man's place in the world and his ultimate destiny, is enshrined in the works of a series of *auctores* and that the skilled exegete, by effectively utilizing the tools extant in the *trivium* and the *quadrivium*, could interpret the meaning of the *auctoritates*.[2]

It was also understood very early that interpretation involves not only reading but also writing. Writing seems naturally to follow reading as well as preceding it. Reading an interpretation arouses the need for further writing and further interpreting.[3] But in the Middle Ages, such writing was a re-thinking of existing material for the purpose of extracting or making clearer previously existing meanings.[4] This writing was not conceived as an innovative extension of the frontiers of knowledge in the modern sense, which views human mental horizons in spatial terms that are basically limitless. The medieval writer was much more of an outliner and compiler than an original thinker.

Medieval culture was aware of the problem of falsification. A coin could be minted without the precious metal that would lend it value. An individual could camouflage true intent and cleverly deceive an opponent.[5] The rhetorical colors could be used to paint an attractive surface upon something not so appealing in its essence. Falsification is referred to for the processes of interpretation, reading, and writing, but it is referred to in terms that fully reflect the tradition of authority and that of the text. The reader or writer could add to the accumulated meaning of a particular idea or sign, but only while fully respecting the integrity of that tradition and by being careful not to adulterate that tradition. To do otherwise would be to falsify.

The "text" of the physical world and a "text" composed of a long series of writings, compilations, and commentaries beginning with the Bible and including, by the thirteenth century, many Classical *auctores*, were present to the world, and thus available for interpretations in a discourse of signs. Such sign systems were necessary, according to St. Augustine, because of a dislocation of human consciousness resulting from the Fall (Brown, 261). Although the hermeneutic process related to the "text" of the physical world was one fraught with difficulty, the signs involved therewith were at least fairly inviolable. Those that were "conventional," those having to do with writing and other human semiotic systems that could be altered either willfully or by mistake, posed a problem for the interpreter on two levels. What was the conventional meaning of the sign in the first place? and second, Had that conventional significance been adjusted with ulterior motive?

The Middle Ages tended to think of every human being in grammatical or logical terms as a subject that had to be related through a predicate toward some final state, which in this world was the fulfillment of the role appropriate to one's hierarchical status and which, for the other world, would be salvation. The successful completion of the earthly mission was seen as proleptic, in many ways, to the achievement of the second goal. For that individual whose status was in some manner that of thinker, the discourse of signs was the medium of primary concern. For others, the media of daily life and daily existence would be more relevant. One concept of enormous importance for all, whether of low or

high estate, was love or desire. Desire affected everyone and possessed an awesome power for transforming things that, if un-
checked, could change the individual from his status of subject
in this world into the final condition of object in hell. It is for
this reason that in the discourse of writing, desire in its various
forms is often the subject of discussion.

Two Spanish works, roughly contemporary with one another
and both from probably the first half of the fourteenth century,
are dedicated to a study of the world and its media, the falsification or misuse of such media, and the manner in which the
Christian aspiration for success in this world and salvation in the
next should deal with these media. The *Libro del Conde Lucanor*
(1335) takes what might be termed a more practical approach to
those interchanges that affect the individual in his everyday life.
The book appears to be a kind of meditation upon the problem
of the medium, a meditation designed to guide the reader induc-
tively to an awareness of the problem with media and to an understanding of how to deal with these problems. The *Libro de buen
amor* in its so-called final version (1343) is concerned with the
hermeneutics of desire, how the reader interprets a wide variety
of situations and phenomena, particularly literary discourse, according to his own predispositions and inclinations.[6]

The first part or book of the *Conde Lucanor* consists of fifty
framed examples plus an epilogue, which are presented as an
interchange of question and answer between Count Lucanor and
his advisor.[7] In the second part or book of proverbs, the author,
responding to a complaint that the mode of exposition in the first
part has been too open, presents a series of proverbs ever more
complex and enigmatic as one proceeds through the three sub-
divisions of the book. This book has a long epilogue, which some
critics have also taken as a separate division of the whole work.
After a section of doctrinal explanations, the author explains that
man alone among creatures must learn to utilize his intelligence
in conjunction with a number of naturally occurring as well as
contrived media if he is to survive. "You should well believe, Sir
Count, that among all the animals which God created in the
world, and among all corporeal things, he created none so com-

plete or so lacking as man. And the completeness which God gave him exists for no other reason save for his understanding, reason, and free will . . ." (518). But even with this understanding, man finds himself in a most difficult situation because he must depend upon a group of secondary media for his survival: ". . . for man has nothing of his own by means of which he may live. But the animals are all clothed, with skins or hair or with shells or with feathers with which they protect themselves from cold and heat and the contrary elements . . ." (522). This dependence upon physical items is paralleled by metaphysical structures that govern and control his conduct. "Also, all the animals know how to govern themselves and have no need for someone to arrange such for them; but men cannot govern and control themselves without the aid of someone else and they are unable to learn how to live if someone doesn't show them . . ." (522). As the individual struggles to attain those physical things necessary for existence and to master and observe those rules that allow him to coexist with his fellows, there arises the problem of desire. "And also as their understanding develops, but is not yet complete, they desire and wish for that which is not good for them and which can even be dangerous for them" (521). Also, those whose intellect has been developed can use their powers to induce those not yet so fortunate to do what they might otherwise not choose to do. What Juan Manuel has stated at the end of the epilogue to the second book is the reason for the composition of the entire work in the first place. Man must learn to master the media.

Richard Dawkins in *The Selfish Gene* has suggested that man's large brain and his disposition to reason mathematically may have evolved as a mechanism of ever more devious cheating and ever more penetrating perception of cheating in others.[8] The *Conde Lucanor* is designed to teach the reader to perceive such cheating and to avoid the consequences of being deceived. The way to cheat effectively is to manipulate the media. The way to avoid being cheated is to know how to interpret the media correctly. The reader must develop his intellectual powers so that he may not be persuaded to do something that is against his best interests.

In the introduction to the work, Juan Manuel tells us that, just as every individual has a face different from the faces of all others, so he also has an intention that is distinct. The face and the outward manner may not signal what that intention is, but there are ways of fathoming it. "And I shall give you some examples so that you may understand it better" (60). The examples are to be presented in a pleasing literary form so that the reader may better appreciate them. The author's illustration of the relation of the attractive form to the content appears to be somewhat naive. He uses the familiar case of bitter medicine sweetened with sugar or honey so that the liver will absorb it. Old Spanish letters are filled with stories of poison being administered in the same way, whether it be in food for a watchdog or in the lovely but venomous damsels of the Alexander legends. But our author is not naive. He is cleverly implying that the reader will even have to probe his ingenuous assurance that his intention in writing the book is positive. He is also preparing the reader for the series of lessons in binary and even more complicated forms of deconstruction that are to follow.

The first example is the story of the king who decides to test his chief advisor by telling him that he has decided to abandon his lofty position to live the life of a poor hermit and will therefore deliver all his wealth into the hands of his advisor. The advisor is at first delighted but, wisely, himself decides to seek counsel. The advice is, shave your head and beard, dress in rags, and proclaim yourself ready to accompany your lord in his self-imposed exile from the world.

This pretended reversal of status in the first *exemplum* is mirrored in the last three by very real changes. Number 49 is the folkloric tale, of such interest to Sir James Frazer, of the individual chosen as ruler and then deposed after a specified period. Juan Manuel has him placed nude on a desert isle. Eventually, one individual sends provisions to the island ahead of time and thus escapes the unhappy fate of his predecessors. Number 50 tells how Sultan Saladin takes up the life of a wandering minstrel to learn what is the best personal attribute that a person can hope to possess. The epilogue, which some critics take as *exemplum* 51, is the story of the overly proud king who dares to reverse the words of the Magnificat so that it is the rich who are exalted. As a punishment, his clothes are stolen from him by an angel while he is at the baths. The angel then takes his place as ruler of the kingdom and refuses to relinquish it until the rightful lord repents and learns humility.

These four *exempla* frame the other forty-seven. The first says that the reverse of a situation may be truer than what seems obvious. The last three demonstrate that the "real" has an obverse side that may well wind up being the final "reality." All four invite the reader to contemplate that which appears to be reality in order to make certain that it is not a mask concealing something else.[9] The high estate of the rulers in the last three *exempla* is not a false medium, but it is certainly not a permanent one. To depend upon such a status would create a false sense of security as unreal as the king's pretended longing for a simpler life in the first *exemplum*.

Juan Manuel also understood a point of enormous importance in regard to a medium. The medium does not exist in a static situation nor create a static situation. It serves as a vehicle for transformation, as a catalyst, that on one level assures that a message moves from point A to point B. As in the grammatical example discussed earlier in this paper, it also can function as predicate relating subject to object and object to subject. It can, of course, shape and influence the final outcome of the transformation. If the honey or sugar used to make the liver absorb the medicine is pure, the results of the process are positive. If poison is mixed in, then the medium becomes negative and destructive.

Juan Manuel returns to a variation on this point in the second *exemplum*. "And well believe that the more intelligent boys are, the more they are capable of making great errors in their affairs; they have the understanding necessary to begin the thing, but they don't know the way to finish it, and for this reason they fall into great error, and there is no one who can protect them from such" (83). The lack of a proper medium is the reason for that failure. The young man must not only understand the danger inherent in certain media, he must also learn to find positive ones so that he will be able to achieve his goals.

The *Conde Lucanor* is a "mirror of princes" that teaches the individual how to deal with the media in all of their complexity. The forty-six *exempla* after number 2 and before the final three, which imprint the frame with the theme of reversal, are a kind of *distinctio* that present the problem from a wide variety of perspectives. In some of the *exempla*, such as number 6—that of the swallow and other birds who saw a man sowing flax—one must learn to become proficient in interpreting the merest physical sign. "For he is not intelligent who sees the thing once it has occurred, but he is intelligent who by a sign or some small movement understands the danger that can happen to him and thereby takes counsel so that it doesn't happen to him" (118). In number 11, "Concerning what happened to a dean of Santiago with don Yllan the great master of Toledo," everything that occurs is an illusion. But it is an illusion that the Dean of Santiago as well as the astute reader should have foreseen. Just as Don Yllan is about to take the Dean into the caverns under the Tagus and initiate his illusory ascent to the Papacy, he tells a servant to prepare partridges for dinner that evening but not to begin to roast them until later. The partridge was widely used in the Middle Ages as a sign and symbol of deceit.[10] Juan Manuel was placing a sign in the text to advertise the deceit that would be forthcoming. Or then there is the *exemplum* of the king's new clothes where, in effect, the medium of clothing is expressed as a negative sign. Here the social circumstances, the absolute necessity of legitimate succession, become the vehicle that allows the deceit.

In *exemplum* 20, which tells what happened to a king deceived by a man who says he knows how to do alchemy, Juan Manuel deals specifically with the theme of the counterfeit. The pseudo-alchemist takes filings from gold coins and shapes them along with other substances into small pellets. The mask is here in part verbal, because the rogue gives the name of the pellets as *tabardíe*, a word derived from an Arabic verb *barada* meaning to file.[11] Eventually, after the king has seen gold derived from a process that uses the pellets, he sends for the false alchemist, who cleverly deceives one and all. "And the scoundrel, although he gave signs that he wished to hide his knowledge and to imply that he did not know alchemy, in the end gave the impression that he did know how . . ." (97). (This, of course, was his intention all along.) The rogue flees after securing an excellent price for the false secret, but he leaves a letter in which he explains his deception.

All of the material utilized by Juan Manuel is a kind of intertext. The author has arranged a large number of traditional tales and stories as a means of teaching the young prince how to understand and utilize the media. Some of the *exempla*, such as the one just referred to, deal with the theme of falsification. But the forgery always refers back to the problem of intention and how it is portrayed. The forgery itself, literary or material as in the coins, is of lesser interest.

The "curse of mediacy," to borrow a phrase from Cassirer[12]— the necessity of learning to judge the media so that one does not make terrible mistakes—appears to be the primary concern of Juan Manuel. He cleverly incorporates the idea of the binary nature of the world, the true and the untrue, into the *Conde Lucanor* with the carnivalesque reversal of status. To apply the term "deconstructionist" to the process by which he teaches is not anachronistic, because it is a process allied to the same tradition that inspired the twentieth-century deconstructionists. Whether it is the Muslim savants hoping to arrive at the *batin* or interior, hidden meaning of things, or Jewish students of the *Kabbala*, or the Christian exegete, the method used is remarkably similar.

The *Libro de buen amor* is a work that also deals constantly with the media and with the problem of the counterfeit meaning attached to the medium. But the final intention of the poet, to uncover that which determines what is false and what is true, what is counterfeit and what is genuine, never becomes clear. Juan Ruiz appears to have dealt with the problem by constantly shifting his ground, by implying the negative pole at precisely the moment when he is asserting the absolute validity of the positive one.

Marina Brownlee has recently posed the *Libro de buen amor* within the tradition of the positive rewritings of the *Confessions* of St. Augustine.[13] Juan Ruiz is concerned with a problem, how-ever, that, although inherent in the work of the Bishop of Hippo, did not interest him very much. If it is impossible to posit such a thing as a universal reader, and Brownlee would argue that St. Augustine understood this problem, then the conversion paradigm presented in the *Confessions* cannot logically function for anyone who is not predisposed to receive it in the first place. Juan Ruiz takes this difficulty and makes it the centerpiece of his book. "Indeed, it is precisely this paradox (positing the existence of a universal reader, but realizing that he doesn't exist) which gen-erates the bifocal tension found with the Libro."[29] Juan Ruiz is not, therefore, striving to give a model for reforming the syntax of selfhood, to present a book serving as a predicate for a subject in the hope of attaining a desirable objective end. His work is rather a poetic reflection upon the difficulty that he understands as present in his audience. It is for him a given that some of his readers will interpret his text in terms of earthly love. He therefore allows his text to demonstrate graphically and constantly the two possible ways of understanding.

In addition, I suspect that "the curse of mediacy" is also a difficulty for the Archpriest. Juan Manuel understood that the media present mankind with great problems of understanding and interpretation, but he obviously believed that such were soluble, since he wrote a treatise dedicated to this question. In the last analysis, it may be that Juan Ruiz despaired of ever finding a way to deal adequately with the media in this fallen world. Doña Garoça, one of the many women avidly pursued by the shifting narrative "I" of the poem, observes to Trotaconventos that "the world is woven out of worthless scraps. . . ."[14] Such a view, if it were finally that of the poet, could not hold that something worthwhile could or should be realized from the worthless scraps. The world would be counterfeit, a falsification undependable in the extreme.

One of the reasons, doubtless, why St. Augustine might not have been so concerned with his unpredisposed reader could have

been that he believed in ancient notions concerning the thera-
peutic, thaumaturgic power of language, a power redemonstrated
in the Gospel of St. John. In line with another ancient concept,
that of sympathy and antipathy (surely also not foreign to the
Bishop of Hippo), language, particularly if divinely inspired language, could have been understood as producing a beneficial,
salutary effect in any hearer or reader.

Malcolm K. Read, in his recent study on the language of the
Libro de buen amor, points out that the invocation to the Trinity
and to the Godhead in stanzas 11–13, stanzas that formed the
beginning of the *Libro* in the so-called first version, has something
of the same effect.[15] The invocation is more than just words. This
is a prayer to result in and produce an effect. "You, Lord and my
God, who formed man, inform and help me, your Archpriest, so
that I may write this book on good love which shall gladden men's
bodies and benefit their souls" (13). Next, after a two-stanza
reference to his poetic skill, the poet turns to the traditional
hermeneutic posture of the Middle Ages. "Do not think that this
is a book of foolish nonsense, and do not take as a joke anything
that I recite in it, for, just as good money can be stowed in a
worthless purse, so in an ugly-looking book lies wisdom that is
not uncomely" (16).

Following two further stanzas of *amplificatio* in the same vein,
Juan Ruiz turns to the Virgin, the beginning and root of all good,
and salutes her with two delightful poems on the theme of her
seven joys. The first is, of course, Gabriel's visit and the *Ave* that
linguistically reverses "quod Eva tristis" [that which sorrowful Eve
(did)]. This particular phrase, "quod Eva tristis," is used by Juan
Ruiz in his parody of the Canonical Hours later on in the *Libro
de buen amor* and is drawn from a hymn from Lauds for the Marial
Feasts.[16] "And if the girl is one of those who do not dare to walk
about in the narrow streets, have your panderess lead her out into
fields to gather red roses; if the silly girl believes her words and
her advice, she will garner *what sorrowful Eve* did from *whomsoever
hath desire*: blighted fruits" (378; emphasis mine).

The new beginning of the *Libro*, ten stanzas based loosely on
the ritual prayer for the dead—the *Ordo commendationis animae*

(Joset I,1)—in effect reverses the hermeneutic theme of the old beginning. The poet, instead of urging his readers to probe beneath the surface for true meaning, pleads to be lifted from circumstances that appear to have lost their significance for him. The key word here is *sacar*, "remove me." To summarize: just as you, Lord, got the Children of Israel out of Egypt, Daniel from the lion's den, St. Marina from the belly of the dragon and Jonah from the whale, etc., etc., deliver me [*sácame*] from this prison where I lie. Even if the passage refers to a real jail, which I think unlikely, the effect is the same. In the penultimate two stanzas of the introduction, the Archpriest refers twice to the name foretold in prophecy, Emmanuel, and once to the salutation of Gabriel, both suggestive of the Incarnation of the *logos* through the medium of the Virgin in Jesus Christ. In a last fervent entreaty to the Virgin before he begins his sermon in prose, the Archpriest uses the enigmatic word *mescladores*, which most critics accept as meaning in a general sense "slanderers." "Give me grace, Queen of all queens; withdraw your displeasure from me; dispel spite from me; turn everything against my slanderers; help me, Blessed Mother of sinners" (10). *Mescladores* derives from the verb *mesclar*, "to mix." Its meanings extend from the tale-bearers who destroy love affairs through an equivalence to the *mestureros*, who lie about the Cid so that he is banished. "Por malos mestureros de tierra sodes echado" [because of evil meddlers you are sent into exile (15)].

Malcolm Read feels that Juan Ruiz was suffering a "crisis of language," that the influences of nominalism were forcing him to doubt the real connection between signifier and signified and that this lack of certainty resulted in the tension apparent in the book. If Read is correct in his assumptions, one wonders if Juan Ruiz would not have included among his *mescladores* those who were doing away with the old sign systems and the old understanding of the Word. For Juan Manuel, the signs and the media are reliable and valid as conveyors of knowledge and as intermediaries between what is real and what is imitation. One has to learn to interpret them correctly. Juan Ruiz may have reached an opposite conclusion.

Raymond Willis, who studied the *Libro de buen amor* for many years, accepted the idea of two versions of the work. He felt that the 1330 rendition expressed the full gamut of love, including that involving mortal sin, as an integrated system under the rubric *buen amor.* All was present; all had been worked into the text. Recently, Monique de Lope in her study of the journey to Segovia through the Sierra (also present in the 1330 version) reached a conclusion similar to that of Willis in regard to love.[17] The story of the Archpriest's trip is an elaborate integrated intertext involving everything from folkloric happenings to the higher liturgical functions of Catholicism. The journey itself is a kind of mediation, a *rite de passage,* that demonstrates, and one might say establishes, that there is no opposition nor rupture between the most basic of the human environments and the most sacred.

Willis felt that the integrated view of love changed in the 1343 version with the introduction of new material. "The simple logic (and the historical authenticity) of the new bi-polar scheme imposes itself strongly: love, we are made to feel, must be divine and good, or carnal and wicked, with no compromise in principle, although Juan Ruiz equivocates" (xxxvi). A new interpolated episode appears where the poet seeks out Urraca as his go-between and proceeds to tell us that, if success is to be expected from such an old woman, the correct nomenclature must always be used. "Never call such a messenger a mace; whether she warbles well or badly, never call her a magpie, decoy, lid, sledge-hammer, breast plate, door-knocker, shoehorn, halter, or shovel, or tongs, or fishhook" (924). But does a rose by any other name smell as sweet? The long list of appelations for the go-between, which one suspects must have come out of the Spanish folk tradition, serves as a kind of natural indication of her true nature and character and that of those like her. The name *Buen Amor* is a counterfeit, one not even conventional in its application but chosen *ad placitum* to fulfill the desire of the old bawd for good standing and respectability and that of the Archpriest for her aid in achieving his somewhat nefarious ends.

One has the feeling that the "text" is still whole and complete with the 1330 version of the *Libro de buen amor,* as it was for Juan

Manuel. But the new intertext in the 1343 account may have had the effect of unbinding the book, of segmenting the scroll so that what was written was no longer necessarily of one piece. Authority has given way to invention in what is approaching the newer sense of the word. The intention of the poet is no longer to teach that the media can serve if one learns to deal with them adequately. It now is to emphasize that the material of the literary medium is fictive and that this fact must be recognized and understood by the reader. The reader can take pleasure from fictions and even learn from them, but they are fictions and not the real stuff of the world, no longer congruent to it and sympathetically part of it. The medium will begin more and more to convey its own message intertwined with that associated with the intention of the author. The writer will become more and more responsible for reassembling language itself, broken down into its barest words and phrases, if he is to avoid being termed a plagiarist and if his work is not to be designated as an ironic commentary upon a previously existing piece.

Giuseppe Mazzotta

Theologia Ludens
Angels and Devils in the *Divine Comedy*

In the *Summa Theologiae*, St. Thomas Aquinas asks whether or not play can ever be a moral virtue ("utrum in ludis possit esse aliqua virtus").[1] Aquinas proceeds to probe the issue by reviewing, first, the position of St. Ambrose who, on the authority of the Biblical verse ("woe to you who laugh now, for you shall weep") denies that any virtue can lie in playing games. Ambrose's position is confirmed by Chrysostom's belief that the devil, not God, sends us to sport. It is further supported by the opinion of Aristotle who, in his *Ethics* (X,6), states that playful acts have no purpose beyond themselves, and, therefore, no virtue is engaged in playing. St. Thomas's response is that pleasure (*delectatio*) is a remedy for the weariness of the soul. But although he allows for this kind of solace, he sounds some warnings. The first is to avoid jokes that are shameful or obscene. Just as we do not give children complete liberty to play, so the light of a sound mind should be cast on our very fun. This sense of propriety, good manners, and reasonableness is what Aristotle calls *eutrapelia*, a playful disposition that must always be consistent with the dignity of the subject. Since theology is about matters of greatest moment, Aquinas follows St. Ambrose in banishing jocularity ("iocum") from theology, though not from social converse: "Although sometimes decent and pleasant jokes ("ioca") are abhorrent to the Church's doctrine and discipline, for how can we adopt practices not found in the Scriptures?"

Eutrapelia is listed in the *Convivio*, which is admittedly in the tradition of Aristotle's *Ethics*, as one of the eleven moral virtues Dante would probably have discussed had the treatise been completed. In *Convivio* IV.xvii.6, *eutrapelia* is a virtue that ". . . modera noi ne li sollazzi facendo, quelli usando debitamente."[2] But in the *Divine Comedy* there is hardly any room, predictably enough, for playful or humorous words and deeds toward which to turn in order to soften the edge of attention. A small vestige of the virtue of *eutrapelia*—and its painful spiritual limits—is possibly to be found in Limbo, the playground of classical wisdom where Dante meets "la bella scola" (*Inferno* IV, l.94) of poets— Homer, Horace, Ovid, Lucan, and Vergil himself. The Latin "schola," from the Greek *schole*, retains what the etymology designates: the time and space of leisure and pleasant conversation. The lines embodying the principle of decorous discrimination, as to what is or is not proper, unmistakably suggest Dante's understanding of how dignified the pagan spirits' pastime is in their shadowed *locus amoenus*: "parlando cose che 'l tacere è bello, / si com'era 'l parlar colà dov' era" (*Inf.* IV, 104–105).[3] [Speaking of things which were fitting for that place, and of which it is well now to be silent.] But this leisure, which for the pilgrim is the soul's provisional solace, for the poets is a spiritual trap.

Another humorous interlude occurs, in a deliberate symmetry to the scene of Limbo, in *Purgatorio* IV, where Belacqua's ease, his unwillingness to undertake promptly the Purgatorial ascent, moves the pilgrim ". . . un poco a riso" (l. 122). Ease is definitely out of place in this metaphoric land of longing and unquiet hearts, just as good manners would have been incongruous in the harsh confrontations between pilgrim and sinners in hell. All in all, *eutrapelia*, which is a social-moral virtue, is of questionable value in the *Divine Comedy*. There is, nonetheless, in Dante's poem a pattern of figurations and concerns that dramatize how far beyond St. Thomas's prudence and constraint about play Dante's vision can stretch. I shall argue here, as a matter of fact, that Dante takes to task exactly the terms St. Thomas or St. Ambrose had discussed and bracketed: poetry "plays" in the highest realm, and thereby it focuses on the decisive role of play in theology and how play and theology are unthinkable except in their imaginative interaction.

It must be stressed at the outset that nowhere in the critical *corpus* on the *Divine Comedy* do we find an extended, systematic exploration of *theologia ludens*. The reason for this striking gap, it is fair to say, lies in the common perception of Dante as a stern moralist, the poet of stark moods who subordinates the pleasures play entails to the majesty of moral ends. Such a perception is not entirely wrong. As a poet, Dante wills to reverse, and in fact he did reverse, the role *jongleurs* played as truants, itinerant per-formers of troubadoric songs in the courts of Provence and Italy. Yet, it is wrong to believe that Dante's concern with play might be taken as a sign of intellectual frivolity or an escape into the unserious. On the contrary, his figuration of the world *sub specie ludi* stems from his vision that play is the activity that best un-covers God's deepest being.

The language of play in the *Divine Comedy* is not always so heavily charged, though it appears with frequency throughout the text. In *Inferno* XV, to recall a prominent instance, Brunetto Latini races to rejoin his fellow sinners and, in this foot race, he looks like a winner, though he is ironically, like the rest of them, the loser. The scene is imaged by a reference to the annual run-ning game held in Verona ("Poi si rivolse, e parve di coloro, / che corrono a Verona il drappo verde / per la campagna; e parve di costoro / quelli che vince, non colui che perde" [ll. 121–124] [Then he turned about and seemed like one of those that run for the green cloth in the field at Verona, and he seemed not the loser among them, but the winner].) The play metaphor certainly conveys Brunetto's delusive triumph and, beyond that, the deluded sense he has of himself as, literally, the pre-cursor. It also radically turns around, I would like to suggest, St. Paul's metaphor of athletics. In 2 Timothy 4, in a context in which false teachers— teachers who suit their own liking—are exposed, St. Paul sum-marizes his life's work: "I have done my best in the race. I have run the full distance, and I have kept the faith. And now there is waiting for me the prize of victory awarded for a righteous life." The Pauline gloss ironizes the claims of Dante's own teacher; but there is another ironic contrast to Brunetto that is articulated through a play image. In *Paradiso* XVI, Cacciaguida, the athlete of Christ, mentions the last ward reached during the Florentine "annuale gioco" (l. 42) to evoke his own birthplace. Unlike Brunetto, Cacciaguida mentions the spot not as the triumphant finish line for his race but as the point of departure to Jerusalem.

Play metaphors do not simply figure, however, in such a fragmentary way, as symbolic, discrete counters to various moral experiences. In *Purgatorio* XV, in a language that resembles Hyginus' *Poetica Astronomia*, the ecliptic—the yearly revolution of the sun across the sky, which dodges now to one side, now to the other of the equator—is called the circle that plays like a child: "che sempre a guisa di fanciullo scherza" (l. 5). This imaginative bond between astronomy and play hints that play is more than a moral question to be determined (though it certainly is also that); it is the essence of the workings of the cosmos and of God's creation.

The play activity of God emerges explicitly in *Purgatorio* XVI where Marco Lombardo explains to the pilgrim the origin of evil. Evil does not originate in the stars but in man's own moral conduct. At the moment of creation, Marco says, the soul issues forth from her Maker's hand like a child who is later led astray by false pleasures:

> Esce di mano a lui che la vagheggia
> prima che sia, a guisa di fanciulla
> che piangendo e ridendo pargoleggia,
> l'anima semplicetta che sa nulla,
> salvo che, mossa da lieto fattore,
> volontier torna a ciò che la trastulla.
>
> (ll. 85–90)

From his hand who regards it fondly before it is, comes forth, like a child that sports, tearful and smiling, the little simple soul that knows nothing, but moved by a joyful Maker, turns eagerly to what delights it.

In the economy of the narrative, the idyllic picture of the soul's creation is in sharp contrast to the confusion of the world Marco Lombardo goes on to evoke. More to the point, the harmonious playfulness binding the creator and his creature is a miniature representation of what is called *theologia ludens*—the view of God as the playmaker, waiting for the soul to return home to play. When the soul returns, which is a transparent allusion to the

Platonic *reditus animae,* it has the delight of play as the reward God grants. To think of play as constitutive of the divinity implies both some historical questions as well as a number of theological corollaries.

In historical terms, as I have just implied, the metaphor is Platonic and mythical, not Biblical. The Feast of the Gods, the pleasures, conviviality, and laughter on Olympus, certainly is a strain of the imagination of *theologia ludens.* There is very little play, in effect, and almost no laughter in the Bible. A story was told in the Middle Ages, for instance, about the ruminations of a theologian, Petrus Cantor, as to whether Christ ever laughed. There are, nonetheless, Biblical passages that disrupt or shed further light on what seems the uniformly high seriousness of the Judaic ethos. Isaac, whose name is etymologized as laughter, was seen playing with Rebecca. And at least two other passages focus on a theological understanding of play. The first is from Proverbs 8:27–31:

When he established the Heavens, I was there . . . When he marked out the foundations of the earth, then I was beside him, like a little child, and I was daily his delight, rejoicing before him always, rejoicing in his inhabited world and delighting in the sons of men.

The second passage, which inspires one of Dante's examples of humility in *Purgatorio* X, is from 2 Kings 6:5 and 21, where we are told of David dancing before the ark. These two Biblical passages were pulled together by the Greek and Latin fathers to convey divine creation as an esthetic construction, with Divine Wisdom playing or dancing. Tertullian speaks of Divine Wisdom as "modulans cum ipso" [ordering the world with him]; Origen interprets the lines from Proverbs to say that "in this wisdom that was always with the Father there is prefigured creation." Gregory Nazianzen crystallizes the esthetic-theological speculations when he writes that "the Logos on high plays, stirring the whole cosmos back and forth, as he wills, into shapes of every kind."[4]

From a substantial point of view, barely hidden in Dante's metaphor of play, is the metaphysical conviction that the creation of man and of the universe is not an act of necessity, the consequence of inexorable Tyche, but one of free, spontaneous choice. This point is borne out by the textual fact that *Purgatorio* XVI is the context in which Marco Lombardo asserts unequivocally man's free will. At the same time, the view of *Deus Ludens* makes play a *sacer ludus*, a sacred activity, which, as such, puts work in its proper place. From this standpoint, it can be said that work is no longer understood as the *telos* of life; play, rather, is both the foundation and the aim of life. Further, since the creation of the soul is grounded in God's play-activity, to play is to accept rules established by God. Man is not to play God, but let God play as he lets the soul play.

It is well known that Plato refers to man as the "plaything of God." The definition signals that man's nobility, indeed the highest perfection within a creature's grasp, comes forth while man is engaged in play. The process of *paideia* is truly successful when the human soul attains "the lightness and freedom of the spirit"— qualities that are associated with play. But this is not to say that men are mere marionettes, as the aging Plato will come to believe in the *Nomoi*. For Dante, the soul is neither a toy in the hands of the gods nor a spectator in the divine game of the Logos, whom many call chance, as Philo says, with no part to play in a scheme of things that transcends him. The epithet that qualifies the soul, "semplicetta," allows us to perceive a somewhat different story. The word primarily designates the soul as an entity without guile or deceit. In strictly theological terms, however, simplicity is the attribute of the Divinity, for a good that alone is simple and, therefore, unchangeable, is God. Those things that are truly divine are called simple, because in them quality and substance are identical. In short, the epithet of simplicity suggests a likeness between the soul and God, and a passage from St. Augustine's *City of God* explains the substantial identity between Creator and creature: "It is suitable to say that the immaterial soul is illumined with the immaterial light of the simple wisdom of God, as the material air is irradiated with material light, and that, as the air when deprived of this light, grows dark . . . so the soul, deprived of the light of wisdom, grows dark."[5] For St. Augustine, as for Dante, when the original likeness dims into dissimilitude, man is playing a dangerous game, for he can choose either to be like the angels or to be God's antagonist; but this second choice puts him in touch with the devil. For Dante, as we shall see shortly, the world of play is primarily the activity of demons and angelic intelligences.

The place where the joy of divine play is experienced is in *Paradiso*, which is thoroughly organized and represented through play metaphors. The domain of play is vast, and it involves the most disparate esthetic manifestations. In *Paradiso*, the music of the spheres is heard; the Heavenly City is a garden of delights and an amphitheatre; the blessed sing and dance; the universe laughs; the heavens themselves rhythmically whirl around the divine being, and the "chorus angelorum" called "angelici ludi" engaged in "tripudi," "giochi . . . e canti," celebrates the harmony of creation; stars dance and woo each other with a weight of love that keeps the universe from falling asunder. These play activities are a sign of the pleasures of beatitude; they are also the various dimensions of esthetic beauty whose aim, like that of play, is pleasure.

That esthetics, as the disinterested, playful faculty that makes available the beauty and pleasure of creation, is the structuring principle of *Paradiso* is suggested at the very outset of the text. In *Paradiso* I, Beatrice explains the shape and order of creation, and these two terms, "ordine" and "forma," account for the likeness between God and the universe (ll. 103–105). The two words are to be understood in their technical sense as, respectively, "ordo," a criterion of beauty, and "forma," beauty itself. Because in the Middle Ages one cannot find discussions of the autonomy of beauty, of subjective esthetic judgments and taste, it has been said that the period did not produce a genuine theory of esthetics. It has become increasingly clear, however, that at no time was philosophical thinking more permeated with esthetics. The universe was considered an esthetic construction built with mathematical rigor. Its symmetrical arrangement and harmonious relations are conveyed by the verses from the Book of Wisdom: "Omnia in mensura, pondere et numero fecisti." The careful reconstruction of the thought of the Victorines, with its focus on light, sound, and color, as well as the complex speculations on beauty by Albert the Great, St. Thomas Aquinas, and St. Bonaventure, decisively display how much the esthetic faculty loomed in metaphysical and ethical questions.

Aquinas's assertions on beauty, its threefold properties of *claritas* (radiance), *consonantia* (proportion and order), and *integritas* (the perfection of being), are too well known to be detailed here. Equally well known is his understanding of form (the *splendor formae*), the inner essence that shines through and gives an intelligible shape to the phenomenal materiality of objects. What is probably less well known is that St. Thomas can sound remarkably like Plato or Plotinus when he reflects on beauty. "Without beauty, what would become of being," wonders Plotinus. For Thomas, beauty, which he defines as "id quod visum placet" [that which being seen gives pleasure], is a transcendental category; it is the formal perfection of being and the quality that makes an essence appear for immediate perception and pleasure.

In his *Commentary on the Divine Names*—a text that became the focus of extended meditations for Scotus Eriugena as well as for a Victorine such as Hugh—beauty is the attribute of the person of the Son and, along with *Bonum* and *Verum*, one of the Names of God: "Pulchrum, quod est Deus." For Aquinas, this transcendental notion of beauty, whereby God finds all things beautiful, makes talking about esthetic beauty, which deals with contingent subjective perceptions, problematic. On the other hand, Dante's poetic thinking claims the preeminence of the cognitive value of *aisthesis*, the theory of appearance, for he makes visible in the space of his representation both the bewitchment of beauty in *Inferno* and *Purgatorio* and the goodness of beauty, the *kalokagathia*, in *Paradiso*.

At a doctrinal level, this doubleness of beauty is kept rigorously distinct in the *Divine Comedy*. In *Inferno* XXXI, Dante encounters the giants, who are the offspring of the fallen angels' copulating with the daughters of men. In this topsy-turvy world that parodies the hierarchical order of Paradise, the giants are the intermediate beings in the scale of evil that finds in Lucifer its epitome. There is no trace now in Lucifer of his original beauty and splendor, and the line, "La creatura ch'ebbe il bel sembiante" (*Inferno* XXXIV, l. 17) [the creature who had the fair look], seals this loss of pristine beauty. In *Inferno* XXXI, Dante compares the face of Nimrod, the proud builder of the Tower of Babel, to the huge bronze pine cone that stood in Rome and adds that his other bones were ". . . a sua proporzion" (l. 60), in proportion to the face. The word "proporzion" is to be taken in its esthetic sense, since proportion, according to Aquinas, is one of the three requisites of beauty, or, as Dante says in *Convivio*, "Quella cosa dice l'uomo esser bella cui le parti debitamente si rispondono . . . ," and "chè l'ordine debito de le nostre membra rende uno piacere non so di che armonia mirabile" (IV, xxv, 12). Dante's oblique allusion to the beauty of Nimrod is not a startling innovation. As a matter of fact, St. Augustine in his *City of God* remarks exactly on the beautiful appearance of the giants:

And it pleased the Creator to produce them, that it might thus be demonstrated that neither beauty, nor yet size and strength, are of much moment to the wise man, whose blessedness lies in spiritual and immortal blessings, in far better and more enduring gifts, in the good things that are the peculiar property of the good, and are not shared by good and bad alike. It is this which another prophet confirms when he says "These were the giants, famous from the beginning, that were of so great stature, and so expert in war." (XV, xxiii)

In the *Divine Comedy*, Nimrod's is a grotesque beauty, an extinct art of Nature ("Natura certo, quando lasciò l'arte / di sì fatti animali, assai fé bene / per tòrre tali essecutori a Marte" [ll. 49–51] [Nature, assuredly, when she gave up the art of making creatures such as these, did right well to deprive Mars of such executors], which engenders horror and fear in the pilgrim as once they did to the gods (*Inferno* XXXI, l. 95).

By contrast, *Paradiso* XXVIII and XXIX, which focus on angelology, feature a world of order and play created and established by God for the spirits. The "ordine," which Dante emphasizes in *Paradiso* XXIX, l. 31, is both an esthetic *and* a theological-moral conception, and he binds them together. In doctrinal terms, the poet's speculation on angels is primarily placed within the Neo-Platonic theory of the plenitude and continuity of God's creation, the so-called Great Chain of Being, which translates rank into value and which posits the necessary presence of intermediate hierarchical grades between the oneness and simplicity of God and the materiality of contingent forms. The enumeration of the nine angelic orders, from the Seraphim, Cherubim, Thrones, to Archangels and Angels, occurs in *Paradiso* XXVIII, and it follows the account given by Dionysius's *The Celestial Hierarchy*. The present account, as is well known, is a correction of the views held by both St. Gregory and Dante himself in *Convivio*. As a follow-up to this intellectual self-correction, Beatrice discusses the nature and function of the angelic intelligences. The exposition is punctuated by the language of esthetics, which is not merely a technique of describing the mode of angelic existence but is the perspective from which Dante mounts a critique of the major theological and philosophical conjectures on angelology.

The divine act of creation is restated in terms of God's pleasure, not necessity. Time, we are told, began with the creation of the material universe, when the eternal love ". . . come i piacque" (*Paradiso* XXIX, l. 17) [as he pleased] opens in "nuovi amor" (l. 18) [new loves]. The opposition in the same line between "nuovi amor" and "etterno amor" addresses, and effectively discards, the Averroistic doctrine of the eternity of the world, which Averroes accepts on the authority of Aristotle's *Physics*. The opinion that the world is eternal and the concomitant belief that there never was a first man were condemned as heretical by Bishop Tempier in 1270. This proposition saw the two major exponents of thirteenth-century theology on opposite sides of the question. Aquinas knew that the eternity of the world, asserted by Averroes, could not be philosophically demonstrated, and although he allows that it is a possibility, he chooses to follow Albert the Great's belief in creation *ex nihilo*. Bonaventure, on the other hand, attacks Averroes on this issue by arguing that since the number of souls is finite, the universe must have a beginning.

These doctrinal disagreements over the eternity of the world extend to the debate on the nature of angels. The debate, actually, is the watershed between Christian philosophy and pagan conceptions, because the very notion of the intelligibility of the universe depends on it. Philo speaks of pure spirits peopling the air, who are called demons by the philosophers and angels by Moses. Porphiry and Jamblichus count angels among the demons. The Pseudo Dionysius argues for the total incorporeity of the angels, and the immateriality of the angels is also Dante's view, who calls them "puro atto" (l. 33), whereas matter, as pure potentiality (l. 34), lies at the foot of the ladder of creation. This notion of the angels' absolute transcendence, which to Petrus Olivi seemed to make deities out of these separate substances, is Aristotle's and Averroes's. Dante's major agreement with Averroes, let me add, comes to the fore when he identifies the angels with the intelligences that move the spheres, for it is in this operation wherein lies their perfection ("Non concederebbe che i motori / sanza sua perfezion fosser cotanto" [Paradiso XXIX, ll. 44–45] [It cannot be allowed that the movers of the heavens should be without their perfection]). Finally, Dante departs from Philo's and Porphiry's identification of angels with demons. Consistent with canonical church teachings, he distinguishes between rebellious, fallen angels and the faithful ones (ll. 52–55).

This configuration of textual strains is a mark of Dante's syncretism, of the prodigious, multiple vibrations in his magisterial voice. Much is at stake in this style of fabulation. In a primary way, it is as if he peeks into the stubborn contradictions housed by divisive philosophies and juggles them into his own master version of the angelic myth. But the harmonization Dante produces is not the mechanical, and finally reductive, compendium of heterogeneous fragments; rather, he inserts within his borrowings from disparate philosophical speculations that which his sources bypass or never acknowledge: the fact that their systematic, mutually exclusive philosophical broodings are not and cannot be construed as the truth. They are polemical, partial glimmers of the total light, or at best, resilient imaginative constructions akin to an esthetic vision that only a poet such as Dante is empowered to deliver. The esthetic turns into a genuine source of knowledge and is the perspective from which to unveil the arbitrary claims of philosophy.

Dante's awareness that the esthetic imagination is the ground of cognition is shown by his insistent deployment of the language of play and music in his rendition of the mode of angelic existence. Thus, the faithful angels, called "sustanze . . . gioconde" (*Paradiso* XXIX, l. 76) [jocund substances], are said to experience delight in their "arte . . . da circuire" (ll. 52–54), their contemplation and dancing around God to the implicit tune of the spheres, the melodious sound that is caused, as Macrobius puts it, by the rapid motion of the spheres themselves. This Neoplatonized myth of the harmony of the universe, known as *musica mundana*, is the imaginative point of convergence between theological order and esthetic order.

In and of itself, the heavenly music of the angelic songs and dances echoes the motif of the harmony of the spheres announced in *Paradiso* I: "Quando la rota che tu sempiterni / desiderato, a sé mi fece atteso / con l'armonia che temperi e discerni . . ." (ll. 75–78) [When the wheel which you, being desired, makes eternal held me intent on itself by the harmony you attune and distinguish . . .]. More to our concern, this Pythagorean theme, which Boethius elaborates, provides the dramatic rationale within which to account for the ludic metaphors Dante deploys in the cantos. He speaks of "angelici ludi" (*Paradiso* XXVII, l. 126); the angels' performances are called "tripudi" (l. 124), and, later in *Paradiso* XXX, their feast is "il triunfo che lude" (l. 10) [the triumph that plays]; above all, the angelic choirs are introduced as they sing in unison a ceaseless song of praise, "io sentiva ossanar di coro in coro" (XXVIII, l. 94) [I heard Hosanna sung from choir to choir].

In the liturgy of the Church, in which man is seen as part of the cosmic whole, "Hosanna" prefaces the worship of the whole universe, a worship in which sun and moon and stars will take part. The motif of cosmic worship has its lyrical articulation in St. Francis' *Laus creaturarum*, but it is codified in the liturgy, for instance, of St. James: "Him do praise the Heavens . . . and their concerted might, sun and moon and all the singing galaxies of stars, earth, sea and all they contain . . ... the spirits of just men and apostles, angels and archangels."

From the standpoint of this liturgical worship, there is an ethos to music: the *harmonia*, which in Greek is an agreement and accord of disparate parts, aims at producing a moral order, figured by music, in the individual soul. The notion is central to Plato's theory of education, and Macrobius states with great clarity the ethical character of music:

> Every soul in the world is allured by musical sounds so that not only those who are more refined in their habits, but all the barbarous people as well, have adopted songs by which they are inflamed with courage or wooed to pleasure; for the soul carries with it into the body a memory of the music which it knew in the sky, and is so captivated by its charm that there is no breast so cruel or savage as not to be gripped by the spell of such an appeal.[6]

Macrobius's mixture of ethics and music is the brunt of Dante's *theologia ludens*. To be sure, music, which to Dante is linked to poetry, has its own esthetic lure. In the encounter with Casella, the distraction that Casella's song engenders in the pilgrim certainly echoes the sense of how deceptive the pleasures of even Church melodies seem to Augustine's ear (*Confessions* X, 33). But the moral ambiguity of music is muted in Paradise. Music, the art that makes time audible, is now the vibration of God's light. Dante, in a way, makes clear what in Macrobius is muted. If there is an ethics of beauty, then esthetics is a supreme theory of value; it is the faculty that transforms essences into images. Here, in effect, lies the radical, potentially subversive threat of beauty (and, indirectly, the reason for the philosophers' effort to circumvent or contain play and esthetics): as beauty translates an essence into an appearance, it displaces the essence into the imaginary. Few poets have understood, as Dante has, this trickiness of beauty—tricky because it can never be perceived if not as a dazzling image. Readers of the *Vita nuova* should hardly need to be reminded of the power of the image of beauty to engender a vanishing epiphany in the commonplace density of the daylight world or even to generate a tremendous nightmare in which the ordinary consistency of the world is swallowed up.

This dangerousness of appearance figures in *Paradiso* XXIX in a roundabout way. There is, actually, toward the end of the canto an angry counterpoint to the play of the angels. Beatrice states that the angels have no memory: they have no need to recall the past since they see eternal present in God's eyes. She then attacks those who philosophize on earth and who are attracted by the love of show:

> sì che là giù, non dormendo, si sogna,
>   credendo e non credendo dicer vero;
>   ma ne l'uno è più colpa e più vergogna.
> Voi non andate giù per un sentiero
>   filosofando: tanto vi trasporta
>   l'amor de l'apparenza e 'l suo pensiero!
>
>   (ll. 82–87)

Thus down there men dream as they are awake, believing and not believing that they speak the truth—but in the one case is the greater blame and shame. You down there do not proceed along a single path in your philosophizing, so much does the love of show and the thought of it carry you away.

Because of this love of show, reemphasized a few lines down in the text ("Per apparer ciascun s'ingegna e face / sue invenzioni . . ." [ll. 94–95] [Each tries for display, making his own inventions . . .]), the philosophers neglect and pervert Scripture (ll. 88–90) while they concoct improbable reasons for the solar eclipse at Christ's passion. The burden of the attack is on the sleep of reason and the eclipse of faith in "le vostre scole" (l. 70), which never probe beneath, but actually wallow in appearances and forget what is essential. At the same time, the world of appearances comes through in its unavoidable power to derealize the world, since images do not merely give a replica or a disclosure of the reality that underlies them. Rather, images obscure or elide the reality they replace.

In *Paradiso* XXIX, Dante does not quite confront the radical inconsistency of appearances—the way appearances hollow out substances. It is in the area of fraud in *Inferno*, however, that we encounter the diabolical caricature of angelic play and, more generally, the representation of hoaxes and counterfeits as threats to the hard core of reality. In *Inferno* XXI and XXII, where the barrators are punished, Dante features the grotesque activity of demons, the so-called *commedia dei diavoli*: the devils' "nuovo

ludo" (*Inferno* XXII, l. 118) [new sport], their mode of leaping—
a parodic dance, tricks ("buffa," l. 133), scuffles in a boiling pond,
scatological sounds (which are a *musica diabuli*)—these are the
wares of comic laughter as well as the details of the devils' play.

That this is the context within which the two cantos should
be read is made manifest by Dante's reference to "la mia comedia"
[my comedy] at the start of *Inferno* XXI (l. 2), as well as by the
extended images of tournaments and jousting that open *Inferno*
XXII ("Io vidi già cavalier muover campo, / e cominciare stormo
e far lor mostra, / e talvolta partir per loro scampo; / corridor vidi
per la terra vostra, / o Aretini, e vidi gir gualdane, / fedir tor-
neamenti e correr giostra" [ll. 1–6] [I have seen before now horse-
men move camp, and open the attack, and make their muster,
and at times go off in flight; I have seen scouts over your land,
Aretines; and I have seen the movements of raiding-parties, clash
of tournaments and running of jousts]). This grotesque mixture
of horror, play and laughter (the sinners are tortured, the devils
roar with laughter, the pilgrim is scared of being thrown down),
is punctuated by images recalling the trivialities of the *carmina
potatoria* and *lusoria* ("ma ne la chiesa coi santi / ed in taverna
coi ghiottoni" [*Inferno* XXII, l. 15] [but in church with saints and
with guzzlers in the tavern]). It is also punctuated by the rhetoric
of the *sermo jocosus* that the *poeti giocosi*, such as Cecco, Folgore,
Meo dei Tolomei, and Dante himself, deployed.

From one point of view, Dante rejects the profanities of that
style and its implicit moral abjection as he assigns them to this
place of evil. By so doing, he suggests that sports and laughter
are experiences of moral degradation standing in sharp juxtaposition to the upward movement of the pilgrim. In this sense,
Dante absorbs the attacks unleashed against the immorality of
spectacles and theater by the early apologists of the Church such
as Tertullian, Cyprian, St. Augustine himself, and John of Salisbury. Spectacles, in their view, are immoral because they trap
the mind in an experience of illusion and sham and because they
hold it back from its spiritual askesis. From another point of view,
it can be said that these blasphemous, vulgar sports bring forth
the presence of a reality that escapes those who are caught in the

natural world: the sports reveal the supernatural, the persistent presence of a sacred reality, albeit in its demonic shape. Dante's ethical judgment of these esthetic forms is unequivocally firm, but his poetry rescues them from his own judgment.

There is in the twelfth century a bold moral defense of the ugly and horrid worth mentioning. Hugh of St. Victor believed that God can be more easily discovered in ugly forms than in externally beautiful ones. The pure appearance of beauty, one can say, chains the mind to the sensible world, but what one experiences as ugly forces one away from the contemplation of it and urges one to transcend it. Hugh writes: "Quando per pulchras formas laudatur Deus, secundum speciem huius mundi laudatur. . . . Quando vero per dissimiles et a se alienas formationes laudatur, supermundane laudatur, quoniam (tunc) nec idem esse dicitur nec secundum id sed supra id totum aliud per quod laudatur."[7] [When God is praised by means of beautiful forms, he is praised in terms of this world. . . . But when he is praised by means of forms that are dissimilar and foreign to him, he is praised in transcendent terms, because then he is not said to be the same as, or in conformity to, but rather above all those other forms by means of which he is praised.] Hugh's Neoplatonic esthetics is confirmed by other medieval estheticians who assert, for instance, that ". . . just as the beauty of a picture may be enhanced by a dark color in the proper place, so the beauty of the universe is enhanced by moral errors." This is exactly the paradox dramatized in the comedy of the devils: Dante's ethical stance rejects the universe of sham and hoaxes as morally wrong, but he retrieves their ethical power in the mode of rejecting it.

Dante's moral judgment of these illusory forms depends, no doubt, on his insight into the dangerousness of esthetics, and I would like to look briefly at two instances in *Inferno* where the play metaphors are used. The first case occurs in *Inferno* XX, where Dante sees Michael Scott, "che veramente de le magiche frode seppe il gioco" (ll. 116–117) [who truly knew the game of magic frauds]. The other case occurs in *Inferno* XXIX, the canto of alchemists and impersonators, where Griffolino, "parlando a gioco" (l. 112), promised Albero da Siena he would teach him the art of flying, to be a "Dedalo" (l. 116), and was burned for being unable to keep his promise.

The reference to Daedalus, which commentators generally neglect, may shed considerable light on the issues at hand. The story of Daedalus, the artificer who escapes from the labyrinth he had built for Minos, is the mythical Neoplatonic paradigm for the flight of the soul and its final deliverance from the world of matter. As such, for all its jocular force, the recall of Daedalus hints at the eerie bond between alchemy and Neoplatonism. The alchemists, who believe that there is a secret, valuable core beneath the world of deceptive appearances, are like Platonists who seek to transcend the illusions of nature. But these alchemists—just as the magician Michael Scott—never penetrate the veil of appearances and abide in coverings and disguises. Griffolino and Michael Scott are both masters of illusions: their "gioco" is, quite literally, the illusory doubling and counterfeiting of being. Or, to say it in the Neoplatonic language the text evokes, their art is ". . . di natura buona scimia" (Inferno XXIX, l. 139) [a good ape of nature], for it is an artifice of raw simulation. From this standpoint, all the sinners of fraud, the falsifiers of words and deeds, counterfeiters, hypocrites (who are like actors on the stage), impersonators (who suffer a disfiguration of skin—in an overtly parodic reversal of the etymological meaning of pulcher), are players for whom reality is an optical illusion.

In a way, the fraudulent sinners tread the same path the mystics and angels do, though they move in the opposite direction. The mystics, as hinted in the discussion of Peter Damian, and the angels are convinced that the image is false, and, therefore, they attempt to tear the image from themselves, to experience direct vision or attain a dazzling blindness. The fraudulent sinners, convinced that images are illusory and that there is nothing behind them, plunge into them, manipulate them at will, and in the false glare of their alchemies and other simulations, they unveil (ironically, at the same time) both the illusoriness and the resistance of matter. One thing is nonetheless certain: as the sinners of fraud seek to hollow out the solidity of reality, they effectively signal how substances are dissolved into pure emptiness. In short, these evil-doers are esthetes whose sparkling imitations suggest that their tricks and simulations are shadows of the play of the world. But their imitations also destroy the natural order of work and production.

As is often the case with the *Divine Comedy*, talking about one issue inevitably leads one into its polar opposite: the pastoral to history, utopia to exile, ethics to esthetics, play to work. In the metaphoric reversal from play to the morality of work it appears that one is playing a losing game. More precisely, I have argued that esthetics, which is God's activity, is the ground of ethics and of all knowledge, but, paradoxically, it is subordinated in the poem to ethics. One is led to the unavoidable conclusion that whereas God plays, man is enjoined to work, and that there is a wide gap between God's being and man's life. It could be answered, as a way of accounting for this gap, that esthetics has a double value, that its property lies exactly in this doubleness, to be indistinguishable from ethics. This identity cannot be viewed in optimistic terms; for that very reason, it is also capable of effacing ethics.

The predicament the above formulation entails is not final in the *Divine Comedy*, for Dante still explores possible continuities between the playing of God and the playing of man. The Garden of Eden—the original realm of play and ease, the golden age dreamed by poets—is imaginatively recalled as the fixed time and place of play with binding laws that were nonetheless breached by man's sin. In this Garden, pleasure holds sway ("lo tuo piacere omai prendi per duce" [*Purgatorio* XXVII, l. 131] [henceforth take your pleasure for guide]). Matelda is seen singing, picking flowers, laughing and moving with dancelike steps (*Purgatorio* XXVIII, ll. 40–54). The reference to Psalm 91, "Delectasti" (l. 80), which, as St. Augustine calls it, is a "psalmus cantici in diem sabbati" (a psalm, that is, of tranquility and rest), heightens the quality of the place as a play-world where a song of joy and praise is given to God's name, his constancy and love ". . . to the music and the harp, to the melody of the lyre." In short, the pleasure the pilgrim experiences is what Aristotle in his *Ethics* calls the crown of the activity, that which comes to man once the work is completed.

In the world of history, play is available to man in the liturgy of the Church. More than that, Franciscan spirituality, the practice of the *ioculatores Domini,* as the Franciscans are called, embodies the theology of play in action. The model for this theology is Jesus himself on the cross, whose mantle and crown mock the regal *insignia* of the world. Among Francis's successors, one could mention Iacopone da Todi's vision of love as "amor de riso e ioco," or even the Franciscans' reputation as "friars of the cornet," as Salimbene speaks of them. Their reputation as troubadours of poverty and *jongleurs* of God springs from the legend of St. Francis himself, who, as one reads in the second *Vita* by Celano, "when the sweetest melody of spirit would bubble up in him . . . he would burst into songs of joy in French which express the breath of the divine whispers his ear perceived. . . . He would make, out of the stick he would pick up from the ground, a violin, and pretending he would pluck unseen strings he would sing in French."[8] Dante had dismissed the poets—tumblers of Provence— but he assents to Francis's theology of play.

Unlike Aquinas, who even acknowledges the legitimacy of the theater and the acting profession but contains play within Aristotelian boundaries, St. Bonaventure, who speaks of the Scriptures as being "citharae," responded to St. Francis's insight into the playfulness of God, into playfulness as the aim and the means to go to God. In *Paradiso* XI, Dante fully grasps the essence of that insight. What St. Francis conveys in *Paradiso* XI, through his exuberant jests, parody of institutions, and laughter, is the vision, at the same time militant and prophetic, of the religious imagination capable of crossing all boundaries of commonplace values, of yielding to God's summons to a radical homelessness, of peering in delight at the things of the world that have equal standing with one another in God's eye.

Dante's own text, which fuses work and play, stems from such a vision. Never before or after has poetry played such a visionary role in encompassing the most diverse contradictions and experiences in man's life. The *Divine Comedy* witnesses the breakdown of human projects and human bonds, and the mockery of justice, but it knows that tragedy may not be real—no more, at any rate, than the night is real for the mystic who knows all along that the dark is not dark but only the shadow of the light. It evokes the feast of thinking by which man plays and meets the Playmaker; but it knows that play can be the shakiest of illusions—the bottomless dream of man's long night.

Nancy S. Struever

Machiavelli, Montaigne, and the Problem of External Address in Renaissance Ethics

I would like to place this discussion of Machiavelli and Montaigne in the context of a larger project, a project that attempts an account of serious ethical investigation in the Renaissance. The use of the qualifier "serious" vastly simplifies this task, for it eliminates the considerable number of Humanist moral treatises that seem devoid of intrinsic interest. To be sure, naive appropriations, such as the reissue of a Ciceronian rhetorical-political program by Baron's Civic Humanists, remain of great historical interest. But further, key Humanist figures were themselves devoid of interest in ethical issues. Recall Grafton's account of Politian: Politian rejected civil and moral issues as a means of safeguarding or assuring patronage for the philological project itself.[1] My working hypothesis is that important changes in Renaissance ethical inquiry were changes in the ethics *of* inquiry, changes in the definition of what constitutes proper moral work. Thus, every revision of investigational topic is, at the same time, a revision of investigational practice, of the modes of discursive exchange, by the investigators.

There were three major stages of strategic development. In the first stage, we notice tactics of detachment, disjunction, dislocation. Francesco Petrarca, I would argue, relocates inquiry outside the academy, or university, and outside of a dysfunctional academic or university discourse. When he claims in letter XIII,4 of the *Familiari* that the single important issue is encapsulated in the question, "How should one live?", he claims at the same time

that the issue is ignored in contemporary inquiry.[2] The *Letters* as
a whole expound this simple yet difficult issue, and, at the same
time, embark on a program of detaching the investigational community from the institutions and institutionalized discursive
forms: it is, in sum, a deinstitutionalizing moment. Here, "intimacy" is value; *amicitia,* friendship, is the new site of worthwhile
investigation, and the familiar letter is the hegemonic genre. The
ethical significance of this strategy is obvious; the new constraint
on inquiry is the insistence on the immediate personal worth of
insight and information, the direct use of classical text or Christian devotional exercise in intimate arrangements. Friendship is
privileged as at once the most difficult and the most accessible
domain for thought experiment.

In the second stage, investigators accept relocation but modify
drastically the notion of intimacy in insisting on a new, rigorous
internal discipline, that is, a discipline internal to inquiry. In the
careers of two of the more rigorously inclined investigators of the
fifteenth century, Lorenzo Valla and Nicolaus Cusanus, the primary disciplinary tactic is a near-sighted focus on the formal grid
that invests discursive practices; their concern is with linguistic
capacity and communicative tactics. This concern has direct and
specific relevance to their interest in ethical values. Valla embarks
on a lexical revision, a critique of Aristotelian, classical voca-
bularies as dysfunctional, as distorting Christian moral values.
Cusanus, on the other hand, focuses not on word but on figure;
it is the use of metaphor and image that fascinates him. The
primary genre is a meditative genre, and the primary strategy is
a meditation on metaphor. The devotional exercise is posed as a
request to the reader to attend to his use of figure; the figures
have sequential steps, and the reader, in following sequence, becomes aware of the limits of figure, and thus the limits of inquiry.
Cusanus prefers mathematical figures because their greater precision
lends greater precision to our knowledge of the limits of mind. A
notion of the limits of freedom, a map of the boundaries of responsible command in the domain of free inquiry, is the result.[3]

In the third stage, the investigators accept the relocation of
inquiry, accept the need for a revised discipline, but focus pri-

marily, and most usefully, on the relation between the internal discipline of the investigators and external address to a larger community. Dominant in the ethical inquiry of the sixteenth century is the problem of good counsel, a dominance authenticated by the spectacular solutions offered in, say, Erasmus's *Praise of Folly*, More's *Utopia*, Castiglione's *Courtier*, and Rabelais's *Gargantua and Pantagruel*. These texts seem to acknowledge that conventional counsel has produced conventional, and therefore dysfunctional, moral-political behavior; addressing a political elite as ideally rationalist produces an inadequate rational idealism. Their artful prose diagnoses social dysfunction; the difficult "intimacy" at the centers of power represents both a problem to be surmounted and an unusual opportunity for address.[4]

MACHIAVELLI: NARRATIVE AS ARGUMENT

The most spectacular solutions to this sixteenth-century problem are Machiavelli's *Prince* and Montaigne's *Essais*. The *Prince* both revises the notion of what constitutes good counsel and redefines the role and act of giving counsel. The *Prince* is, of course, a complex project: it attempts a radical change in the conventions of political advice; it is yet recognizably "Humanist," if we accept the definition of a Humanist program as the invention of a classical edifying past and the presentation of this past in edifying prose; and, finally, it is morally perspicacious prose. Certainly, reading the *Prince*, judging by the long history of strong, acerbic, and even hysterical reader response, does not blunt the moral sensibilities. My argument is that by both retaining the Humanist premise that the past edifies and at the same time instigating gross changes in topics and modes of address, Machiavelli produces a text that, in its extraordinary combination of sophistication and naiveté, redefines investigation as moral work.

K.-H. Stierle has described Boccaccio's *novelle* as "problematizing" the medieval moral *exemplum* by complicating characters and thickening plots.[5] Just so, the strategies of characterization and emplotment in the notorious chapter 7 of the *Prince* present

Cesare Borgia in a problematizing vein, for Machiavelli narrates not a simple story but different and contradictory versions of Borgia's disgusting political choices. The narrative miniatures within the text of the *Prince* provide an episodic, discontinuous frame; like the picaresque novel, the structure of the *Prince* is formally open, but ideologically closed. The pícaro, C. Guillén has pointed out, learns, but does not improve, through episode.[6] Both the fictional rogue and the confected, artificial prince are disallowed maturational, unitary development—each is constantly forced back on the task of reinventing his role. And if, like Boccaccio, Machiavelli has rejected the narrative example as simple, transparent illustration of a moral paradigm, he also rejects the narrative example as segment of a historical project, a single frame of a unitary historical truth. The prince is perpetually engaged in event, but incapable of being regenerated by means of it, within a continuous structure, or of generating history as meaningful continuity.

I shall now argue that the function of the narrative *exempla* is argumentative, and that the argument defines a hypothetical rather than a historical domain. Machiavelli, indeed, pursues in the *Prince* a "bracketing-off" strategy that distinguishes between political discourse and political investigative discourse. In a letter to Guicciardini, Machiavelli notes that ". . . always, as far as I can recall, war has either been going on or it has been talked of. Now it is being talked of; in a short time it will be carried on; and when it is finished it will be talked of again, so that there never will be a time for thinking of anything. . . ."[7] "Thinking" is not a continuation of political activity but constitutes a distinct project. Therefore, the *Prince* as thought-project requires formal analysis of a "philosophical" sort, in the sense of the description of logical modes, of argumentative forms, of the status of terms. Analysis would reveal a pervasive commitment to "bracketing" tactics, since his project is marked by a rich development of the hypothetical, by the use of the "subjunctive" to illuminate a problematic "indicative." In another letter to Guicciardini, Machiavelli describes a letter to Strozzi in which he had ". . . debated three propositions: one, in spite of the treaty the king would not be free; two, if the king is freed, he will keep the treaty; three, he will not observe it. I did not say which of the three I believed, but I did decide that from any of these Italy would have war."[8] The letter stipulates "existence" as predicate as totally irrelevant; what is important is the demarcation of realms of political possibility, realms that, because of their purely formal status, are capable of exhaustive description. Since the claim is that the description of adjacent, possible worlds resituates meaning within a timeless, "real" present, modern possible world semantics presents a useful analogue; in both the Machiavellian and the modern projects the exploration of adjacency is a tactic to redesign control of the factual, the "real" that eludes us in undisciplined talk.[9]

Or, to use a Renaissance analogue, I would suggest that Machiavelli's use of narrative *exempla* has the same type of motivation as the fourteenth- and fifteenth-century philosophers' involvement with invalid arguments and with the difficulties of paradox. Although Machiavelli deals with structures of willed and unwilled events rather than with structures of valid and invalid inference, the *Prince*, in the form of its content, is a collection of *sophismata*.[10] The function of the narrative of Borgia is not protoscientific or pseudo-historical, but has a status like that of the hypothetical cases of philosophical discussion; it is much closer to statements of the order of "the present King of France is bald" than to Humanist philological reconstructions of historical event. Further, since only difficult statements are worthy of analysis, Machiavelli's formal analytic program motivates his pervasive reductive strategies. The spare and precise narratives are the results of a process that strips the exemplary accounts of every condition and capacity of rule that simply acts in a self-fulfilling manner. Once Machiavelli rejects the easy congruences of a moral-ontological paradigm with political conduct, the "reductive" depiction of the theoretically interesting "powerlessness" of the Prince follows. He must delimit an artificial political sphere drained of noumenal, customary constraints; he strives for clarity of definition of political capacity, stripped of nonpolitical, ceremonial justifications, the institutional constraints that are self-fulfilling, simply reproductive. The organizational choices of the *Prince* as text engage a relentless process of elimination of circularities of the type: "Lovable behavior inspires love." Machiavelli rejects as unworthy of treatment every condition of rule that acts as question-begging premise: "The hereditary prince enjoys ritual safeguards," or "Happy republics are the scene of republican virtues."

If the Borgias did not exist, Machiavelli would have to invent them; Cesare Borgia's career and "the present King of France is bald" share the capacity for clearly pointing to difficulty and ambiguity, and share extremity. The papacy is frame for Borgia's career, and what political entity could be as fraught with discontinuity and structural difficulty as the papacy, a polity that by rule ceases with the cessation of life in an unending sequence of old men? Still, there is no sense in which the analytic example conjures an "imaginary" as opposed to "hypothetical" quality. Rather, we find that both Machiavelli and the philosophers have the same taste for technical virtuosity, for "contentless" issues,[11] and for the confrontation of structural and factitious necessity. Just as "the present King of France is bald" refers to and clarifies the facts of natural languages, so Cesare Borgia refers to and clarifies political events. Thus, the exemplary Borgia and bald French king constrain in the same way; that is to say, the constraints work positively, not negatively, in the sense that they add to our knowledge of the capacity of structure. It is not a very pleasant experience of constraint, to be sure; Machiavelli peddles basic, not superficial discomfort. Just as grammatical structure, in the sense of the presuppositional nature of language, which is the issue addressed by the bald French king, allows us the disturbing capacity to speak seriously and logically of untruth, of fiction, so political structures, as described by Machiavelli, allow us to speak seriously and logically of the unethical.[12] Machiavellian analysis discloses no gap between politics and ethics, but a very strong tie; it is simply not the one we want.

Croce's general impression of Machiavelli's "dolorous and austere" moral conscience,[13] then, should be related to specific patterns of distinction and connection, hypothesis and assertion. We must appreciate the tight, elliptical syntax that controls a stringent account of diminished moral capacity accompanied by increased responsibility. There is no diminution of the coherence and pertinence of the moral value system; ethical values remain intact, the system integral, the judgments inescapable. Machiavelli's strategy of projecting adjacent, possible worlds maintains the moral system as a contiguous, possible realm that demands political mastery but wherein there is no automatic enhancement of political power: adjacency does not guarantee reciprocity. Thus, if we recall the argument of chapter 15, which insists on the separation of the domain of "is" from the domain of "ought," we recall not only that the domain of "is" is a realm of appearances of virtue and vice rather than of substance, but also that the combination of this distinction with the major distinction of *virtù* from *fortuna* as causes results in the formulation that the prince as virtuoso is responsible for all appearances while in control of only half the events. Further, the peculiar double explanation of chapter 7 of Borgia's failure to achieve a stable state hinges on the co-occurrence of two events: the death of Cesare's father, Pope Alexander, and his own sickness. One event conveys excuse, the other blame, since Cesare did not foresee and prepare for illness. The events are inextricably connected, since the excusing circumstance is also the condition of blame. But further, the hypothetical is enmeshed with the actual: Borgia is responsible for the subjunctive as well as the indicative, since *virtù* is defined as total, exhaustive control. The effect of the Borgia example is thus to extend responsibility across the entire range of possible worlds; if it *can* be thought, it *must* be thought.

If hypotheses are used to enlarge responsibility, then assertions attenuate performance; Machiavelli's assertive statements about human nature can be read as versions of the more unsettling of the constructs developed in modern analytic philosophy of ethics. On the one hand, Machiavelli, like Donald Davidson, gives a bleak and plausible psychological account of "incontinence"—of acting contrary to judgment—as normal and endemic in human affairs. On the other hand, Machiavelli, like Davidson, generates a pessimistic account of "pluralism," where "principles, or reasons for acting, are irreducibly multiple" and therefore intractable to the simple hierarchic orderings of classical and Christian moralities.[14]

The modal and generic choices of Machiavelli, I have been arguing, are deliberate interventions, tamperings with the rules and conventions of Classical-Christian advice literature. The narrative exemplary forms dictate a drastic pruning away of moral opportunity and moral self-justification; therefore, Machiavelli does not need to include easy polemical indictments of moral failure, since he has effectively reduced the possibilities of easy moral success. To assume difficult constructs such as "incontinence" and "pluralism" complicates; it forces changes in the strategies of address, the ways of mobilizing the knowledge shared by advisor and advisee.[15] The interventions suggest that the fundamental contribution of Machiavelli to ethical inquiry is meta-discursive and meta-critical, and that the proper analysis of the *Prince* is pragmatic analysis—in the technical sense of analysis of use—of the relation of text to speaker/listener. Certainly he speaks directly to the issues of the use of knowledge, and his innovations are innovations in inquirer's usage. Attempts to validate the *Prince* as political science or political history simply pursue the old, standard strategy that focuses on the acquisition, not the use, of knowledge, and on the validity of techniques of acquisition; they can reveal Machiavelli only as having little to offer in the way of prescientific methodology. Machiavelli does speak, however, in a most stimulating fashion to the pragmatic issue: How do you use exemplary narrative and logical connection in an argument that is both psychologically persuasive and logically compelling, that forces consideration, and that interferes with the reader's beliefs and dispositions concerning civil values and acts?

MONTAIGNE: THE WEB OF BELIEF

For Montaigne, as well as Machiavelli, the relation of internal discipline to external address is a central one, and, as with Machiavelli, the imperatives of address and the rigors of discipline reciprocally affect one another. But where recent scholarship (making, I believe, anachronistic attributions to Montaigne of twentieth-century literary-philosophical interests in self-subversion, deconstruction, and destabilization) has focused on the negative, skeptical aspects of Montaigne's discipline, I shall emphasize the positive force: the project is not so much the constitution of an impregnable skeptical position as the reconstitution of a proper set of beliefs. A primary object of Montaigne's inquiry is to form a web of belief in Quine's sense of a repertoire of dispositions to act or of qualities of mind, referred to by Montaigne as his "*complexion.*"[16]

I shall argue for the sophistication and complexity of his project. The notion of belief to be derived from his text is not that of belief as inadequate knowledge, opinion that is not yet knowledge; and it touches upon, but is not entirely explained by, reference to belief as Christian faith. Rather, of Paul Ricoeur's three primary historical concepts of belief—opinion (Greek *doxa*), religious faith (Christian *foi*), and personal assent (Cartesian *assentiment*)—Montaigne's usage comes closest to the Cartesian.[17] Montaigne's project, then, focuses neither on the adequacy of belief as knowledge, nor on the orthodoxy of belief as faith; rather, Montaignian inquiry presents itself as a simple, familiar, and humble mental task of assessment and repair of the web of belief. Simple, yet difficult; for it is a web that, like Quine's, represents a heterogeneous and transitory, an untidy and informal set of qualities and dispositions, a spectrum of beliefs that may be ill-assorted and contradictory but that relates to the entire spectrum of significant and insignificant action and engagement—for Montaigne complicates his already complicated task by his formulations of beliefs as knit into our civil practices. Montaigne seems to both anticipate and resolve the modern argument over belief as primarily interactional and belief as solipsist. Belief as *assentiment* is radically internalized, closely held; no one assents for you. But certification of belief is communal; the origin of the force of belief is external. As H. Parret notes: "The 'force' of belief systems does not depend on production conditions in the 'believing subject,' seen as a subjectivistic atom, but rather on linguistic interaction or transaction in the community of believers."[18] Thus, on the one hand, Montaigne insists on the ineluctably first-personal nature of belief; on the other hand, Montaigne presents an interactional model of the effective presence of belief systems in living situations. Every specification of belief, every investigative act of refinement and discrimination is at the same time a specification of possible interactivity, of a possible ethical competence. Every characterization of the intractability of our web of belief is at the same time an address, an invocation to a reader to recollect the places the web of belief impinges on the social frame. This intractability does not diminish, but exacerbates responsibility.

The essays *"De la praesumption"* and *"Du repentir,"* which seem to investigate balancing states of mind, seem to offer a balanced account of Montaigne's tactics of specification of belief. His inquiry into what it is to presume and repent puts into place two seemingly contrary but, in effect, interlocking strategies: formalization and familiarization. The only criteria of inquiry are formal criteria: Montaigne specifies again and again the values of *"ordonnance,"* of self-regulation, of tranquility of opinions, of circumspection (1.658; 2.809; 2.1110).[19]

Formality as a valuable trait is at once respect for the integrity of belief, and dictated by the intractability of belief. While Montaigne prides himself on his capacity to maintain his beliefs against attack from without, "de n'assubjectir aisement ma creance" (1.658), his protective gestures simply reinforce immutable facts. *"Du repentir"* focuses on beliefs, habits, qualities of mind deeply enracinated, anchored; so rooted, in fact, that they are not subject to contradiction (2.808). He speaks of habits as *incorporées* (1.633), and therefore inaccessible to introspection; one masks, but does not extirpate them: "on n'extirpe pas ces qualitez originelles, on les couvre, on les cache" (2.810). From this argument follows the inadequacy of normal disciplinary responses; Montaigne claims he knows only the names of the liberal arts (1.651). He distrusts a philosophical program of confecting systematic rationality; not only is reason a double-edged sword (1.654; 2.1026), but knowledge as product, not life as question, presents a "labyrinth of difficulties" (1.634). But Montaigne distrusts as well the central rhetorical strategy of decorum as exclusive focus on adaptability, as appropriateness of response. He does not regard his mind as vivacious and supple (1.649, 658), and he distrusts suppleness (2.1034). Montaigne, far from looking for opportunities for self-subversion, prefers self-presentation as the sure-footed, steady agent confronting circumstances of flux and variety, rather than as an agent of dizzying vivacity, countering dogmatic rigidity. To be sure, the reduction of intellectual value to formal value, the representation of intellectual goal as a tranquil and ordered carapace enclosing beliefs, attenuates the notion of investigative response; this is, perhaps, one of the sources of Pascal's reaction to Montaigne as not strenuous enough, as nonchalant.[20]

But Montaigne's essay on repentance emphasizes not only the formality of the remedy but the familiarity of the vice. Montaigne specifically focuses on the type of sin that is at home in us, "qui loge en nous comme en son propre domicile" (2.808). At the same time, intimate behavior, the unwitting witness of "exercitation basse et obscure," tests our perception of virtue most severely and usefully; Socrates, rather than Alexander, edifies (2.809).

Familiarization is investigative procedure as well as topic and witness; a "pratique de familiarité et privée acointance" (1.660) is the vital and often missing link in the process of educating the young. In adult enterprise, however, Montaigne forces the connection between intimacy and risk-taking that Petrarch imposed on the readers of his *Familiari* long before. Thus Montaigne on the subject of his own virtues achieves the most intimate of tones—vulnerability. He seems deliberately to court being perceived as an egoist; his description of his virtues are as persuasive, as seductive, as his descriptions of his vices.

But intimacy can function as devaluation of classical currency as well. His tactics distort the standard classical *exempla*; when he cites Alcibiades' lisp as exemplary of a propensity so individual, so incorporated that it cannot be recognized by the individual, he encourages anecdotal, gossipy use (1.633).[21] He reduces the *sententiae*, maxims of *ancienneté*, to complicitous maneuvers. Human vanity, he claims, is the domain for "*le beau jeu*" of philosophy; philosophical maxims most charm when combatting presumption (1.634). Here, of course, familiarity combines with formality; the Montaignian gesture both domesticates and empties the philosophical enterprise as pleasant game.

Both formalization and familiarization, then, dispute normal stipulations of authority; they rearticulate discursive possibilities, revalue the competence of classical authors, and question the authoritarian strategies of educational institutions, as well as the manipulative vacancies of doctrines. Certainly it is the case that Montaignian strategies permit some very interesting, indeed novel, statements. The essay on presumption ends with a series of remarks about contemporary great men, employing a rhetorical *gradatio* that culminates with praise of his adopted daughter, Marie de Gournay le Jars, for the "*sincerité et la solidité de ses moeurs*" (1.661). Here he both notes and cancels the issue of gender as incapacity, while he makes a case for the formal virtues of an intimate. None of her acts have the public quality that is the normal and unremarkable qualification for classical exemplarity. Her exemplarity, like that of Alcibiades' lisp, gives pause; it reorients attention to familiar obscurity as ethically significant context.

The reconstitution of the web of belief as a simple and intimate task does, indeed, free ethical speculation from routinization. A remarkable confirmation of this enabling strategy is that Judith Shklar can publish a book in 1984 on *Ordinary Vices* both structured and energized by Montaignian strategies.[22] Indeed, Shklar's use of Montaigne raises our original issue—How serious is Renaissance ethical inquiry? Or, to put it another way, can we make a case for sustainable advance, initiatives that enable further, perspicacious discoveries?

I argue that the work of Montaigne constitutes a sustainable advance precisely because it connects strategies of specification of belief to strategies of address; the reconstitution of belief as task thus impinges on changes in the conception of address as task. To express this point more floridly, Montaigne's account of belief combines the boldest empiricism pertaining to Quine's depiction of the web of belief with the important civil emphasis of Michel

De Certeau's definition of belief as relational engagement.[23] When de Certeau begins his account by citing Benveniste's etymology of *credo* as referring to commerce, to reciprocal obligation, he not only argues the importance of the original meaning of belief as engagement but also claims that belief as a contractual practice, an *énonciation*, becomes only an *énoncé* when it ceases to be a relational engagement. The belief, originally denoting a strategic place of communication, is transformed into ideology, into doctrinal system.

De Certeau's differentiation between belief and doctrine, between *énonciation* and *énoncé*, diagnoses sustainable advance in the Montaignian strategies of maintaining the propriety of the ethical relation of the self to the community. Beliefs are both public and closely held; all responsibility is ineluctably individual, but all process and value is social. Thus we note Montaigne's preference for custom, for shared rule rather than individual choice as guide; he follows "l'ordre public du monde" in the sense of custom or local practice (1.656).[24] Prudence, he claims (and surely this is a counterintuitive move), plays little part in his actions. At the same time, the essays are replete with assertions regarding the isolation of the self. Montaigne thus depicts beliefs as a matrix for action, as at once products of interactional certification and objects of solipsist possession.

This double premise, I now argue, permits a clarification of the sustainable advance found in sixteenth-century refinements in strategies of address. The clear gain of the Renaissance Humanist initiatives was the rearticulation of how inquiry impinges on public exchange. Petrarch's relocation of inquiry, the innovations in internal discipline, are consolidated in shifts in strategies of address. Every change in the notion of what is worthwhile to investigate is, at the same time, a change in the notion of worthwhile presentation, of discursive practice. Montaigne, like Machiavelli, renegotiates the relation of counselor, counsel, and counselee. Montaignian practice stipulates detachment from academic modes and, at the same time, rigorous, disciplined analysis of the web of belief, as well as great tact in address: the reader, only hypothesized, replicates Montaigne in being both aware of incompleteness and desirous of *ordonnance*.

To state it more baldly, the crucial shift was the predication that ethics is *only* a practice. A confirmation of the well-motivatedness of this shift can be found in Bernard Williams's recent book, *Ethics and the Limits of Philosophy*; indeed, I find an almost uncanny resemblance between Williams's and Humanist strategies.[25] Williams's effort is revisionary, an attempt to regain the investigational momentum in ethics, now lost in the swamps of fine analytic discriminations, in the high grass of countless detailed linguistic expositions. In his first chapter, Williams begins his revision of ethical investigation by reformulating the major issue, in order to undercut the standard academic philosophical preoccupations with foundationalism and deontology. His choice of the Socratic question—"How should one live?"—has, of course, its precise analogue in the original Petrarchan formula, "The only question of importance left is, How should one live?" (*Fam.*, XIII, 4,57; IX, 5,114). In chapter 2, Williams makes it clear that the choice of the question was designed to demarcate the limits of professional philosophical competence. And just so, Petrarch had explained the dysfunction of fourteenth-century academic ethics as the product of the refusal to focus on this question. For both, academic failure is rooted in the temptation of academic communities to deal primarily with the problems amenable to their specialist procedures and discourse. Also for both, just as a more exclusive definition is more powerful, so the exclusive focus on the *"vivere"* project enhances the investigative project; it enhances by rejecting the temptations to create labyrinthian systems of moral obligations, duties, or rights with "objective" foundations. Moreover, Williams's primary strategy in this chapter is to turn to the quintessentially rhetorical issue of external address. His strong claim is that there is no easy transfer from reflection to practice, no transparency of ethical activity to theorizing; therefore, the philosophical research that assumes transparency and tries to move directly to moralization and to the production of moralistic discourse is improperly motivated. In this chapter, Williams devotes himself to the questions: From whence is the philosopher speaking? To whom does he address himself? and, Against what does he argue? Here the similarities with Renaissance rhetorical initiatives are obvious; it is precisely the function of rhetorical analysis of philosophical discourse to delineate the limits of philosophical competence, to demarcate the ethical force of ethical inquiry (22–23). Rhetoric limits, and thus strengthens, philosophy. It is this kind of analysis that strengthens the program of Petrarch and Valla, Machiavelli and Montaigne.

The basic initiative of both Montaigne and Machiavelli is to discriminate between proper moral work and moralism. The hinge on which the arguments of Montaigne, Machiavelli, and Williams turns is antimoralism: it is a repudiation of a powerful and dysfunctional classicizing intellectual style. The reorientations of classical *exemplum* and classical maxim in both Machiavelli and Montaigne are responses to their own pragmatic exigencies. Neither one denies classical values, but both deny that easy transparency between moral theory and moral practice presumed by the exemplary mode, which tends to reduce events to a set of instantiations of classical moral-political maxims.

There are simple antimoralistic positions in Montaigne; recall the self-denial in the "*Du repentir*" of the statement, "je n'enseigne poinct, je raconte" (2.806). In the "*De la praesumption*," Montaigne eschews prescription; he is a poor preacher to the populace, "Mauvais prescheur de commune" (1.637), and his express prescriptions do not work even for himself: "si je m'ordonne de le faire par une expresse et prescrite ordonnance, je ne le sçay plus faire" (1.650). Injunction interferes with action. When he defines a third, proper audience, neither "*sçavans*" nor vulgar—the audience of "*les belles ames*" (1.652)—I believe he treats it as an empty class.[26]

It is no accident that Montaigne's only explicit reference to Machiavelli appears in the "*De la praesumption*," that in this most programmatic of all essays, he considers not simply Machiavelli's work but the work as address and the infelicitous reaction to the work. Recall that Villey claimed that Montaigne responds here not only to the *Discorsi* but to I. Gentillet's *Anti-Machiavel* of

1576.[27] "Les discours de Machiavel, pour example, estoient assez solides pour le subject; si, y a-il eu grand aisance à les combattre; et ceux qui l'ont faict, n'ont pas laissé moins de facilité à combattre les leurs" (1.655). [Machiavelli's arguments, for example, were solid enough for the subject, yet it was very easy to combat them; and those who did so left it no less easy to combat theirs (trans. Donald M. Frame).] The connection between Machiavelli's solidity, Machiavelli's risk, and receptive infelicity is no accident either; solidity provokes dishonesty, Montaigne claims, for the attackers of Machiavelli simply recycle in moralistic schemes the strictures they attacked when expressed in his solid and obvious prose. It is also no accident that the description of the infelicity of Machiavelli's reception is followed by Montaigne's modest estimation of his own possible reception; he is aware, he says, that his "exercitation" will bring little praise or fame, "peu de nom" (1.657).

Further, in the "Considerations sur Ciceron," Montaigne repudiates the easy Humanist solution to the problem of felicitous address; Montaigne claims that he does not write intimate letters, because he has no one to write to, and he disclaims any talent for public letters, the letters of "*négoce.*"[28] When he states that letters require an *adresse forte et amie* (1.252), he refers, I believe, both to authorial skill, or address, and to the *destinataire.* When he denies his possession of address, he questions the facile assumption of familiarity as tone in classical practice. This denial impugns, I would argue, the facile solution of Erasmus who stretches the construct of *amicitia* to include hundreds of correspondents in an epistolary practice that amounts to a reinstitutionalization of Humanist inquiry.

The central strategy is a redefinition of the fiduciary nature of investigative practice. Erasmian ethics required the premise of free will to secure moral responsibility; Montaigne, on the other hand, specifies himself as accountable but not competent. Montaigne's redefinition of fiduciary trust is based on a discrimination between the necessary task of tending a web of beliefs and an unnecessary rhetorical task of "making believe"—*facere fidem,* in Quintilian's words.[29]

Beliefs do not travel; they are heavily circumscribed. The essay "*Des boiteux*" is a wide-ranging discussion of belief that stipulates the first and simplest rule: one should believe only that which pertains to the human—"soit cru de ce qui est humain" (2.1031) —and believe of the supernatural only that authorized by supernatural "*approbation.*" But within the first boundary, there is another circumscription: beliefs are not transportable. Recall that Montaigne argues for the radical contingency of "*bon avis*"; it succeeds or fails according to circumstance, but it is good or bad according to its freedom and clarity. Successful counsel is an accident, good counsel, formally correct, eschews resonant response (2.814).[30] Montaigne describes his discursive mode as a "*maniere de devis,*" not a "*maniere d'avis*" (2.1033). More specifically, he impugns the project of confecting belief; he himself does not care to produce faith in, to *give* credence to his discourse— "*donner creance et authorité*" (2.1028). Indeed, he connects the central rhetorical function, "*facere fidem,*" with creating authority by means of violence, where "adjoustons le commandement, la force, le fer, et le feu" (2.1028). Further, an attempt to create belief would damage his project, make him less courageous: "Je ne serois pas si hardy à parler s'il m'appartenoit d'en estre creu" (2.1033).

Montaigne's investigation of belief uses Williams's two postulates of intransivity and enclosure. Williams stipulates that "the excellence or satisfactoriness of a life does not stand to beliefs involved in that life as premise to conclusion. Rather, an agent's excellent life is characterized by *having* these beliefs" (154). Beliefs are not contingent effects, but intrinsic investment—close to Montaigne's construct of "universal stain, dye" of the soul (2.813). Williams also insists that "practical deliberation is first personal, radically so" (67); therefore, the moralistic discourse that shifts from first person to third person, from "I should" to "they ought," is illegitimate (61f.).

Likewise, both Machiavelli and Montaigne block those shifts and pursue "bracketing-off" strategies. Where moralism assumes the transparency of experience to moral theory and the easy transition from moralistic stricture to practice, antimoralism insists that ethics is only a practice and isolates investigative activity as a special practice. The strategies of address are therefore central, not peripheral, issues; the investigation, like any other practice, must be assessed for its motives and postures, its interactional structures. Here both writers develop a paradigm that disbars moral interference with others and assigns the excoriating and isolate role of the inquirer into civility. The fiduciary role of both Machiavelli and Montaigne stipulates that they must continue their moral work; at the same time, reflexive awareness makes it clear that invention and argument do not support moralistic harangue of a large community, and that inventive investigation proceeds "as if" that large community does not hear.

Machiavellian practices of circumscription develop not fictional but hypothetical accounts of political action; the new tactics of characterization and emplotment, when combined with the old injunction to imitate these inimitable plots and characters, forces the reader into theoretical practice, into a hypothetical realm.[31] Machiavelli rejected as delusive or trivial the thesis that rational idealism begets ideally rationalist practice; Machiavelli, although gloomily expecting refusal, invites his audience to join him in investigative practice as the most useful ethical practice. The only adequate riposte to Machiavelli's theorizing is to do theory. A moralistic response is insufficiently theoretical, uncritical; like Gentillet's response, as Montaigne indicated, it is both naive and dishonest.

Montaigne's investigation is, again, a severely circumscribed practice. It is not a skeptical, negative project but a multilayered, positive program of securing beliefs in which mechanisms of doubt and suspension of judgment form only one layer. It is private thoughts about public virtues; radically first-person speculation about a web of belief that characterizes and defines excellent life. The essay as discursive practice for this investigation is an enclosure; the fiction of the audience is that the audience is a fiction. The world, others, but not Montaigne, are always vis à vis (1.657).

Notes

Introduction (pp. 1–19)

1. For the Text/Work distinction and an overview of Structuralist and Post-structuralist contributions to literary theory, see the introduction by Josué V. Harari to *Textual Strategies: Perspectives in Post-Structuralist Criticism* (Ithaca: Cornell University Press, 1979), pp. 17–72.

2. Michel Foucault, "What Is an Author?" in Harari, *Textual Strategies,* pp. 141–60.

3. For an exploration of the relation between the historical and the theoretical dimensions of counterfeit, see Walter Stephens, "Mimesis, Mediation and Counterfeit," in *Mimesis in Contemporary Theory: An Interdisciplinary Approach. Vol. 1. The Literary and Philosophical Debate,* ed. Mihai Spariosu (Philadelphia/Amsterdam: John Benjamins, 1984), pp. 238–75.

4. David Quint, *Origin and Originality in Renaissance Literature: Versions of the Source* (New Haven: Yale University Press, 1983).

5. John Freccero, "The Fig Tree and the Laurel: Petrarch's Poetics," *Diacritics* 5 (1975):34–40.

6. See Harold Bloom, *The Anxiety of Influence: A Theory of Poetry* (New York: Oxford University Press, 1973); and Claude-Gilbert Dubois, *Le Maniérisme* (Paris: Presses Universitaires de France, 1979), pp. 28–35.

7. In this context, see also Thomas Greene's notion of textual "vulnerability" as set forth in "Erasmus's *Festina lente*: Vulnerabilities of the Humanist Text," in *Mimesis: From Mirror to Method, Augustine to Descartes,* eds. John D. Lyons and Stephen G. Nichols (Hanover/London: University Press of New England, 1982), pp. 132–48.

8. See Malcolm K. Read, *The Birth and Death of Language: Spanish Literature and Linguistics: 1300–1700* (Madrid: Porrúa, 1983), pp. 27ff. See also Marina Scordilis Brownlee, *The Status of the Reading Subject in the "Libro de buen amor,"* UNCSRLL 224 (Chapel Hill: University of North Carolina Press, 1985), pp. 23–35, 74–97.

9. Ernst Cassirer, *Language and Myth,* trans. Suzanne Langer (New York: Dover, 1946), p. 7.

The Vowels of Authority
(Dante's *Convivio* IV.vi.3–4) (pp. 23–46)

The research and writing of this essay were accomplished during part of a six-month EXXON Foundation grant at the Newberry Library in Chicago. I wish to thank Tom Stillinger, Joseph Lowenstein, John Martin, Robert Lerner,

Walter Stephens, and Kevin Brownlee for comments on an earlier draft, which led to substantive revisions for publication.

1. All citations are from Dante Alighieri, *Il Convivio*, 2 vols., eds. G. Busnelli and G. Vandelli, intro. by M. Barbi, appendix by A. Quaglio (Florence: Le Monnier, 1964, 2nd ed.). Translations from the Temple Classics edition (J. M. Dent), slightly modified at times.

2. *Dante and Philosophy*, trans. D. Moore (1949, New York: Harper and Row, 1963), p. 156, cf. pp. 140, 188.

3. Which is not to say that the question is never raised there. See Dante Alighieri, *De Monarchia*, ed. P. G. Ricci (Verona: Mondadori, 1965), esp. I.i.4–5; cf. I.v.2–4, III.iii.14–16.

4. "Auctor, Actor, Autor," *Bulletin du Cange: Archivium Latinitatis Medii Aevi*, 3 (1927):81–86; see also his amplifications in *Toward Understanding St. Thomas*, trans. A. M. Landry and D. Hughes (1950, Chicago: Henry Regnery, 1964), esp. pp. 128–38; Alistair Minnis, *Medieval Theory of Authorship* (London: Scolar Press, 1984), pp. 10–12, passim; entries for "autentico," "autentin," "autore," and "autorità" in the *Enciclopedia Dantesca*, 5 vols., dir. U. Bosco (Rome: Istituto dell'Enciclopedia Italiana, 1970–1976). The distinction is commonplace and numerous sources are listed in the above. For easy consultation see Isidore of Seville, *Etymologiarum sive Originum Libri XX*, 2 vols., ed. W. M. Lindsay (Oxford: The Clarendon Press, 1911), IX.iii.16, iv.34 and X.i.2; and Guilliel-mus Brito, *Summa Britonis sive Guillelmi Britonis Expositiones Vocabularum*, eds. B. A. Daly and L. W. Daly (Padua: Antenore, 1975), vol. 1, p. 75.

5. See the *Enciclopedia Dantesca* entry for "Uguccione," vol. 5, pp. 800–802. For a sketch of Hugutio's political views in the context of the medieval debate, see Brian Tierney, *The Crisis of Church and State, 1050–1300* (Englewood Cliffs: Prentice-Hall, 1964), pp. 116–26.

6. The relevant passages from the *Derivationes* are quoted in the *Enciclopedia Dantesca*, vol. 1, p. 457. Isidore (VIII.vii.3) applies *veio* to the poet as *vates*, i.e., as divinely inspired prophet, but does not make the link to *auieo*/autore.

7. "Nomina sunt consequentia rerum" (*Vita Nuova*, ch. 13). See E. R. Curtius, *European Literature and the Latin Middle Ages*, trans. W. R. Trask (1948, Princeton: Princeton University Press, 1953), pp. 495–500. More recent and detailed is R. Howard Bloch, *Etymologies and Genealogies: A Literary Anthropology of the French Middle Ages* (Chicago: University of Chicago Press, 1983), esp. pp. 54–58.

8. Strictly speaking, even medieval theology, in the wake of Augustine's *De Doctrina Christiana*, esp. bk. 1, would have considered the identification of *res* with *verba* idolatrous, since the only true "thing-in-itself" is God.

9. *"De Inventione," "De Optimo Genere Oratorum," "Topica,"* trans. H. M. Hubbell, in the Loeb Classical Library (Cambridge, Mass.: Harvard University Press, 1949). Cf. Chenu, *Understanding St. Thomas*, p. 130; *Enciclopedia Dantesca*, vol. 1, p. 456.

10. *Topica* XX.78: "in the case of man [as opposed to the gods] it is the opinion of his virtue which is most important in winning faith" (cf. XX.73). Throughout, Cicero is more concerned with the rhetorical effectiveness of a witness (*auctor*) than with his actual veracity.

11. Curtius, *European Literature*, p. 464.

12. See *De Monarchia* III.xv.15; *Convivio* IV.ix.3; St. Thomas, *Summa Theologica*, I^a, 33,4,ad.1; cf. *Enciclopedia Dantesca*, vol. 1, p. 458. For the relation of human *auctores* to divine *Auctor*, the precedence of the latter over the former, see *Summa Theologica* I^a, 1, 8 (cf. I^a,1,10, resp.); Minnis, *Medieval Theory of Authorship*, p. 81, passim; Chenu, *Understanding St. Thomas*, pp. 128, 138.

13. Chenu, *Understanding St. Thomas*, p. 128; cf. Minnis, *Medieval Theory of Authorship*, p. 114. Dante, *De Monarchia* III.iii, defines the derivation of authority precisely so he can impeach the credibility of the Decretalists, who are farthest from the divine source.

14. *Enciclopedia Dantesca*, vol. 1, p. 457. Isidore also applies "augere" to a specifically political *auctor* (IX.iii.16).

15. Cf. Curtius, *European Literature*, pp. 51–52.

16. See Minnis, *Medieval Theory of Authorship*, p. 94, for a fourfold distinction among *auctor, scriptor* (scribe), *compilator,* and *commentator.* Chenu sketches the canons for reinterpretation and reconciliation of the *auctores* as they emerged from Abelard to Aquinas (*Understanding St. Thomas*, pp. 139–45). The standard format for presenting authoritative texts, from the Bible on down, was surrounded by commentary and, usually, preceded by an *accessus* that introduced the *auctor* and his *intentio,* including the structure and/or meaning of the work. On this score, see Edwin Quain, "The Medieval *Accessus ad Auctores,*" *Traditio*, 3 (1945):215–64; Minnis, *Medieval Theory of Authorship*, pp. 9–39; Judson Allen, *The Ethical Poetics of the Later Middle Ages* (Toronto: University of Toronto Press, 1982), pp. 67 ff., passim. More generally on the role of the audience in constructing a work's meaning, see Allen, pp. 289–90.

17. This account of the *auctor* apparently reinforces the cliché of medieval anti-historicism and anti-intellectualism. And it is true that the cult of *auctores* was often stultifying; but it was also enabling (cf. Chenu, *Understanding St. Thomas*, p. 83), especially in the twelfth and thirteenth centuries. Moreover, in the early post-Classical period, the "Dark Ages," *auctoritas* clearly was a necessary strategy for conserving the remnants of the great Latin and Greek political-intellectual traditions from impending cultural chaos.

18. Tierney, *Crisis of Church and State*, pp. 1–5, 21–22, passim. Dante attacks this position in the *Monarchia* (III.x.1–4) and gives an alternate account, asserting that the Empire, like the Church, derives its authority directly from God (cf. *Conv.* IV.iv). On Aquinas's discussion of the subordination of reason to revelation see Chenu, *Understanding St. Thomas*, pp. 64–65. See also Gilson, *Reason and Revelation in the Middle Ages* (New York: Scribner's, 1938).

19. See Tierney, *Crisis of Church and State*, pp. 7–13, passim.

20. E.g., I Corinthians 1:18–22. In the thirteenth century, such attacks were often launched by the radical Franciscans. In the fourteenth and early fifteenth centuries, the Christian humanism of Petrarch and others directly opposed the Pauline-Augustinian problem of the fallen will to scholastic rationalism, perhaps under the influence of Nominalist epistemology.

21. See again Tierney, *Crisis of Church and State.* Dante's engagement with this problem in the *Monarchia,* the *Commedia,* and several *Epistolae* needs no rehearsing here.

22. For the ethics/metaphysics hierarchy, see *Conv.* II.xiv and Gilson, *Dante and Philosophy*, pp. 99–109. Explicit references suggest that the fourteenth book

would have been on Justice (I.xii.12; IV.xxvii.11), the fifteenth on Liberality (I.viii.18), the seventh, more conjecturally, on Magnanimity or Temperance (IV.xxvi.7–8); all among the virtues listed in IV.xvii.4–6. Barbi, "Introduzione" in *Convivio*, p. xli, is skeptical about this hypothesis, while Mario Trovato, "Il primo trattato del *Convivio* visto alla luce dell'*accessus ad auctores,*" *Misure Critiche* 6 (1976):14, accepts it. My argument is that Books I to III are all clearly preliminary, while Book IV defines *nobiltà* as the seed of all the virtues (IV.xvi.10), especially the moral virtues that are particularly apt for Dante's chosen audience. One of Dante's primary sources/analogues for the *Convivio*— Egidio Colonna, *Del Reggimento de' Principi,* ed. F. Corazzini (Florence: Le Monnier, 1858)—uses a similar list of the Aristotelian virtues as a structural principle (esp. bk. I, pt. 2).

23. Allen argues that all medieval poetry was actually not poetry at all, but a branch of ethics. This position should be tempered by consulting Winthrop Wetherbee, *Platonism and Poetry in the Twelfth Century* (Princeton: Princeton University Press, 1972), who explores Chartrian attempts to understand poetry as a mode of metaphysical speculation; Glending Olson, *Literature as Recreation in the Later Middle Ages* (Ithaca: Cornell University Press, 1982), who cites medical and other evidence for the special value of specifically *literary* pleasure; and, finally, Minnis's elaborate treatment of the medieval analogy between theological and literary *auctores.* This essay suggests that Dante clearly separates poetry from other fields, even as he assimilates it now to one, now to another.

24. Busnelli and Vandelli, note to *Conv.* IV.vi, state that Aristotle is cited more than fifty times throughout the work.

25. In the *De Vulgari Eloquentia,* ed. A. Marigo (Florence: Le Monnier, 1968), I.i.4, written at roughly the same time, Dante takes the opposite view, and by the end of *Conv.* bk. I he has shifted his ground considerably (I.x.12–13, xiii).

26. Curtius, *European Literature,* pp. 515–18. Cf. Paul Zumthor, *Essai de Poétique Médiévale* (Paris: Seuil, 1972), pp. 64–69, 172–74. See also the contrasting arguments of Leo Spitzer, "Notes on the Poetic and Empirical 'I' in Medieval Authors," *Traditio* 4 (1946):414–22; and Peter Dronke, *Poetic Individuality in the Middle Ages* (Oxford: The Clarendon Press, 1970).

27. The two projects have an obvious point of convergence—it is Dante's authority that makes him a good teacher of others. See *Convivio* III.i.5; IV.viii.3, for references to the basis of other-love in self-love. Seth Lerer, *Boethius and Dialogue: Literary Method in the "Consolation of Philosophy"* (Princeton: Princeton University Press, 1985), esp. pp. 203–36, discusses the *Consolation* in terms of the construction of *auctoritas* via references to poetic and philosophical *auctores.* Dante's strategy is very different from that of Lerer's Boethius.

28. Cf. Allen, *Ethical Poetics,* p. 257.

29. On the Dante/Christ analogy, see Daniel J. Ransom, "*Panis Angelorum:* A Palinode in the *Paradiso,*" *Dante Studies* 95 (1977): esp. p. 89.

30. See n. 15 above. Dante's basic models are the Biblical glosses (the *Glossa Ordinaria* and the commentaries on individual books), literary commentaries such as the *Ovide Moralisé,* and the philosophical commentaries, above all those of Aquinas on Aristotle. See Bruno Nardi, "Osservazioni sul medievale 'accessus ad auctores' in rapporto all'*Epistola a Can Grande,*" in *Saggi e Note di Critica*

Dantesca (Milan-Naples: Ricciardi, 1966), pp. 268–305, for Dante's use of that tradition. See Trovato for its specific relevance to *Convivio* bk. I.

31. Curtius, *European Literature*, p. 221, gives one minor precedent for auto-commentary. Boethius's *prosimetrum* is the nearest acknowledged analogue, though Dante is obviously fusing several structural models.

32. Despite a citation of Guinizelli's "Al cor gentil ripara sempre Amore" (IV.xx.7), the *Convivio* revises the Guinizellian concept of *gentilezza/nobiltà* as simultaneous with the loving heart of the *Vita Nuova* (esp. chs. 19–20). In the *Convivio*, it is love of wisdom rather than love of a woman that ennobles—and the disposition to nobility specifically *precedes* such love. For the range of views available to Dante, see the entry "nobiltà e nobile" in the *Enciclopedia Dantesca*, vol. 4, pp. 58–62; and Maria Simonelli, "Il tema della nobiltà in Andrea Capellano e in Dante," *Dante Studies* 84 (1966):51–64.

33. Clearly, the very special political climate in Florence around 1300 conditioned Dante in at least two ways: (1) by allowing him to conceive easily of relative political-intellectual independence from authorities; but also (2) by instilling in him an urgent sense of the need for hierarchical authority to restore lost order. Cf. *Enciclopedia Dantesca*, vol. 4, p. 58; Simonelli, "Il tema della nobiltà," pp. 56–58.

34. *Enciclopedia Dantesca*, vol. 1, p. 457.

35. For basic historical background, see Ernst Kantorowicz, *Frederick the Second, 1194–1250* (New York: Richard Smith, 1931). For Dante, Frederick was closely identified with a series of radical crises of authority: positively, as the virtual father of Italian lyric poetry (cf. *De Vulgari Eloquentia* I.xii.4–5) and as an implicit model for the perfection of a dialect both "aulicum et curiale," such as would have been spoken of at a central Italian court if one had existed (I.xvii.1, xviii.2–5) (as it had *almost* existed in Frederick's Sicily); and negatively, both as a heretical enemy of the Catholic *fede* (cf. *Inf.* X) and as a reminder of the effective collapse of legitimate imperial authority (cf. *Convivio* IV.iii.6). So this reference is not "simple" after all.

36. Note how the belief in an authoritative name converges on the problem of etymology raised earlier. It is no coincidence that this crucial passage (IV.vi) intertwines etymology and authority, complicating both.

37. According to Chenu, *Understanding St. Thomas*, pp. 140–41, this is exactly how apparent contradictions among *auctores* were dealt with.

38. In the *Monarchia*, Dante is talking about the conservation of institutional authority through genealogical descent, where family and *ricchezza* are crucial. In the *Convivio* he avoids any serious problematization of the relation between individual and institutional authorities, thus marginalizing a central question of medieval politics. See Kantorowicz, *The King's Two Bodies: A Study in Medieval Political Theology* (Princeton: Princeton University Press, 1957), on the systematic relation/separation of human king and institutional kingship.

39. No direct source attributing these words to Frederick has been found. However, the point is not that Frederick did not say it, but that Aristotle *did*, and that Dante almost certainly knew he did. Allen Gilbert, "Had Dante Read the *Politics* of Aristotle?" *PMLA* 43 (1928):603–13, answered that he had not. The entry under "Politica" in the *Enciclopedia Dantesca* argues persuasively that he had (vol. 4, pp. 585–86). In any case, the quotation in the *Monarchia* bears

the unmistakable traces of Aquinas's commentary on the *Politics*, where the *ingenuitas* of the available Latin translation had become Dante's *nobilitas*—see St. Thomas Aquinas, *In Libros Politicam Aristotelis Expositio*, ed. R. Spiazzi (Rome: Marietti, 1951), bk. IV, lect. vii, n. 612. In the *Convivio*, Dante also quotes the *Politics* at IV.v.5. Moreover, in the very same section of the *Politics*, Aristotle again raises the matter of the credibility of popular opinion, which Dante does explicitly attribute to him.

40. Opinions about the depth or nature of Dante's attachment to Aristotle vary somewhat, though there has been more discussion about *whose* Aristotle he prefers (Albertus's? Aquinas's? Siger's?). In the *Convivio*, there is only one explicit disagreement, on a point of astrology (II.iii.3–4). One might actually argue that the implicit repudiation of faith in Aristotle as *auctor* is a natural consequence of thirteenth-century neo-Aristotelian rationalism. If *autorità* is a matter of *fede*, St. Thomas assigns to Aristotle and philosophy the domain of reason as distinct from faith, even while recurring to *auctores* himself at every turn. In *Summa Theologica* I^a,1,8, he states that argument from (human) authority is the weakest kind of argument—and cites Boethius to prove it! Chenu (*Understanding St. Thomas*, p. 138), is keenly aware of the paradox in Thomas. Dante too speaks explicitly of "la virtude de la veritade, che ogni autoritade convince" (IV.iii.10) [the power of the truth, which confutes all authority]. One might be tempted to assert that, rather than offering a new, "proto-Renaissance," approach to authority, Dante is simply repeating or extending a constituent paradox of the great intellectual-cultural revolutions of the twelfth and thirteenth centuries. But this is a point that I cannot, or will not, settle.

41. Dante distinguishes between the "natural" and the "theological" causes of nobility with an odd, potentially unorthodox, equivocation. Just *before* turning from "natural" disposition of body and soul to "theological" infusion from above, he attributes to an unspecified set of thinkers, "alcuni di tale oppinione," the idea that a perfect natural disposition to receive nobility would result in another man-God, a second Christ (IV.xxi.10). In light of my discussion, the failure to cite an *auctor* for this notion, with the recourse to general "oppinione," makes this claim a particularly suspicious and interesting one.

42. Republic II.376e–III.403b, X.595a–608b. The argument is not that Dante knew these texts directly, which he did not, but that he was dealing with the same basic configuration of authorities. He *was* familiar with the neo-Platonic, Christian attacks against poetry as worthless fiction—represented by St. Augustine (*Confessiones* I.16–18, III.2, passim) and Aquinas himself (*Summa Theologica* I^a,1,9). On the Dantean "defense of poetry" against this tradition, see Dennis Costa, "Dante as Poet-Theologian," *Dante Studies* 89 (1971):81–82; Robert Hollander, "Dante *Theologus-Poeta*," *Dante Studies* 94 (1976):97–99, 118; and Ransom, "*Panis Angelorum*," p. 82.

43. "The Unfinished *Convivio* and Dante's Rereading of the *Aeneid*," *Medieval Studies* 13 (1951):41–64. See also Hollander, "Dante's Use of *Aeneid* I in *Inferno* I and II," *Comparative Literature* 20 (1968):142–56.

44. See especially Giuseppe Mazzotta, *Dante, Poet of the Desert* (Princeton: Princeton University Press, 1979), pp. 256–68. See also Hollander, "Dante's Use of *Aeneid* I," pp. 144–45, for the analogy/contrast between Virgil as *autore* in *Inferno* I.85 and IV.113 and God as *Autore* in *Paradiso* XXVI.26, 40, 47.

Mazzotta demonstrates various ways in which the *Commedia* limits and even undercuts the *autorità* that it initially confers on Virgil (pp. 90, 154–55, 190, 222). Quotations are taken from *The Divine Comedy*, 3 vols., ed. and trans. Charles S. Singleton (Princeton: Princeton University Press, 1970–1976).

45. See Aquinas, *Summa Theologica* Iᵃ 13, 9, resp. and 13, 11, ad.1. For a somewhat more recent reworking of this problem, see Arthur Rimbaud's "Voyelles."

46. See Charles S. Singleton, *Dante's "Commedia": Elements of Structure* (1954, Baltimore: The Johns Hopkins University Press, 1977), esp. pp. 1–17, 84–98, for Dante's discussion of the "allegory of theologians" in the *Convivio* (II.i) and the *Epistola* to Can Grande and for his use of it in the *Commedia*. See also Hollander, *Allegory in Dante's "Commedia"* (Princeton: Princeton University Press, 1969), and "Dante *Theologus-Poeta.*"

47. Pietrobono, "Filosofia e Teologia nel *Convivio* e nella *Commedia*," *Giornale Dantesco* 41 (1938):13–71. See Barbi and Gilson for the opposition, and Leo, "The Unfinished *Convivio*" pp. 42–46, for a summary of the earlier debate. Freccero, "Dante's Prologue Scene," *Dante Studies* 84 (1966):1–25; "Casella's Song (*Purgatorio* II.112)," *Dante Studies* 91 (1973):73–80. Materials from the *Convivio*, as we know, constantly reappear in the *Commedia* and, just as constantly, are altered and revised in crucial ways: *Conv.* IV.xii–xiii introduces key motifs that become the framing moments of Dante's journey with Virgil (*Inf.* I and *Purg.* XXVII; cf. Freccero, "Dante's Prologue Scene," and Hollander, "Dante's Use of *Aeneid* I"); Guido de Montefeltro (*Conv.* IV.xxviii.4 and *Inf.* XXVII) and Cato (*Conv.* IV.xxviii and *Purg.* I–II); the motif of the "pan degli angeli" (*Conv.* I and *Purg.* II; cf. Ransom, "*Panis Angelorum*"); Beatrice versus the "donna gentile" (*Conv.* II and *Purg.* XXX and XXXIII; cf. Pietrobono); the canzone "Voi ch'intendendo il terzo cielo movete" (*Conv.* II and *Par.* VIII–IX; cf. Rachel Jacoff, "The Post-Palinodic Smile: *Paradiso* VIII and IX," *Dante Studies* 98 (1980):111–22); not to mention lunar spots, angelic hierarchies, and so on. A question to ask is, How do we differentiate the conversion-palinodes of the *Commedia* from Dante's penchant for self-revision and/or contradiction in *all* his works; for instance, the shift on the Latin/Italian question from the *Convivio* to the *De Vulgari Eloquentia* or the change in the definition of nobility between *Convivio* and *Monarchia*?

48. Cf. n. 21 above. For celebrations of the "dignitas hominis," see III.ii.14, iii.5ff., viii.1–2, IV.xix.6–7, xx.3. For the limits of human language and reason, see III.canzone, iii.13–15, iv.1–4, viii.14–17. The crucial point is that human knowledge, unlike the pure intellection of angels, is always mediated by images derived from sense experience by the fantasy and stored in the memory (III.iv.9–11; for the same question in the *Commedia*, see Mazzotta, *Dante, Poet of the Desert*, pp. 260–268, passim).

49. "When Love inspires me, I take note, and go setting it forth after the fashion which he dictates within me" (trans. Charles S. Singleton, slightly modified). On the trinitarian character of the poetics in *Purg.* XXIV, see Mazzotta, *Dante, Poet of the Desert*, pp. 202ff.

50. Ransom, "*Panis Angelorum*," esp. pp. 86–90.

51. Singleton, *Dante's "Commedia,"* p. 62. My reading of allegory in the

Commedia is influenced by Mazzotta, *Dante, Poet of the Desert,* pp. 227–74 (esp. p. 252).

52. Hollander, "Dante *Theologus-Poeta,*" pp. 111–112. But perhaps Dante expected us to see how extreme and extremely improbable this insistence on literal veracity is.

53. It can be argued that the poetic *note* of XVI–XVII is set in specific relation to the "notational" poetics of *Purg.* XXIV, which shifts the burden of authorization from Dante's own words to God's Word. See my discussion of this question in *Ariosto's Bitter Harmony: Crisis and Evasion in the Italian Renaissance* (Princeton: Princeton University Press, 1987), pp. 264–304. If such an evolutionary internal narrative of Dante's poetics is to be credited, however, one must ignore the crucial pilgrim/poet distinction on which the notion of a privileged theological perspective ultimately depends; that is, if the poet is what the pilgrim becomes after completing his journey, there is no reason why his poetics should be partial or incomplete at an earlier stage of the writing. His access to divine inspiration should be full from the beginning, in *Inferno* as well as in *Purgatorio.*

54. Minnis, for instance, argues that the thirteenth century sees a marked shift from divine to human author (*Medieval Theory of Authorship,* esp. pp. 94–103). He develops for a different historical period a theme treated more generally by such critics and theorists as Robert Durling, *The Figure of the Poet in Renaissance Epic* (Cambridge, Mass.: Harvard University Press, 1965); M. H. Abrams, *The Mirror and the Lamp* (New York: Oxford University Press, 1953); Northrop Frye, *Anatomy of Criticism* (Princeton: Princeton University Press, 1957); Kenneth Burke, *The Rhetoric of Religion* (Berkeley: University of California Press, 1970); Frank Kermode, *The Sense of an Ending* (New York: Oxford University Press, 1967); and Roland Barthes, "The Death of the Author," in *Image, Music, Text,* trans. S. Heath (1968, New York: Hill and Wang, 1977), pp. 142–148.

55. David Quint, *Origin and Originality in Renaissance Literature: Versions of the Source* (New Haven: Yale University Press, 1983). On the question of imitation and originality, see also Thomas Greene, *The Light in Troy: Imitation and Discovery in Renaissance Poetry* (New Haven: Yale University Press, 1982).

56. See Quint's excellent concluding remarks on *Paradise Lost* in an "Epilogue," *Origin and Originality,* pp. 207–20. See also John Guillory's extended treatment of Milton in *Poetic Authority: Spenser, Milton and Literary History* New York: Columbia University Press, 1983).

Vico's New Critical Art and the Authority of the Noble Lie (pp. 47–59)

1. *La Scienza nuova seconda,* vol. 4 of *Opere di G. B. Vico* (Bari: Laterza, 1911–1914), pp. 369–90. English translation: *The New Science of Giambattista Vico,* trans. Thomas Goddard Bergin and Max Harold Fisch (Ithaca: Cornell University Press, 1968). The numbers used in citations refer to the paragraph enumeration common to the Laterza and Cornell editions. Vico gives the list of several principal aspects of his science as corollaries in his presentation of "poetic metaphysics" (385–99). In this list, "a philosophy of authority" is called the second principal aspect, as it is in his introduction to the idea of the work (7). In the section on "Method," "a history of human ideas" is termed the

second principal aspect, and "a philosophy of authority" is presented in third place (although it is not called third). "A history of human ideas" appears as third in Vico's full list of seven.

2. For Vico's criticism of Hobbes, see *Scienza*, 179. Max Fisch suggests in his introduction to the English translation of Vico's *Autobiography* that there may be a connection between Vico's ideas and later British thinkers, including Hume: "Hume's natural history of religion, for instance, is up to a point eminently Vichian" (*The Autobiography of Giambattista Vico*, trans. Max H. Fisch and Thomas G. Bergin [Ithaca: Cornell University Press, 1975], p. 82). An interpretation of Hume that makes Hume compatible in many respects with Vico is Donald Livingston, *Hume's Philosophy of Common Life* (Chicago: University of Chicago Press, 1984). Livingston writes: "Hume, like Vico, was working towards a reform of philosophy that takes history, not natural science, as the paradigm of knowledge" (ix).

3. Donald Phillip Verene, *Vico's Science of Imagination* (Ithaca: Cornell University Press, 1981).

4. Giambattista Vico, *Autobiografia*, ed. Mario Fubini (Turin: Einaudi, 1970), 80 ff.

5. See Ernst Cassirer, "The Influence of Language upon the Development of Scientific Thought," *Journal of Philosophy* 39 (1942):309–27.

6. For a discussion of this concept, see *Vico's Science of Imagination*, ch. 3.

7. See also Donald Phillip Verene, "Vico's New Critical Art and the Muses," *New Vico Studies* 1 (1983):21–38.

8. *The Republic of Plato*, trans. F. M. Cornford (New York: Oxford University Press, 1945), pp. 68 and 106n.

Homer's Virgilian Authority: Ronsard's Counterfeit Epic Theory (pp. 63–75)

A shorter version of this article was presented as a paper at the National Conference of the Renaissance Society of America at the Huntington Library, on Saturday, March 23, 1985. I wish to thank Professor Marc Bensimon for organizing a special section for Ronsard's quadricentennial celebration (1585–1985).

1. "Entre Homere et Virgile, ainsi qu'un demy-Dieu /Environné d'esprits j'ay ma place au milieu." "Elegie à Louis Des Masures," in: Ronsard, *Oeuvres Complètes*, ed. by Paul Laumonnier, vol. 10 (Paris: Droz, 1939):369, ll. 123–24. All translations are mine.

2. "La plus chère ambition de Ronsard était précisément de doter la France d'une épopée, qui, jetant une belle lumière sur notre poésie, ne manquerait pas d'en immortaliser l'auteur." P. Laumonier in his "Introduction" to Ronsard's *Oeuvres Complètes*, vol. 16 (Paris: Nizet, 1983):v. All subsequent references to *La Franciade* are to volume 16 of this edition. On the epic poem in French Renaissance theory, see Thomas Sebillet, *Art Poëtique Françoys*, ed. by F. Gaiffe (Paris: STFM, 1910), II, xiv; Joachim Du Bellay, *La Deffence et Illustration de la langue françoise*, ed. by H. Chamard (Paris: Didier, 1948), II, V, pp. 127 sq.; Jacques Peletier du Mans, *Art poétique*, ed. by A. Boulanger (Paris: Belles-Lettres, 1930), pp. 194–210.

3. "J'ay patronné mon oeuvre . . . plustost sur . . . Homere que sur Virgile . . ." *Epistre au Lecteur* (1572), Ronsard, *Oeuvres*, vol. 16, p. 5. This statement will be analyzed in detail in the following pages.

4. "Ses (Ronsard's) préférences politiques le portaient peut-être davantage vers l'âge d'Auguste qui pouvait devenir le support d'un mythe." D. Ménager, *Ronsard: Le Roi, le poète et les hommes* (Geneva: Droz, 1979), section IV, "La Tentative épique," p. 65, note 1. "Ronsard's principal model seems clearly to have been the *Aeneid*—certainly the *Aeneid* furnished him the context and general lines of the story." Bruce R. Leslie, *Ronsard's Successful Epic Venture: The Epyllion* (Lexington, Ky.: French Forum, 1979), p. 111.

5. *Virgil and Ronsard* (Paris: Champion, 1923), p. 99. Storer's belabored point is of course biased by the very onus of his thesis, which forces him to find as many parallels as possible between the two poets.

6. *Ronsard and the Hellenic Renaissance in France*, vol. 1, *Ronsard and the Greek Epic* (Saint Louis: Washington University Press, 1961), p. 433.

7. "Virgile . . . conceut ceste divine Aenide qu'aveq toute reverence nous tenons encores aujourd'huy entre les mains." Ronsard, *Oeuvres*, vol. 16, p. 7. All references in parentheses in the text will be to this volume.

8. "Suy Virgile qui est maistre passé en composition et structure des carmes: regarde un peu quel bruit font ces deux icy sur la fin du huictiesme (chant) de l'*Aeneide*. (*Ae.* VIII, 689–90). Tu en pourras faire en ta langue autant que tu pourras" (347).

9. *Art Poétique*, ed. Boulanger, Chapter "De L'Imitacion," pp. 95–104.

10. As Isidore Silver puts it, *Ronsard and the Greek Epic*, p. 34, note 156.

11. "Virgile à imité ce qu'il à vù d'admirable en Homere. Mes il l'à chatiè an plusieurs androetz. E ici metrè quelque nombre de poinz, léquez Virgile n'à pas trouuèz bons an Homere, e dont il s'et gardè." Peletier, *Art Poétique*, p. 98.

12. Ibid., pp. 98–99.

13. Ibid., p. 102. "Quandoque bonus dormitat Homerus . . ." *Ars poetica*, l. 359.

14. Peletier, *Art Poétique*, p. 98.

15. "Considere, si l'Eneide ùt etè fete auant l'Iliade, que c'et qu'il an faudroet dire." Ibid., p. 98.

16. "Disons Virgile imitateur par euuidance: e Homere invanteur, par jugemant e opinion." Ibid., p. 98.

17. "Si et-ce que je trouve Virgile etre tombè an samblable faute." Ibid., p. 99.

18. "Il n'et si grand, qui ne tombe an faute." Ibid., p. 102.

19. "Qu'il sache que c'et qu'il doèt imiter e quoe non." Ibid., p. 98.

20. "C'est le seul (Virgile) qu'il (Peletier) veut voir imité par les poètes français. Pour lui, comme pour Vida, il n'est de salut que dans l'imitation de ce prince des poètes. Sa doctrine du poème épique n'est donc que la pratique de l'*Enéide* réduite en art et en principes. Il était d'ailleurs d'accord sur ce point avec la majeure partie du public français qui, une fois tombée la première flambée d'enthousiasme pour l'hellénisme, s'attachait presque uniquement aux Latins et faisait de Virgile son dieu domestique." A. Boulanger on Peletier's theory of "original imitation," in Peletier, *Art poétique*, p. 42. For H. Chamard and I. Silver, Peletier's admiration for Virgil stems from a theoretical flaw ("a critical

weakness"), namely the belief that the *Aeneid* is superior to the *Iliad* because it is an improved imitation of Homer, "as though the imitating poet were *always* superior to the imitated one." Cf. Silver, *Ronsard and the Greek Epic*, pp. 36 ff.

21. "De Merové, des peuples conquereur, / Viendra meint prince, & meint grand empereur / Hault eslevez en dignité supresme: / Entre lesquels un Roy CHARLES neufiesme, / Neufiesme en nom & premier en vertu, / Naistra pour voir le monde combatu / Desous ses pieds, d'où le soleil se plonge, / Et d'où ses rais sur la terre il allonge, / Et s'eslançant de l'humide sejour / Aporte aux Dieux & aux hommes le jour." *Franciade*, in *Oeuvres*, vol. 16, p. 41, ll. 247–56.

22. Only Christ, when He comes again to judge the living and the dead, will be able to establish a perpetual, universal, and worldwide kingdom. Ronsard's eulogy of the French king may appear to be sacrilegious in its obvious extremism. His Jupiter speaks like God himself in the Christian *Credo*.

23. "Je m'asseure que les envieux caqueteront, dequoy j'allegue Virgile plus souvent qu'Homere qui estoit son maistre, & son patron: mais je l'ay fait tout expres, sçachant bien que nos François ont plus de congnoissance de Virgile, que d'Homere & d'autres Autheurs Grecs." *Oeuvres*, vol. 16, p. 342.

24. Ménager, *Ronsard*, p. 292.

25. For a summary of the reasons given for the "failure" of *La Franciade*, see Silver, *Ronsard and the Greek Epic*, pp. 418–20; Leslie, *Ronsard's Successful Epic*, pp. 111–14; Ménager, *Ronsard: Le Roi*, p. 312.

26. Leslie, *Ronsard's Successful Epic*, p. 111.

27. "Imitant toutefois a mon possible de l'un & de l'autre, l'artifice & l'argument plus basty sur la vraysemblance que sur la verité." "Suivant ces deux grands personnages, j'ay fait le semblable." *Oeuvres*, vol. 16, pp. 5 and 7.

28. "Imitant ces deux lumieres de Poësie, fondé & appuyé sur nos vieilles Annales j'ay basti ma *Franciade*, sans me soucier se cela est vray ou non, . . . me servant du possible, & non de la verité." *Oeuvres*, vol. 16, p. 340.

29. "Si je parle de nos Monarques plus longuement que l'art Virgilien ne le permet, tu dois sçavoir, Lecteur, que Virgile (comme en toutes autres choses) en ceste-cy est plus heureux que moy, qui vivoit sous Auguste, second Empereur, tellement que n'estant chargé que de peu de Rois & de Cesars, ne devoit beaucoup allonger le papier, où j'ay le faix de soixante & trois Rois sur les bras." *Oeuvres*, vol. 16, p. 5.

30. "Au reste j'ay patronné mon oeuvre (dont ces quatre premiers livres te serviront d'échantillon) plustost sur la *naïve facilité* d'Homere que sur la *curieuse diligence* de Virgile." *Oeuvres*, vol. 16, p. 5.

31. "Et hercule ut illi [Homero] *naturae caelesti* atque immortali cesserimus, ita *curae et diligentiae* vel ideo in hoc [Vergilio] plus est, quod ei fuit magis laborandum, et quantum eminentibus vincimur, fortasse aequalitate pensamus." *Institutio oratoria*, X, I, 86. Translation by H. E. Butler (Cambridge, Mass.: Harvard University Press, 1936), vol. 4, p. 49.

32. Cf. Sebillet's earlier dictum: "Le Poëte naist; l'Orateur se fait." *Art Poëtique Françoys* (1548), ed. Gaiffe, p. 25.

33. Ed. H. Chamard, pp. 103–105. Cf. Grahame Castor, *Pléiade Poetics* (Cambridge: Cambridge University Press, 1964), p. 44.

34. "Par le conseil de mes plus doctes amis j'ay changé, mué, abregé, alongé beaucoup de lieux de ma *Franciade* pour rendre plus parfaite, & luy donner sa

derniere main. Et voudrais de toute affection que noz François daignassent faire le semblable: nous ne verrions tant d'ouvrages avortez, lesquels, pour n'oser endurer la lime & parfaite polissure requise par temps, n'aportent que deshonneur à l'ouvrier, et à nostre France tres mauvaise reputation." *Oeuvres*, vol. 16, p. 3.

35. "Vingt fois sur le métier remettez votre ouvrage; / Polissez-le sans cesse et le repolissez; / Ajoutez, quelquefois, et souvent effacez." *Art Poétique* (1669–74), ll. 172–4. *Oeuvres poétiques*, ed. by F. Brunetière (Paris: Hachette, 1914), p. 196.

36. "Tu enrichiras ton Poëme par varietez *prises de la Nature*, sans extravaguer comme un frenetique. Car pour vouloir trop eviter, & du tout te bannir du parler vulgaire, si tu veux voler sans consideration par le travers des nues, & faire des grotesques, Chimeres & monstres, & non une *naifve & naturelle poesie*, tu seras imitateur d'Ixion, qui engendra des Phantosmes au lieu de *legitimes & naturels enfans*." *Oeuvres*, vol. 16, p. 334.

37. *Deffence*, ed. Chamard, II, 5 "Du Long Poëme Françoys," p. 127.

38. On *mimesis* and *imitatio*, see Castor, *Pléiade Poetics*, pp. 72–73.

39. "La guerre Troyenne a esté feinte par Homere, comme quelques graves auteurs ont fermement assuré: les fables qui on sont sorties depuis sont toutes puisées de *la source de cest Homere* . . . Autant en faut estimer de Virgile, lequel lisant en Homere, qu'Aenée ne devoit mourir à la guerre Troyenne . . . , conceut ceste divine Aeneide." *Oeuvres*, vol. 16, pp. 6–7.

40. D. Quint, *Origin and Originality in Renaissance Literature. Versions of the Source* (New Haven: Yale University Press, 1983), pp. 23 ff.

41. "O qu'il i ùt ancore un Auguste pour voèr s'il se pourrèt ancore trouver un Virgile!" Peletier, *Art Poétique*, p. 210.

42. "Certainement si nous avions des Mecenes & des Augustes, les Cieux & la Nature ne sont point si ennemis de nostre siecle, que n'eussions encores des Virgiles!" Du Bellay, *Deffence*, pp. 132–33.

43. "Suy Virgile qui est passé maistre en composition & structure des carmes." *Oeuvres*, vol. 16, p. 347.

44. "Mon Passerat, je ressemble à l'Abeille / Qui va cueillant tantost la fleur vermeille, / Tantost la jaune: errant de pré en pré / Volle en la part qui plus luy vient à gré, / Contre l'Hyver amassant force vivres. / . . . Ainsy courant & feuilletant mes livres, / J'amasse, trie & choisis le plus beau, / Qu'en cent couleurs je peints en un tableau, / Tantost en l'autre: & maistre en ma peinture, / Sans me forcer j'imite la Nature." *Oeuvres*, ed. Laumonnier, vol. 15, p. 252.

45. Castor, *Pléiade Poetics*, p. 72.

46. "J'ai patronné mon oeuvre . . . sur la naïve facilité d'Homere." *Oeuvres*, vol. 16, p. 347.

47. "En ce laborieux ouvrage de la *Franciade*, l'Autheur s'est proposé la façon d'escrire des Anciens, & sur tous du divin Homere." Ronsard, *Oeuvres*, vol. 16, p. 14.

48. "Combien qu'en ce premier livre il ait principalement imité Homere et Virgile, si est-ce que l'embarquement de Francus est à l'imitation d'Apolloine Rhodien." *Oeuvres*, vol. 16, p. 14.

49. "Il ressamble à l'abeille, laquelle tire son proffit de toutes fleurs pour en faire son miel: aussi sans jurer en l'imitation d'un des Anciens plus que des

autres, il considere ce qui est en eux de meilleur, dequoy il enrichist (comme toujours il a été heureux) nostre langue françoise." *Oeuvres*, vol. 16, p. 14.

50. This conception had been forcefully criticized by Jupiter in Ronsard's *Ode à Michel de L'Hospital*, ll. 395–408.

51. Quint, *Origin and Originality*, p. 30.

52. *"Gallica se quantis attollet gloria verbis!"* Here one recognizes a line from *Aeneid* IV, 49: "Punica se quantis attollet gloria rebus." To what heights will Punic glory soar!

Author/Narrator/Speaker: The Voice of Authority in Chrétien's *Charrete* (pp. 76–96)

1. See Rupert T. Pickens, *"Estoire, lai* and Romance: Chrétien's *Erec et Enide* and *Cligés,"* *Romanic Review* 66, no. 4 (1975):247–62 [262]; on general characteristics of the *lai*, see Jean Frappier, "Remarques sur la structure du lai: Essai de définition et de classement," in *La littérature narrative d'imagination* (Paris: PUF, 1961), pp. 23–37.

2. *Sens and Conjointure in the Chevalier de la Charrette* (Paris/The Hague: Mouton, 1966).

3. The epilogue is found in mss. C (B.N. f. fr. 794), T (B.N. f. fr. 12560), and V (Vatican 1725) (Manuscript sigla are those, generally accepted, from Wendelin Foerster's *Der Karrenritter* [Halle: Max Niemeyer, 1899]). In the fourth manuscript, F (B.N. f. fr. 1450), which also contains the romances of *Troie, Eneas, Brut*, and *Dolopathos*, the scribe has, interestingly enough, chosen to interpolate Chrétien's five romances in the middle of Wace's *Brut* at the moment when Arthur has established his universal peace, as though the knightly adventures were taken to illustrate a "pause" in the otherwise unrelenting movement of universal history. Of the five, the *Charrete* appears last, and the scribe, accordingly, adapts the first lines of the romance epilogue to form a narrative transition with the continuation of Wace's previously interrupted narrative voice (fol. 225r):

> Segnor, se io avant disoie
> Ce ne seroit pas bel a dire.
> Por ce retor a ma matire . . .

[My lords, were I to speak any further it would not be a seemly discourse. Therefore, I am returning to my matter.]

Curiously enough, whereas we might speak of distinct narrators when dealing with discrete works, the context of the manuscript compilation possibly suggests, as here, that the scribe's narrative "voice" encompasses and supersedes that which is attributable to the individual poem, thus bespeaking a global intentionality behind the work of compilation itself.

4. References to the *Charrete* are taken from Mario Roques's edition in the Classiques Français du Moyen Âge series (Paris: Champion, 1958), largely a transcription of ms. C. For a recent discussion of Chrétien's continuator, Godefroy de Leigni, see David J. Shirt, "Godefroi de Lagny et la composition de la 'Charrete,'" *Romania* 96 (1975):27–52; and its companion piece, "How much

of the Lion can we put before the Cart?", *French Studies* 31, no. 1 (January 1977):1–17.

5. Cf. Kelly, *Sens*, pp. 33–35; Marie-Louise Ollier, "The Author in the Text: The Prologues of Chrétien de Troyes," *Yale French Studies* 51 (1974):26–41; and Pierre Gallais, "Recherches sur la mentalité des romanciers français du moyen âge: les formules et le vocabulaire des prologues," *Cahiers de Civilisation médiévale* 7 (1964):479–93; and 13 (1970):333–47.

6. For an excellent review of the manuscript tradition, see Alexandre Micha, *La Tradition manuscrite de Chrétien de Troyes*, Publications romanes et françaises 90 (Paris: Droz, 1939), to which must be added the recent fragments discovered at Princeton (Garrett 125), q.v., Leonard Rahilly, "Le manuscrit Garrett 125 du *Chevalier de la Charrette* et du *Chevalier au Lion*: un nouveau manuscrit," *Romania* 94 (1973):407–10; and "La tradition manuscrite du *Chevalier de la Charrette* et le manuscrit Garrett 125," *Romania* 95 (1974):395–413.

7. For a convenient summary and discussion, see Shirt, "Godefroi de Lagny," 36–37; Alison Adams provides an unconvincing argument for situating the break in the two parts at a point much earlier than is typically conjectured in her "Godefroi de Leigni's Continuation of *Lancelot*," *Forum for Modern Language Studies* 9 (1974):295–99.

8. Shirt, "How much of the Lion," esp. pp. 6–12.

9. See especially, in addition to Ollier and Gallais (note 5 above), Pierre-Yves Badel, "Rhétorique et polémique dans les prologues de romans au moyen âge" *Littérature* 20 (1975):81–94; and Michel Zink, "Une mutation de la conscience littéraire: Le langage romanesque à travers des examples français du XIIᵉ siècle," *Cahiers de Civilisation médiévale* 24 (1981):3–27.

10. For important statements supporting and refuting the influence of school rhetoric upon vernacular prologue material see, respectively, Tony Hunt, "Tradition and Originality in the Prologues of Chrestien de Troyes," *Forum for Modern Language Studies* 8 (1972):320–44; and James A. Schultz, "Classical Rhetoric, Medieval Poetics, and the Medieval Vernacular Prologue," *Speculum* 59 (1984):1–15.

11. Quoted from Ulrich Mölk, *Französische Literarästhetik des 12. und 13. Jahrhunderts* (Tübingen: Max Niemeyer, 1969), p. 92.

12. Cf. Peter Haidu, *Aesthetic Distance in Chrétien de Troyes: Irony and Comedy in Cligés and Perceval* (Geneva: Droz, 1968).

13. Ed. Léopold Constans, *Société des Anciens Textes Français*, vol. 1 (Paris: Firmin Didot, 1904), ll. 132–37.

14. Cf. Gallais, CCM 13 (1970):338–42.

15. For a fuller discussion of this methodological problem, see my *Self-fulfilling Prophecies: Readership and Authority in the First Roman de la Rose* (Cambridge: Cambridge University Press, 1986), pp. 10–104.

16. That Chrétien's romances were commonly viewed by the medieval public in this way is confirmed, on the one hand, by B.N. f. fr. 1450's subordination of his entire *oeuvre* to the wider historical vision of Wace (see note 3 above) and, on the other hand, by the reconception of the *Lancelot* and *Perceval* romances through a vision of universal history in the lengthy prose *Lancelot-Graal* of the thirteenth century.

17. This hypothesis has been advanced by Roger Dragonetti in his *La Vie de la lettre au moyen âge* (Paris: Seuil, 1980), pp. 13–17, although it is left largely undeveloped and unsubstantiated.

18. For a restatement of the prologue's "classic" interpretation, see Jean Frappier, "Le prologue du *Chevalier de la Charrette* et son interprétation," *Romania* 93 (1972):337–77, which is a response to a series of polemical articles published by Jean Rychner: "Le prologue du 'Chevalier de la charrette,'" *Vox Romanica* 26 (1967):1–23; "Le prologue du *Chevalier de la charrette* et l'interprétation du roman," *Mélanges offerts à Rita Lejeune* (Gembloux: Duculot, 1969), pp. 1121–35; and "Encore le prologue du 'Chevalier de la Charrette,'" *Vox Romanica* 31 (1972):263–71.

19. See, however, Norris J. Lacy, *The Craft of Chrétien de Troyes: An Essay on Narrative Art*, Davis Medieval Texts and Studies, 3 (Leiden: Brill, 1980), p. 57; and Matilda Tomaryn Bruckner, "Le Chevalier de la Charrette (Lancelot)," in *The Romances of Chrétien de Troyes: A Symposium*, ed. Douglas Kelly (Lexington, Ky.: French Forum, 1985), pp. 132–81 [133].

20. As Rychner has noted ("Le prologue du *Chevalier de la Charrette*," p. 3), line 4, "come cil qui est suens antiers," is repeated verbatim in line 5656, and there refers to Lancelot's submission to Guenevere.

21. The term *gré* has understandably received little attention in discussions of Chrétien's technical vocabulary, since he does not actively exploit or discuss it in that context. Nonetheless, it seems to denote a type of mental activity, or attitude, that is neither covered by the term *sens*, suggestive of some vague sort of transmissible meaning or message, nor by the term usually translated as "intention," *entencïon*, which, as Ollier reminds us ("The Author," pp. 32–33), "denotes the creative effort itself" and is generally associated with a dynamic expression or decoding of meaning. Between these two terms, there is a rhetorical space left open for personal attitudes that can neither be coded in denotative language as an active expression of will nor directly transmitted as though they were goods or commodities. It is this intangible passive or ambiguous personal attitude, sometimes at odds with expressed intentions, that is, I submit, covered by the term *gré*.

22. This peculiar scene has either been passed over or misread by the critics. To summarize the "meaning" of the episode out of context, as does Kelly (*Sens*, p. 146: "Guenevere . . . nearly loses her self-control for joy"), is to neglect for a large part the eccentric qualities of Chrétien's narration. David Shirt, on the other hand, simply misreads the account: "C'est au cours de cet épisode (v. 6807–53) que Lancelot et Guenièvre se voient pour la première et pour la dernière fois dans le travail de Godefroi" ("Godefroi de Lagny," p. 41). On three other occasions in the same article (pp. 41, 43, 44), he refers to this moment as their "dernière rencontre," when they are not in fact described by the narrator as coming together, or even seeing each other, at all!

23. Cf. Gerard J. Brault, "Chrétien de Troyes' *Lancelot*: The Eye and the Heart," *Bulletin Bibliographique de la Société Internationale Arthurienne* 24 (1972):142–53.

24. Cf. Shirt, "Godefroi de Lagny," p. 43.

Widowed Words: Dante, Petrarch, and the Metaphors of Mourning (pp. 97–108)

1. *Vita nuova* 31.2. Throughout this essay, Dante's text appears as in Fredi Chiappelli's edition (Milan: Mursia, 1965). All translations are my modifications of those of Mark Musa (Bloomington and London: Indiana University Press, 1973) and Barbara Reynolds (Harmondsworth, England: Penguin, 1969). All future references to the *Vita nuova* (*VN*) will be by chapter and section (not line) number and will be indicated in the text.

2. *Rime sparse* 268.78–82. Throughout this essay, quotations from Petrarch's *Rime sparse* (*RS*) appear as in Robert Durling's edition and translation (Cambridge, Mass.: Harvard University Press, 1976). All future references are indicated in the text.

3. See, for example, Ezio Chiorboli's edition of the *Rime sparse* (Milan: Trevisini, 1924), p. 620.

4. In *Le Maniérisme* (Paris: Presses Universitaires de France, 1979), pp. 28–35.

5. Bloom's argument is most thoroughly articulated in *The Anxiety of Influence: A Theory of Poetry* (New York: Oxford University Press, 1973).

6. *Familiares* 23.19, as cited by Thomas Greene, *The Light in Troy: Imitation and Discovery in Renaissance Poetry* (New Haven: Yale University Press, 1982), p. 95. Greene's discussion of Petrarch's theory of imitation, as well as of the broader implications of the concept of *imitatio*, are singularly illuminating.

7. For the use of the term "città dolente" in reference to hell, see *Inferno* 3.1 and 9.32.

8. See Chiorboli, *Rime sparse*, p. 608; and Thomas P. Roche, Jr., "The Calendrical Structure of Petrarch's *Canzoniere*," *Studies in Philology* 71 (1974):153, n. 2.

9. See Durling, "Petrarch's 'Giovene donna sotto un verde lauro,'" *Modern Language Notes* 86 (1971):1–20; Martinelli, "'Feria sexta aprilis': la data sacra nel Canzoniere del Petrarca," *Rivista di storia e letteratura religiosa* 8 (1972):449–84; and Roche, "Calendrical Structure," pp. 152–72.

10. See Martinelli (ibid.) for his debate with Calcaterra on this issue.

11. For the variants, see Chiorboli, *Rime sparse*, pp. 618–19. All translations from the variants are mine.

12. On the significance of Dante's use of the term "poeta," see Kevin Brownlee, "Why the Angels Speak Italian: Dante as Vernacular *Poeta* in *Paradiso* XXV," *Poetics Today* 5 (1984):597–610.

13. For this connotation of the Latin roots of the term "vedova," see the Ernout-Meillet Latin etymological dictionary, s.v. *viduus,-a,-um*.

The Counterfeit Muse: Ovid, Boccaccio, Juan de Flores (pp. 109–127)

1. "Cada escritor crea a sus precursores" ("Kafka y sus precursores," in *Otras inquisiciones* [Buenos Aires: Sur, 1963], p. 128).

2. In this connection, see especially Giuseppe Mazzotta's extremely illu-

minating book, *The World at Play in Boccaccio's Decameron* (Princeton: Princeton University Press, 1986).

3. Vittore Branca (*Boccaccio. The Man and His Works*, trans. Richard Monges [New York: New York University Press, 1976], pp. 29ff.) discusses the myth of Fiammetta. Her obvious fictionality is attested to, for example, by the fact that her date of birth is given as 1310 in the *Filocolo*, 1313 in the *Commedia*, and after 1321 in the *Decameron*. Janet L. Smarr explores the multiple permutations of Fiammetta in her book, *Boccaccio and Fiammetta: The Narrator as Lover* (Champaign: University of Illinois Press, 1986).

4. Thomas G. Bergin, *Boccaccio* (New York: Viking Press, 1981), p. 168.

5. Dante Alighieri, *De vulgare eloquentia*, ed. Pier Vincenzo Mengaldo (Padova: Ed. Antenore, 1968), p. 39.

6. Branca, *Boccaccio*, pp. 80–81.

7. Robert Hollander, *Boccaccio's Two Venuses* (New York: Columbia University Press, 1977), p. 49.

8. Bergin, *Boccaccio*, pp. 169, 179.

9. In its argument, the *Elegia* most closely resembles the second *Heroid*, that of Phyllis and Demophoön.

10. Antonio Prieto (*Morfologia de la novela* [Barcelona: ed. Planeta, 1975], p. 273) is representative of much *Fiammetta* criticism, accepting Boccaccio's statement at face value: " 'Voi leggendo non troverete favole greche ornate di molte bugie, né troiane battaglie . . .' Es decir, no acomodará algo ageno a un presente (como *Amadís* podrá estar acomodado en la historia de Ardanlier), sino que escribirá del presente, *será* presente en el que ir formándose (e informándonos) hasta en particularidades como su nostalgia de Nápoles ('lieta, pacifica, magnifica. . .'), donde intensamente vivió. No se recoge en *Fiammetta* como pasado sino que exclama desde ella su deseo de vevir, *castigando* en Fiammetta lo que pueda detener ese deseo de camino." Cesare Segre, on the other hand, is one of the few modern critics who wisely attempt to consider the poetic potential of Boccaccio's extensive use of myth. See his very thoughtful essay, "Structures and Registers in the *Fiammetta*," in his *Structures and Time*, trans. John Meddemmen (Chicago: University of Chicago Press, 1979), pp. 66–92.

11. All citations to the *Elegia* refer to the *Opere di Giovanni Boccaccio*, ed. Cesare Segre (Milano: Mursia, 1966). English translations are from *Amorous Fiammetta*, trans. Edward Hutton (rpt., Westport, Conn.: Greenwood Press, 1970), this quotation from pp. XLIX–L.

12. "Quantunque volte, graziosissime donne, meco pensando, riguardo quanto voi naturalmente tutte pietose siate . . ." (Giovanni Boccaccio, *Decameron*, in *Opere di Giovanni Boccaccio*, ed. Cesare Segre [Milan: Mursia, 1966], p. 13).

13. Terry Eagleton, *Literary Theory. An Introduction* (Minneapolis: University of Minnesota Press, 1983), p. 104.

14. Classicists tend to consider the *Heroides* proper as being comprised of fifteen verse letters, rather than twenty-one, viewing the last six as pertaining to a different work written at a different time, the so-called "double-letters" of three legendary couples. Yet the twenty-one epistles were transmitted to the Middle Ages as one integral work. Robert A. Day, in his book, *Told in Letters. Epistolary Fiction Before Richardson* (Ann Arbor: University of Michigan Press,

1966), p. 12, succinctly articulates the immense importance of Ovid's twenty-one *Heroides* for modern fiction:

These poetic epistles are one of the most important sources or models for the emotional layer in modern fiction, not alone because of their literary quality, but because of the immense popularity and prestige which Ovid has always enjoyed. Here are letters which express changing and wavering emotions or outbursts of passion, written in the crises of love; further, in the epistles of Helen and Paris, Hero and Leander, and Acontius and Cydippe (*Heroides* XVI–XXI), the technique is carried a step beyond; we find exchanges of letters which carry the burden of a dialogue. The elements of letter fiction are all here, requiring only to be combined and properly developed, though they had to wait centuries for the process to take place.

15. Tzvetan Todorov, "Reading as Construction," in *The Reader in the Text*, eds. Susan R. Sulieman and Inge Crossman (Princeton: Princeton University Press, 1980), pp. 74–75.

16. See, for example, G. Karl Galinsky, *Ovid's 'Metamorphoses.' An Introduction to the Basic Aspects* (Berkeley: University of California Press, 1975); and Brooks Otis, *Ovid as an Epic Poet* (Cambridge: Cambridge University Press, 1970).

17. John D. Lyons, "*The Héptameron* and the Foundation of Critical Narrative," in *Medieval History/Discourse/Literature*, eds. Kevin Brownlee and Stephen G. Nichols, *Yale French Studies* 70 (1986):165.

18. Howard Jacobson, *Ovid's 'Heroides'* (Princeton: Princeton University Press, 1974), p. 354.

19. Florence Verducci, *Ovid's Toyshop of the Heart. 'Epistulae Herodium'* (Princeton: Princeton University Press, 1985), p. 16. Linda S. Kauffman discusses the originality and novelistic implications of the *Heroides* in her book, *Discourses of Desire. Gender, Genre and Epistolary Fictions* (Ithaca: Cornell University Press, 1986).

20. Sharon Cameron, *Lyric Time. Dickinson and the Limits of Genre* (Baltimore: Johns Hopkins University Press, 1979), p. 206.

21. See Eugenio Donato, "'Per Selve e Boscherecci Laberinti': Desire and Narrative Structure in Ariosto's *Orlando Furioso,*" *Barroco* 4 (1972):31.

22. Fiammetta's inability to act is all the more striking given her insistent citation of Senecan texts. See in this connection, Segre, *Structures in Time*, pp. 254 ff.

23. On questions of dating, Boccaccio as subtext, and matters of technique and style, see the insightful introduction to Pamela Waley's edition of *Grimalte y Gradissa* (London: Tamesis, 1971); as well as her article, "Fiammetta and Panfilo Continued," *Italian Studies* 24 (1969):15–31. Also useful, primarily for its information on sources and antecedents, is Barbara Matulka's *The Novels of Juan de Flores and their European Diffusion: A Study in Comparative Literature* (New York: Institute of French Studies, 1931). Another critic who gives lengthy consideration to the question of the *Fiammetta* in relation to the *Grimalte* is Dinko Cvitanovic in his book, *La novela sentimental española* (Madrid: Prensa Española, 1973). I obviously do not share his view (p. 274) that the importance of the Boccaccian subtext is minimal: "La historia de Fiammetta . . . es apenas una parte muy exigua de la obra de Flores, a tal extremo que es su punto de partida o su continuación." For two recent and illuminating studies on the

Iberian reception of the *Heroides/Fiammetta* configuration, see Alan Deyermond, "The Female Narrator in Sentimental Fiction: *Menina Moça* and *Clareo y Florisea,*" *Portuguese Studies* 1 (1985):47–57; as well as his treatment of it in "Las relaciones genéricas de la ficción sentimental española," to be included in an homage volume for Martín de Riquer. Also important to this subject are three fine essays by Olga Tudorica Impey: "Ovid, Alfonso X, and Juan Ridríguez del Padrón: Two Castilian Translations of the *Heroides* and the Beginnings of Spanish Sentimental Prose," *Bulletin of Hispanic Studies* 57 (1980):283–97; "Un dechado de la prosa literaria alfonsí: el relato cronístico de los amores de Dido," *Romance Philology* 34 (1980–1981):1–27; and, "Ovid, Alfonso X and the Literary Emancipation of Juan Rodríguez del Padrón: From the Fictional *Cartas* to the *Siervo libre de amor,*" *Speculum* 55 (1980):305–16. For further thoughts on this problem, or on any other aspect of the *novela sentimental* in general, see the indispensable critical bibliography of Keith Whinnom, *The Spanish Sentimental Romance (1440–1550)* (London: Grant and Cutler, 1983).

24. In this context, see Matulka, *The Novels of Juan de Flores,* pp. 305 ff.

25. Joseph E. Gillet, "The Autonomous Character in Spanish and European Literature," *Hispanic Review* 24 (1956):181.

26. Part 2, Chapter iv: "Nunca segundas partes fueron buenas" (Miguel de Cervantes, *Don Quijote de la Mancha,* ed. Martín de Riquer [Barcelona: Ed. Juventud, 1968], p. 567).

27. "lo fazeys con sperança de yo nunqua bolver, porque quedeys libre" (7).

28. For a very interesting discussion of the important book-within-a-book structure of the *Grimalte,* See Barbara F. Weissberger, "Authors, Characters and Readers in *Grimalte Y Gradissa,*" in *Creation and Re-creation: Experiments in Literary Form in Early Medieval Spain. Studies in Honor of Stephen Gilman,* eds. Ronald E. Surtz and Nora Weinerth (Newark, Del.: Juan de la Cuesta, 1983), pp. 61–76.

29. Indeed, as Waley insightfully observes, "One of Flores' assumptions in both of his novels is that what people say and do does not necessarily coincide with what they think and intend, and the application of this to the action of the novels results in a sophistication of characterization akin to that of *La Celestina*" (*Grimalte y Gradissa,* 1).

30. Translation mine.

31. Of this unexpected development, Waley (*Grimalte y Gradissa,* xxxiii, note 46) is accurate in stating that: "After Fiometa's death Pamphilo changes so radically that he is as different from Flores' presentation of him in the earlier part of the novel as he is from Boccaccio's Panfilo."

32. The few times classical allusion is exploited in the *Grimalte,* it is used by Flores with incongruous hyperbole (bordering on the comical); for example, Grimalte's Jason/Grimalte equation or his Alexander/Pamphilo analogue (p. 27), invoked as he tries desperately to persuade Pamphilo to accept Fiometa. (See also p. 57, where he invokes Priam's daughters, Hecuba, Pentasilea, and Circe.) These examples corroborate Waley's general observation that: "Whereas the *Elegia* abounds in classical allusion, as much to the taste of fifteenth-century Spain as to that of fourteenth-century Italy, Flores not only eschews it almost entirely, but denies the value of classical *exempla.*" In his other novel, *Grisel y Mirabella,* Flores writes: "Si las antiguas hystorias alguna loharon, cada día se

usan cosas nuevas, y si en aquell tiempo usaron nobleza las damas, del contrario os preciáys agora. Y ahun puede acahecer que ninguna cosa de aquellos lohores de Lucrecia y Atalante no fuesse verdad." This is his reply to *De Claris Mulieribus* ("Fiammetta and Panfilo Continued," p. 29). I would, however, underscore the fact that although the *Elegia* makes extensive use of classical mythology, it too "denies the value of classical *exempla*," as my interpretation of the *Elegia* makes clear.

33. The importance of the seemingly anomalous (yet persistent) presence of the wildman (wildwoman) is very suggestively explored by Alan Deyermond, who sees it as a reaction to the untenability of the courtly idiom: "de las cinco novelas sentimentales del siglo XV . . . las más importantes del género, cuatro al menos tienen hombres o mujeres salvajes de una forma u otra, y estos salvajes se asocian intimamente con el amor cortés" ("El hombre salvaje en la novela sentimental," *Filología* 10 [1964]:108).

34. The infernal punishment of women who have abused their lovers is studied by William Allen Nielson in "The Purgatory of Cruel Beauties," *Romania* 29 (1900):85–93.

Structures of Authority in Christine de Pizan's *Ditié de Jehanne d'Arc* (pp. 131–150)

1. Edouard Perroy, *The Hundred Years War* (New York: Capricorn, 1965), pp. 284–85.

2. For an insightful recent consideration of Christine's identity as medieval woman author and the implications of her "feminism" in this context, see Sylvia Huot, "Seduction and Sublimation: Christine de Pizan, Jean de Meun and Dante," *Romance Notes* 25 (1985):361–73. For further discussion of Christine's feminism, see Douglas Kelly, "Reflections on Christine de Pisan as a Feminist Writer," *Sub-Stance* 2 (1972):63–71; Mary Ann Ignatius, "A Look at the Feminism of Christine de Pizan," *Proceedings of the Pacific Northwest Conference on Foreign Languages* 29 (1978):18–21; and Joan Kelly-Gadol, "Early Feminist Theory and the Querelle des Femmes, 1400–1789," *Signs* 8 (1982):4–28.

3. Christine de Pizan, *The Book of the City of Ladies*, trans. E. Jeffrey Richards (New York: Persea, 1982), pp. xxxv–xxxviii.

4. For the structure of the *Ditié* see Christine de Pisan, *Ditié de Jehanne d'Arc*, eds. Angus J. Kennedy and Kenneth Varty (Oxford: Society for the Study of Mediaeval Languages and Literature, 1977), pp. 9–10. See also Therese Ballet Lynn, "The *Ditié de Jeanne d'Arc*: Its Political, Feminist and Aesthetic Significance," *Fifteenth Century Studies* 1 (1978):150–51; and Liliane Dulac, "Un écrit militant de Christine de Pizan: Le *Ditié de Jehanne d'Arc*" in *Aspects of Female Existence*, eds. Birte Carlé et al. (Gyldendal, Denmark, 1980), pp. 118–20.

5. All citations and translations (with selective emendations) from the *Ditié* are from the excellent edition of Kennedy and Varty.

6. The extended narrative of Penthesilea's glorious but tragic death in Part 6 of the *Livre de la Mutacion de Fortune* (1403) is also relevant here (vv. 17561–17896 in the edition of Suzanne Solente, 4 vols. [Paris: Picard/SATF, 1959–1966]). The *Ditié*'s reference to Joan of Arc as more powerful than "Hector

n'Achilles" (v. 287; the poem's only mention of exemplary male warriors from the classical tradition) should perhaps be seen in part as involving a corrective Christian evocation of Penthesilea's noble pagan failure as bellatrix.

7. In terms of historical chronology, it seems that Christine is privileging the Sibyl by including her here. The relevant prophecies attributed to Merlin and to Bede clearly antedate the composition of the *Ditié*. With regard to Merlin, it is a question of two passages in Book 7 (*De prophetiis Merlini*) of Geoffrey of Monmouth's *Historia Regum Britanniae*: (1) "Ad hec ex urbe canuti nemoris eliminabitur puella . . ." and (2) "Ascendet virgo dorsum sagittarii. & flores virgineos obfuscabit" (ed. Acton Griscom [London, 1929], pp. 390–91 and p. 397). With regard to Bede, it is a question of an incorrectly attributed chronogram widely circulated in France during the spring of 1429 and supposed to indicate that year: "Vis comulcoli. bis. septen. se sotiabunt. / Galboni. pulli. bella. nova. parabunt. / Ece. beant. bela. tunc. fert. vexila. puela." See the *Chronique d'Antonio Morosini*, 4 vols., ed. L. Dorez et G. Lefèvre-Pontalis (Paris: Renouard, 1898–1902), vol. 3, pp. 126–127 and vol. 4, pp. 316–27. See also Kennedy and Varty, pp. 68–69; and Deborah Fraioli, "The Literary Image of Joan of Arc: Prior Influences," *Speculum* 56 (1981):817–18. The Sibyl, however, was not associated with prophecies concerning Joan before the composition of the *Ditié*. As Fraioli notes, "The view that Joan of Arc had been heralded in sibylline literature was not articulated until the summer of 1429 in a treatise written by a cleric of Speyer, entitled *Sibylla francica*" (817–18). Indeed, the text of this treatise as found in Jules Quicherat, ed., *Procès de condamnation et de réhabilitation de Jeanne d'Arc*, 5 vols. (Paris: Renouard, 1845–1849), 3:422–68, gives the date "juillet–septembre 1429" (422). An important literary precedent for the association of the Sibyl with Merlin and Bede in political prophecies of French victory in the Hundred Years War is to be found in a ballade of Eustache Deschamps written c. 1385–1386 (number 26 in the edition of Queux de Saint-Hilaire and Gaston Raynaud, 1:106–107).

8. Halina D. Loukopoulos, *Classical Mythology in the Works of Christine de Pisan, with an Edition of L'Epistre Othea from MS Harley 4431*, diss. Wayne State University, 1977, p. 289. See also Charity Canon Willard, *Christine de Pizan. Her Life and Works* (New York: Persea, 1984), p. 99. For Christine's global strategy of feminist rewriting of clerkly sources in the *Epistre*, see Christine Reno, "Feminist Aspects of Christine de Pizan's *Epistre d'Othea a Hector*," *Studi Francesi* 71 (1980):271–76.

9. *Le Livre du Chemin de Long Estude*, ed. Robert Püschel (Berlin: Damköhler, 1887), my translation. Other related points: (1) The Sibyl thus will play the role of the learnèd female teacher to Christine the protagonist, especially during the first part of the journey. This female configuration is important. (2) Within the plot line, Christine attains future knowledge and thus, in a sense, becomes a sibyl herself (pp. 92–95).

10. Maureen Curnow, *The "Livre de la Cité des Dames" of Christine de Pisan: A Critical Edition*, diss. Vanderbilt, 1975, p. 786. All citations are from this edition.

11. Richards, p. 99. All translations from the *Cité* are from this edition.

12. It is suggestive to note in this context that Christine's name appears

twice in this poem, at the beginning (in the first line of the first stanza) and at the end (in the first line of the final stanza).

13. See Mary Louise Pratt, *Toward a Speech Act Theory of Literary Discourse* (Bloomington: Indiana University Press, 1977), p. 82: "The illocutionary act of commanding . . . has an appropriateness condition requiring that the speaker be in a position of authority."

14. Christine is here utilizing the so-called Second Charlemagne Prophecy, current in France since at least 1382. See Kennedy and Varty, *Ditié*, pp. 63–65; and Marjorie Reeves, *The Influence of Prophecy in the Later Middle Ages. A Study in Joachimism* (Oxford: Clarendon, 1969), pp. 320–31. See also Fraioli's astute consideration of the role of the later medieval tradition of political prophecy in contemporary perceptions of Joan of Arc (811 ff.). In terms of the *Ditié*, what is of capital importance is the fact that Christine's tentative and conditional associations of Charles VII with the Second Charlemagne Prophecy (in stanzas 16–18) only become certain and definite when linked to prophecies of Joan of Arc's future achievements (in stanzas 42–43). In this case, as in so many others in the *Ditié*, it is Joan who "authenticates" Charles. It is important to note that this authentification involves a strategic rewriting (and reinterpreting) of the Second Charlemagne Prophecy as it had previously existed. "A blend of several different prophetic strains, this prophecy made promises that had little or nothing to do with Joan's mission as she announced it. It is Christine de Pizan who applied these promises to the mission of Joan of Arc" (Fraioli, 827).

15. See in this connection Dulac's excellent discussion of the *Ditié*'s "militancy": "son rapport étroit avec *l'actualité* et surtout la volonté qui s'y manifeste d'intervenir dans le cours des événements" (127 ff.). Also relevant is Jean-Claude Muhlethaler's analysis of Christine's utilization of the stance and discourse of Old Testament prophecy in "Le Poète et le prophète: Littérature et politique au XVe siècle," *Le Moyen Français* 13 (1983):37–57.

Petrarchan Textuality: Commentaries and Gender Revisions (pp. 151–168)

1. St. Augustine, *On Christian Doctrine*, trans. D. W. Robertson, Jr. (New York: The Liberal Arts Press, 1958), p. 30.

2. See William J. Kennedy, "Petrarchan Audiences and Print Technology," *The Journal of Medieval and Renaissance Studies* 14 (1984):1–20.

3. All quotations from the commentaries in this essay refer to the following editions: *Petrarca con doi commenti. El primo del M. F. Filelfo. L'altro del M. Antonio da Tempo* (Venice: Gregorium de Gregoriis, 1508); *Il Petrarca con l'espositione d'Allesandro Vellutello* (Venice: Erasmo, 1541); *Il Petrarca col commento di M. Sebastiano Fausto da Longiano* (Venice: Francesco di Allesandro Bindoni, 1532); *Il Petrarca colla spositione di M. Giovani Andrea Gesualdo* (Venice: Nicolini da Sabio, 1533); *Sonetti di M. F. Petrarca con breve dichiaratione di Antonio Bruciolo* (Venice: A. Brucioli, 1548); and *Sonetti, Canzoni, e Triomphi con la spositione di Bernardino Daniello da Lucca* (Venice: Nicolini da Sabio, 1549).

4. All quotations from Petrarch refer to *Rime*, ed. Ferdinando Neri et al., La letteratura italiana. Storia e testi. (Milan: Riccardo Ricciardi, 1951). English translations refer to *Petrarch's Lyric Poems*, trans. Robert M. Durling (Cambridge,

Mass.: Harvard University Press, 1976). For commentary on Petrarchan instability see Adelia Noferi, *L'esperienza poetica del Petrarca* (Florence: Le Monnier,
1962); Marco Santagata, *Dal sonetto al Canzoniere* (Padua: Liviana, 1979); and
Nancy Vickers, "The Body Re-Membered" in *Mimesis: from Mirror to Method,*
ed. John D. Lyons and Stephen G. Nichols, Jr. (Hanover, N.H.: University
Press of New England, 1982), pp. 100–109.

   5. All quotations from Louise Labé refer to *Oeuvres complètes,* ed. Enzo
Giudici (Geneva: Droz, 1981). English translations refer to *The Penguin Book
of French Verse,* ed. Geoffrey Brereton, 4 vols. (Baltimore: Penguin Books, Inc.,
1958), vol. 2. For Labé's literary background, see Enzo Giudici, *Amore e follia
nell 'opera della Belle Cordière* (Naples: Ligouri, 1965); for her own textuality see
François Rigolot, "Signature et Signification: Les Baisers de Louise Labé," *Romanic Review* 75 (1984):10–24.

   6. Emile Littré lists two primary senses of *contrôleur*: (1) "Fonctionnaire
chargé de tenir registre de certaines choses ou de faire une vérification";
(2) "Celui qui examine, critique les actions d'autrui." *Dictionnaire de la langue
française,* 7 vols. (Paris: Jean Jacques Pauvert, 1956), 2.817. For the second
sense, Littré cites examples from Montaigne and d'Aubigné.

   7. Quotations from Shakespeare refer to *Shakespeare's Sonnets,* ed. Stephen
Booth (New Haven: Yale University Press, 1977). Booth's analytic commentary
amply illuminates Shakespeare's Petrarchan textuality, as does Booth's *An Essay
on Shakespeare's Sonnets* (New Haven: Yale University Press, 1969). See the
vigorous defense of the orthography of the 1609 Quarto by Thomas M. Greene,
"Anti-hermeneutics: The Case of Shakespeare's Sonnet 129," in *Poetic Traditions
of the English Renaissance,* ed. Maynard Mack and George deForest Lord (New
Haven: Yale University Press, 1982), pp. 143–62.

Saint Paul Among the Amazons: Gender and Authority in *Gerusalemme liberata* (pp. 169–200)

   This article was written during a year at Villa I Tatti, funded by the National
Endowment for the Humanities, Dartmouth College, and the Robert Lehman
Fellowship. Translations are mine except as noted.

   1. C. P. Brand, *Torquato Tasso: A Study of the Poet and of His Contribution
to English Literature* (Cambridge: Cambridge University Press, 1965), p. 205.

   2. Brand, *Torquato Tasso,* pp. 208–209. Brand's whole chapter (205–225)
is a useful synopsis of the legend. For a more recent and more compendious
survey of Tasso's legend in literature and the other arts, see *Torquato Tasso tra
letteratura, musica, teatro, e arti figurative,* ed. Andrea Buzzoni (Bologna: Nuova
Alfa Editoriale, 1985), esp. pp. 363–429 *passim,* containing numerous representations of Tasso and Eleonora by nineteenth- and twentieth-century painters.

   3. See Margaret Ferguson, *Trials of Desire: Renaissance Defenses of Poetry*
(New Haven: Yale University Press, 1983), esp. pp. 120–36; and Sergio Zatti,
L'uniforme cristiano e il multiforme pagano: Saggio sulla "Gerusalemme liberata"
(Milan: Saggiatore, 1983).

   4. Marilyn Migiel, "Tasso's Erminia: Telling an Alternate Story," *Italica* 64
(1987):62–75. Quotations from pp. 63 and 72.

   5. Zatti, *L'uniforme,* p. 37.

6. Migiel's primary target is Kristen Olsen Murtaugh, "Erminia Delivered: Notes on Tasso and Romance," *Quaderni d'Italianistica* 3 (1982):12–25, whom she rightly charges with encouraging us "to interpret the story of Erminia according to the wishes Tasso expressed for Erminia in his correspondence and the wishes he expressed for his epic poem in his theoretical writings on poetry" (Migiel, pp. 62–63). She also criticizes Andrew Fichter, *Poets Historical: Dynastic Epic in the Renaissance* (New Haven: Yale University Press, 1982), pp. 112–55, for "reassur[ing] the reader that Tasso's practice coincides with his theory" and that GL "is ultimately in the service of moral values" (n. 4). However, it is also difficult to agree fully with Migiel's axiomatic deconstructive contention that "[Erminia's] desire threatens the downfall of narrative and interpretive codes in the poem" (64).

7. Maggie Günsberg, "'Donna liberata?' The Portrayal of Women in the Italian Renaissance Epic," *The Italianist* 7 (1987):7–35, quotation from p. 8. This purports to be a Lacanian reading, but it is also infused with a rather facile social criticism that, I suspect, would be styled "Marxist" by its user. Like Migiel, Günsberg has a primary target: L. S. Robinson, *Monstrous Regiment: The Lady Knight in Sixteenth-Century Epic* (New York: Garland, 1985). As for my own "targeting" of studies on Tasso by women, it is perhaps statistically inevitable, given that women critics are now proposing the most provocative readings.

8. Older studies tend to treat "slippage" as poetic incompetence or personal instability: e.g., Brand, *Torquato Tasso*, 99–114; Eugenio Donadoni *Torquato Tasso: saggio critico* (1928, Florence: Nuova Italia, 1952), *passim*, esp. 305–336.

9. Zatti, *L'uniforme*, pp. 41–44, esp. 43: "The reiteration of such identifying stylemes in fact underlines the objective convergence between the opposing spheres of good and evil, of Christian and pagan, of divine and demonic."

10. Torquato Tasso, *Lettere*, ed. Ettore Mazzali, 2 vols. (Turin: Einaudi, 1978), vol. 1, p. 36. This edition reproduces Mazzali's edition of Tasso's *Prose* (Milan: Ricciardi, 1959), pp. 731–1142, the most complete modern text of Tasso's letters since Cesare Guasti's edition in 5 vols. (Florence: Le Monnier, 1854–1855).

11. *Lettere*, 1.36n. The first edition of Speroni's *Canace* was done by Valgrisi at Venice in 1546. There is a modern edition by Christina Roaf, *Canace e scritti in sua difesa* (Bologna: Commissione per i testi di Lingua, 1982).

12. All quotations from *Gerusalemme liberata* follow the edition by Lanfranco Caretti (Turin: Einaudi, 1971). Translations my own. I shall return to these verses of Petrarch and Tasso below, n. 43.

13. As A. Bartlett Giamatti says, "we wince" at Armida's echo of the Virgin. He probably speaks for most twentieth-century critics when he adds that "this echo . . . is too forced. . . . There is something desperate here in Tasso's effort to bring Armida into line with Christianity. The inner conflicts . . . remain to haunt the poem" (*The Earthly Paradise and the Renaissance Epic* [1966, Princeton: Princeton University Press, 1969], pp. 209–210).

14. Altamoro's wife appears in GL 17.26; her words, which refer to their "little son intent on his childish games," clearly recall Andromache's appeal to Hector on behalf of herself and Astyanax in book six of the Iliad (trans. Richard Lattimore [1951, Chicago: University of Chicago Press, 1970], p. 164). Andromache's threnody in book twenty-four quoted from Lattimore, p. 495 (em-

phasis added). Modern commentators follow Tasso's contemporary Guastavini's description of Tasso's "sources" for the Altamoro-Goffredo exchange and thus miss the allusions to Hector and Andromache: see *Luoghi osservati dal Mag. Giulio Guastavini, i quali il Tasso nella sua* Gierusalemme *ha presi, et imitati da poeti, et altri Scrittori antichi* in the edition of Genoa, 1617, p. 33 *ter* and, e.g., the best modern annotated edition by Bruno Maier, 2 vols. (1963, Milan: Rizzoli, 1982) at GL 20.141–42. I have treated the significance of Altamoro's wife for the "desires" of the GL in a paper to be given at the 1989 meeting of the Renaissance Society of America.

15. Migiel, "Tasso's Erminia," p. 64. But Migiel's reasons for this observation differ from mine in repeating it: see n. 6 above.

16. Migiel's analysis of this scene (63–65) is quite good.

17. GL 3.16–20 for Erminia's love for Tancredi; for her attempt to meet him, 6.55.5–7.22.6.

18. "And they were two in one and one in two," *Inferno* 28.125, trans. Charles S. Singleton (*The Divine Comedy* [1970–1975, 6 vols. reprinted in 3 vols., Princeton: Princeton University Press, 1980], 1.301).

19. Compare GL 20.32–35 and 9.68–72.2; one of Clorinda's victims is referred to as *miserabile mostro* in 9.80.6. The connection with Bertran de Born is reinforced by the dependence of Tasso's Argillano episode on the Dantean locus, GL 8.47–62, esp. 60. See David Quint, "Argillano's Revolt and the Politics of the *Gerusalemme liberata*," in *Renaissance Studies in Honor of Craig Hugh Smythe*, 2 vols., ed. Andrew Morrogh et al. (Florence: Giunti Barbèra, 1985), vol. 1, pp. 455–64. Argillano also participates in the complicated body thematics of canto nine, duelling with Solimano and dying at his hand at a distance of only a stanza from the near encounter of Gildippe and Clorinda (9.71.1–72.2; 74.1–88.6). A compendious but rather uncritical treatment of body thematics is in Francesca Savoia, "Notes on the Metaphor of the Body in the *Gerusalemme liberata*," in *Western Gerusalem [sic]: University of California Studies on Tasso*, ed. Luisa Del Giudice (New York: Out of London Press, 1984), pp. 57–70.

20. Torquato Tasso, *Dialoghi*, ed. Ettore Mazzali, 2 vols. (Turin: Einaudi, 1976), vol. 1, p. 91, emphasis added. This edition reprints pp. 3–346 of *Prose* [above, n. 10]). The dialogue, entitled *Il padre di famiglia*, is Tasso's most celebrated precisely because it is set a few months before his imprisonment in Sant'Anna, recalling his abortive attempt to seek "asylum" and employment at the court of Emmanuele Filiberto in Turin (Autumn 1578). It was composed in 1580, probably about five years after the completion of the Gildippe/Odoardo story. This dialogue has an extremely interesting play between open discussion of authority and imitation, and their dramatization by "Tasso" and his interlocutor the patriarch.

21. Tasso's *Dialogues: A Selection, with the Discourse on the Art of the Dialogue*, trans. Carnes Lord and Dain A. Trafton (Berkeley: University of California Press, 1982), p. 79. My disagreements with this translation—which "corrects" Tasso's logical inversions—are in square brackets. For the references to Dante and Petrarch, see Petrarch, *Canzoniere* 214.35; and Dante, *Convivio* 4, *canzone* 3.121–24.

22. See Peter Demetz, "The Elm and the Vine: Notes Toward the History of a Marriage-Topos," PMLA 73 (1958):521–32.

23. Ephesians 5.31, quoted from *Biblia Sacra iuxta Vulgatam Clementinam* (1946, Madrid: Editorial Católica, 1985); for translations, I have used and occasionally modified *The New Oxford Bible with Apocrypha*, 2nd ed. by Herbert G. May and Bruce M. Metzger (New York: Oxford University Press, 1977), in preference to the Douai/Rheims translation of the Vulgate.

24. John A. T. Robinson, *The Body: A Study in Pauline Theology* (1952, Naperville, Ill.: Alec R. Allenson, 1957). Robinson demonstrates (11–33) that Paul's entire notion of the body is a strictly Hebrew one, which neither acknowledges the kind of "mind/body split" Western culture has inherited from Greek thought nor recognizes quite such rigidly defined boundaries between the body of one individual and that of another.

25. "The virtues of a man are prudence, courage, and liberality; those of a woman are modesty and chastity. And with these virtues each can do what is fitting. While chastity is not a masculine virtue, however, a good husband ought to offend the laws of marriage as little as possible. He ought not to be so incontinent that he cannot abstain from the pleasures of the flesh when he is away from his wife, because if he refrains from violating the marriage laws he will strengthen the chastity of his wife. *She by nature is as libidinous and inclined to the pleasures of Venus as he is,* and she is usually prevented from breaking faith with her husband only by shame, love, and fear. Of these [emotions], fear is worthy of both praise and blame, while the other two deserve only high praise" (*Dialoghi* 1.94; *Tasso's Dialogues*, pp. 85–87, emphasis added).

26. 1 Corinthians 10.16–17. As Robinson observes, Paul "directly ground[s] the unity of the Church as the Body of Christ in the sacramental loaf, itself already declared to be the Body of the Lord" (56). The literality of these words cannot be sufficiently stressed: "The whole phrase [of Christ at the Last Supper] 'this is my body . . . my blood' . . . means that Jesus is making over to His followers 'till He come' His actual self, His life and personality. In so far then as the Christian community feeds on this body and blood, it *becomes* the very life and personality of the risen Christ" (57). As Robinson notes, Paul's words indicate that both the Eucharistic host and the "corporation" of believers are *literally* the body of Christ: ". . . to say that the Church is the Body of Christ is no more of a metaphor than to say that the flesh of the incarnate Jesus or the bread of the Eucharist is the body of Christ. None of them is 'like' His body (Paul never says this): each of them *is* the body of Christ. . . . They are all expressions of a single Christology" (51).

Robinson notes "how uncompromisingly physical" is Paul's language about the faithful as body of Christ: it is the language "of sexual union." When Paul refers to a man's being "joined" to a harlot or to God, he uses the same word (*adhaero* in the Vulgate), which has sexual connotations:

. . . the relation of Christians to Christ is that of "one flesh" (cf. Ephesians 5.28–32): they are fused in a single *basar*. This union is as exclusive as that of man and wife. . . . To such an extent is the new union with Christ physical (the word "joined" is again one of sexual union—*kollasthai*; cf. Genesis 2.24, LXX) that immoral sex-relationships can destroy it. It is in their "bodies" (v. 15)—as *somata* and not merely as "spirits"—that Christians are members of Christ. There can be no suggestion that because a Christian has ceased to be "in the flesh" physical relationships have been left behind or become indifferent. . . . Reversion to fornication sunders a Christian from the risen body of Christ, just as much as it would had he actually been married to Christ in the flesh. (52–53)

As regards the relation of the Eucharist to the Church as Body of Christ, "During the early centuries of the Christian era a distinction was maintained between the *corpus Christi,* which was the Church, and the *corpus mysticum,* the Eucharist. About the eighth century, these concepts began to fuse; the Eucharist became the element which mystically unified the Church. . . . By the twelfth century, however, a reversal of terminology had taken place, due largely to the controversy about the meaning of transubstantiation; the Eucharist became the real body of Christ (*corpus naturale*) and the Church became the *corpus mysticum*" (David George Hale, *The Body Politic: A Political Metaphor in Renaissance English Literature* [The Hague: Mouton, 1971], pp. 35–36, quoting Ernst H. Kantorowicz, *King's Two Bodies: A Study in Mediaeval Political Theology* [1957, Princeton: Princeton University Press, 1970], pp. 195–97, who in turn relies on Henri de Lubac, *Corpus Mysticum: L'Eucharistie et l'Eglise au Moyen Age,* 2nd ed. [Paris, 1949], pp. 67–135, esp. 87–88).

The more one follows such developments in Christian thinking after Paul, the clearer it becomes that Tasso's treatment of Gildippe and Odoardo has the same "literality" or nonmetaphoric character as Paul's discourse on the Body and has little to do with later formulations of what Robinson calls the "misleading and unbiblical" notion of a "mystical" body. Curiously, although she perceptively analyzes the "concreteness and density" (65) of Tasso's body-discourse in GL and correctly summarizes Robinson (n. 3), Savoia continually insists on the "metaphoricity" of body discourse in GL, because she sees the poem as "Tasso's conscious participation in his historical environment, . . . his poetic commitment to the Church's ideological view of variety as heresy," that is, to the "mystical" body of later formulations ("Notes on the Metaphor of the Body," p. 67).

27. "Let a woman learn in silence and with all submissiveness. I permit no woman to teach or to have authority [*dominari*] over men; she is to keep silent. For Adam was formed first, then Eve; and Adam was not deceived, but the woman was deceived and became a transgressor. Yet woman will be saved through bearing children, if she continues in faith and love and holiness, with modesty" (1 Timothy 2.11–15).

28. "Wives, be subject [*subditae*] to your husbands, as to the Lord" (Ephesians 5.22); "Wives, be subject [*subditae*] to your husbands, as is fitting in the Lord" (Colossians 3.18). In Titus 2.3–5, Paul instructs Titus to make sure that older women teach younger ones to "be sensible, chaste, domestic, kind, and submissive [*subditas*] to their husbands, that the word of God may not be discredited."

29. A note in the Oxford Bible says that it translates as "veil" the Greek text's *authority* (the Vulgate has *potestas*); another note adds that "Angels were thought of as administering the divine order (see 1 Tim. 5.21 n.). "A woman worshiping in the presence of men with bare head shows disrespect for this order" (p. 1390). On Milton, see *The Poems of John Milton,* ed. John Carey and Alastair Fowler (London: Longmans, 1968), p. 631nn.

30. "Or chi fu il primo feritor cristiano / che facesse d'onor lodati acquisti? / Fosti, Gildippe, tu. . . . / (tanto di gloria a la feminea mano / concesse il Cielo.) . . ." [Who was the first Christian fighting-man to claim praise and honor? Gildippe, it was you. . . . (This much glory did Heaven concede to the hand of a woman.) . . .] As Gildippe's first victim falls, his last sensation is hearing the Christian army cheer in praise of her. In the next moment, the narrator fuses his earlier references to her as *feritor* and to her "feminine hand" by remarking, "Con la destra viril la donna stringe, / poi c'ha rotto il troncon, la buona spada . . ." [Once she has broken her lance, the lady grips her good sword in her virile right hand . . . (GL 20.32.1–33.2)].

31. *Dialoghi*, pp. 91–92; *Tasso's Dialogues*, pp. 79–81. Later the patriarch adds: ". . . women are related to men as desire [*la cupidità*] is to the intellect, and just as desire, which is in itself irrational, is informed by many beautiful and comely virtues when it subjects itself to the intellect, so a woman who obeys her husband adorns herself with virtues that she would not possess if she were rebellious" (*Dialoghi*, p. 93; *Tasso's Dialogues*, p. 85). As Robinson observes (14), "the most far-reaching of all the Greek antitheses, that between *body* and *soul*," is foreign to the Hebrew tradition that animates Paul's body discourse. One misses an awareness of this distinction in Hale (*Body Politic*, esp. 18–47), but I suspect that Tasso was aware of the difference: see Mazzali's notes to these passages.

32. *Dialoghi*, 1.95; *Tasso's Dialogues* 85; emphasis mine. The analogy between the functions of the soul and the social classes of a city is also behind Tasso's *Allegoria* of the GL, where Goffredo is said to represent the intellect: "Però che l'intelletto è da Dio, & dalla Natura constituito Signore sovra l'altre virtù dell'anima, & sovra il corpo; & comanda a quelle con potestà civile, & a queste con Imperio regale. Rinaldo, Tancredi, & gli altri Principi sono in luogo dell'altre potenze dell'animo; & il corpo da i soldati men nobili ci vien dinotato." [Because God and Nature have constituted the intellect as lord over the other powers of the soul, and over the body, and it commands the former with civil authority and the latter with monarchical absolutism. Rinaldo, Tancredi and the other princes are like the other powers of the soul, while the lower orders of soldiers denote the body (edition of Genoa, 1617, p. 34 *ter*).] This of course disagrees with the interpretation several times given in the text of GL, which makes Goffredo the "head" and Rinaldo the "hand" (see esp. 14.13.5–8) and is much more in line with my Pauline analysis. I am convinced that the Platonism of the GL has been exaggerated because of confusion between its Pauline body discourse (head/body) and the Greek philosophical variant (body/soul) of Tasso's theoretical writings. Thus David Quint maintains that the "Platonizing epistemology" of GL cannot "come to terms" with the Incarnation (*Origin and Originality in Renaissance Literature: Versions of the Source* [New Haven: Yale University Press, 1983], pp. 111–17, esp. 116). Tasso and his text are not exactly sanguine about any question relating to life in the body, but Platonism is certainly not the only reason, and perhaps not the most important.

33. GL 20.94: "Gildippe ed Odoardo, i casi vostri / duri ed acerbi e i fatti onesti e degni / (se tanto lice a i miei toscani inchiostri) / consacrerò fra' peregrini ingegni, / sì ch'ogni età quasi ben nati mostri / di virtute e d'amor v'additi e segni, / e co 'l suo pianto alcun servo d'Amore / la morte vostra e le mie

rime onore" [Gildippe and Odoardo, if it be permitted to my Tuscan pen, I will immortalize your harsh fate and your worthy deeds among noble minds, so that every age may point to you as noble prodigies (lit. monsters) of virtue and love, and with his tears, some servant of Love will honor your death and my verse]. As commentators from Guastavini to Maier note, this is a version of the Vergilian narrator's apostrophe to Nisus and Euryalus (*Aeneid* 9.446–49), esp. his characterization of the two friends as *fortunati* (Tasso's *ben nati*). The narratorial apostrophe in the context of a passionate physical friendship also recalls the Homeric narrator's habit of apostrophizing the doomed Patroclus as he fights in Achilles's armor (*Iliad*, bk. 16; Lattimore 330, 346, 348, 350–52). The GL narrator's apostrophe has rewritten the covert sexuality of these male friendships as heterosexual marriage, as he also did, clandestinely and without apostrophe, in the case of Clorinda and Argante's trope of the same "Nisus and Euryalus" topos (in 12.2.8ff.; see Maier's notes).

34. "Pure io femina sono, e nulla riede / mia morte in danno a la città smarrita . . ." [Yet I am a woman, and my death would be no real loss to our bewildered city (12.8.5–6)]. In canto twelve, the narrator executes a cinematic "cut" from Tancredi weeping over the tomb of Clorinda (99) to Jerusalem, which he calls both "la città smarrita," recalling Clorinda's words, and "la rinchiusa terra," recalling her tomb (100.2, 4). The reaction of the women of Jerusalem recalls the reaction of the Trojans to the news of Hector's death (*Iliad* bk. 22; Lattimore 446, esp. vv. 407–11).

35. I am currently at work on a study of GL as a meditation on the body as exemplar of personal, poetic, and cultural unity, specifically in relation to official Counter-Reformation defenses of sacramental bodies: Church, Eucharist, baptism, and marriage.

36. On "mystical" and "political" bodies in the poem, see Fichter (*Poets Historical*, esp. 152 n. 23), Ferguson (*Trials of Desire*, pp. 55–56, 112–113), Savoia ("The Metaphor"), Quint (Argillano's Revolt"), and Zatti (*L'uniforme*, p. 120n.). See also Thomas P. Roche, "Tasso's Enchanted Woods," in *Literary Uses of Typology from the Late Middle Ages to the Present*, ed. Earl Miner (Princeton: Princeton University Press, 1977), pp. 49–78, esp. 57–58, 64; James Nohrnberg, *The Analogy of the* Faerie Queene (Princeton: Princeton University Press, 1976), pp. 19–22, esp. n. 39; Michael Murrin, *The Allegorical Epic: Essays in Its Rise and Decline* (Chicago: University of Chicago Press, 1980), pp. 101–107; Alessandro Martinelli, *La Demiurgia della scrittura poetica: Gerusalemme liberata* (Florence: Olschki, 1983), pp. 112–14, esp. n. 26. Tasso's body discourse in the *Apologia in difesa della* Gerusalemme liberata and *Allegoria* are central to these discussions. See also both Tasso's *Discorsi* on poetry, in *Scritti sull'arte poetica* (reprint from *Prose* [n. 10], ed. Ettore Mazzali, 2 vols. (Turin: Einaudi, 1977), vol. 1, pp. 22–25, 41–42, 81, 139; vol. 2, pp. 225–31, 242–43, 382–83.

37. Revelation 14.1–5; 21.9–14; 21.2. See Jane Tibbetts Schulenberg, "The Heroics of Virginity: Brides of Christ and Sacrificial Mutilation," in *Women in the Middle Ages and Renaissance: Literary and Historical Perspectives*, ed. Mary Beth Rose (Syracuse: Syracuse University Press, 1986), pp. 29–72, esp. 37. This article provides some fascinating examples of the levels on which Pauline body discourse was enacted in real life. In a chapter entitled "Clorinda's Flight

from Egypt," I shall discuss body discourse, scriptural typology, and "wedding" to Christ through baptism.

38. Revelation 21.3–5. Again, compare GL's final verse with that of the *Iliad*: "il gran Sepolcro adora e scioglie il voto" [he worships the great Tomb and fulfills his vow]; "such was their burial of Hektor, breaker of horses" (Lattimore 496).

39. Armida (20.136.7–8) vows that Rinaldo's nod (*cenno*) will be her "law" (*legge*), repeating the vocabulary of Goffredo's election: "Imponga a i vinti *legge* egli a suo *senno* / porti la guerra e quando vole e a cui; / gli altri, già pari, ubidienti al *cenno* / siano or ministri de gl'imperii sui" [May he impose laws on the defeated foes according to his wisdom and carry war whenever and to whom-ever he wishes; the others, once his equals, must now be obedient to his nod and administer his commands (1.33.2–6)]. David Quint also discusses this repetition, *Origin*, pp. 114–16.

40. For Dante's use of the rhyme: *Inferno* 4.98–102 (Dante accepted by the poets), 8.5–7 (Phlegias, burner of the Delphic temple), 16.116–20 (Geryon and the authority of the poem), 21.134–38 (devils' comedy); *Purgatorio* 6.137–41 (Florence vs. Athens and Sparta on law), 19.86–88 (Pope Hadrian V on con-version), 22.23–27 (Virgilio and Stazio on conversion), 27.139–41 (Dante in Eden); *Paradiso* 15.71–73 (Cacciaguida). Other than in sonnet 299.1 and 5, Petrarch is known to have used the *cenno/senno* rhyme only once, in a discarded draft of the *Trionfo della Fama* that Tasso is unlikely to have known (printed in Francesco Petrarca, *Rime, Trionfi e poesie latine*, ed. F. Neri, G. Martellotti, E. Bianchi, N. Sapegno [Milan: Ricciardi, 1951], p. 568).

41. Song of Songs 4.12. The closed garden often appears in exegesis as a symbol of the Church in its role as *sponsa Christi*. D. W. Robertson cites Peter Lombard, *Sententiae* 4.30.2, noting that "Mary was frequently seen as the Sponsa in the Canticle of Canticles, and, in addition, her marriage to Joseph was a familiar type of ideal human marriage" (*A Preface to Chaucer: Studies in Medieval Perspectives* [1962, Princeton: Princeton University Press, 1970], p. 379). On the ecclesiological and ethical significance of the Blessed Virgin as *hortus con-clusus*, see Brian E. Daley, "The 'Closed Garden' and the 'Sealed Fountain': Song of Songs 4:12 in the Late Medieval Iconography of Mary," in *Medieval Gardens*, ed. Elisabeth B. MacDougall, Dumbarton Oaks Colloquium on the History of Landscape Architecture, No. 9 (Washington, D.C.: Dumbarton Oaks Research Library and Collection, 1986), pp. 255–78.

42. "Qualor tenera neve per li colli / dal sol percossa veggio di lontano, / come 'l sol neve, mi governa Amore, / pensando nel bel viso più che humano / che pò da lunge gli occhi miei far molli, / ma da presso gli abbaglia, et vince il core" [When sometimes I see from afar new snow on the hills struck by the sun, Love controls me as the sun does snow, as I think of that face of more than human beauty, which from afar can make my eyes wet but from close by dazzles them and vanquishes my heart]. Francesco Petrarca, *Canzoniere*, ed. Gianfranco Contini (Turin: Einaudi, 1968); translation in *Petrarch's Lyric Poems. The Rime sparse and Other Lyrics*, trans. Robert M. Durling (Cambridge, Mass.: Harvard University Press, 1976), p. 250.

43. Translation of Petrarch's poem 126.33–39 from Durling, p. 245. I say the origin of these verses is "meant to be apparent," but only Fredi Chiappelli

in his edition of GL (Milan: Rusconi, 1982, pp. 196–97n.) appears to have noticed that verse seven comes from Petrarch's poem 366, verse 54. He sees the juxtaposition as a profanation; and so it is, but it prepares the terms within which Armida's salvation will take place. Other commentators, starting with Guastavini (edition of Genoa 1617, p. 8 *ter*), see only the allusion to "Chiare, fresche, e dolci acque" (poem 126), and interpret 4.84.7–8 univocally as a trope of two consecutive verses (38–39) of Petrarch's secular poem: "et faccia forza al cielo, / asciugandosi gli occhi col bel velo."

44. Petrarch 213.1–4 (Durling translation, p. 366). Tasso: "sotto biondi / capelli e fra sì tenere sembianze / canuto senno e cor virile" [under blond hair and amid such delicate appearances, hoary-headed wisdom and a virile courage (GL 4.24.1–3)].

45. Petrarch 213.9–11 (Durling, p. 366). In GL 10.65.5–69.8, Armida appears as a Circe; stanza 68 catalogues the metamorphoses she can effect, and she herself refers to her *imperio* while admonishing the knights to renounce Christianity.

46. Armida's response implies not only Mary's response to Gabriel but also her Magnificat, Luke 1.46–55, esp. 48: "Quia respexit humilitatem ancillae suae."

47. GL 20.128.7, echoing v. 6 of Petrarch's 126: "Clear, fresh, sweet waters, where she who alone seems lady to me rested her lovely body, gentle branch where it pleased her (with sighing I remember) *to make a column for her lovely side*" (Durling, p. 244; emphasis mine). Ironically, Rinaldo's gesture is the same as Odoardo's (20.97.7–98.6), creating another marital resonance for this passage.

48. GL 20.136.3–6; cf. Petrarch 127.43–48 (above, n. 42).

49. Petrarch 366.44–45: ". . . di giustizia il sol, che rasserena / il secol pien d'errori oscuri et folti" (Durling, p. 578). On the *Sol Iustitiae*, see Malachi 4.2.

50. This is essentially the position of Savoia (above, n. 26) and is often implied by studies such as those in note 36.

Counterfeit and the Curse of Mediacy in the *Libro de buen amor* and the *Conde Lucanor* (pp. 203–215)

1. An excellent, overall view of the situation can be found in Peter Brown, *Augustine of Hippo* (London: Faber and Faber, 1967).

2. See Maureen Quilligan, *The Language of Allegory: Defining the Genre* (Ithaca and London: Cornell University Press, 1979); and the superb study of Jesse Gellrich, *The Idea of the Book in the Middle Ages: Language, Theory, Mythology and Fiction* (Ithaca and London: Cornell University Press, 1985), which demonstrates how the "text" of the world in general relates to the written object.

3. Jonathan Culler, *On Deconstruction: Theory and Criticism after Structuralism*, Cornell Paperbacks (Ithaca: Cornell University press, 1983), pp. 85–89, has interesting remarks on the deconstruction of causality, which are suggestive in regard to the circular process of writing and reading and then writing again.

4. See Douglas Kelly, "*Translatio Studii*: Translation, Adaptation, and Allegory in Medieval French Literature," *Philological Quarterly* 57 (1978):287–310.

5. R. A. Shoaf, *Dante, Chaucer, and the Currency of the Word: Money,*

Images and Reference in Late Medieval Poetry Norman, Okla.: Pilgrim Books, 1983) is an excellent, broad study of the whole question of counterfeit in various media.

6. It has been suggested by H. A. Kelly that the work may be as late as 1381. See his *Canon Law and the Archpriest of Hita,* Medieval and Renaissance Texts and Studies 27 (Binghampton: Center for Medieval and Early Renaissance Studies, 1984). Francisco J. Hernández, "The Venerable Juan Ruiz, Archpriest of Hita," *La Corónica* 13 (1984–1985):10–22, gives a rebuttal.

7. Don Juan Manuel, *Libro del Conde Lucanor,* ed. Reinaldo Ayerbe-Chaux (Madrid: Alhambra, 1983). I follow the division of the work into two parts suggested by Ayerbe-Chaux. The translations are my own and are based upon the original on the indicated page in the above edition.

8. Oxford: Oxford University Press, 1976.

9. See James F. Burke, "Frame and Structure in *El Conde Lucanor,*" *Revista Canadiense de Estudios Hispánicos* 8 (1984):263–73.

10. Ibid., p. 265.

11. See James F. Burke, "Juan Manuel's *Tabardíe* and *Golfín,*" *Hispanic Review* 44 (1976):171–78.

12. Ernst Cassirer, *Language and Myth,* trans. Suzanne Langer (New York: Dover Publications, 1946), p. 7.

13. *The Status of the Reading Subject in the Libro de buen amor,* University of North Carolina Studies in the Romance Languages and Literatures 224 (Chapel Hill: University of North Carolina Department of Romance Languages, 1985).

14. I have taken my translations from Juan Ruiz, *Libro de buen amor,* ed. with English paraphrase by Raymond S. Willis (Princeton: Princeton University Press, 1972).

15. *The Birth and Death of Language: Spanish Literature and Linguistics: 1300–1700* (Madrid: José Porrúa Turanzas, 1983), p. 27. An excellent summary of evidence concerning the "two versions" (1330 and 1343) and a discussion of it is available in Willis, *ibid.,* xxiv.–i.

16. Juan Ruiz, Arcipreste de Hita, *Libro de buen amor,* ed. Jacques Joset, 2 vols., Clásicos Castellanos (Madrid: Espasa-Calpe, 1974), p. 142, footnote. This is the accepted edition of the *LBA.*

17. *Traditions populaires et textualité dans le "Libro de Buen Amor"* (Montpellier: Centre d'Etudes et de Recherches Sociocritiques, n.d.).

Theologia Ludens: Angels and Devils in the Divine Comedy (pp. 216–235)

1. *Summa Theologiae,* ed. Instituti Studiorum Medievalium Ottaviensis (Ottawa: Vachon, 1941), II-ii, 168, art. 2.

2. *Il Convivio,* ed. G. Busnelli and G. Vandelli; 2nd ed. by A. E. Quaglio, 2 vols. (Florence: Le Monnier, 1964), IV.xvii.6. All quotations are from this edition.

3. All quotations are from *La Divina Commedia secondo l'antica vulgata,* ed. Giorgio Petrocchi, 4 vols., Società Dantesca Italiana (Milan: Mondadori, 1966–1967).

4. *The Cambridge History of Later Greek and Early Medieval Philosophy* (Cambridge: Cambridge University Press, 1970), p. 447.
5. *The City of God*, trans. John Healey (London: J. M. Dent, 1903), XI, 10.
6. *Commentary on the Dream of Scipio*, trans. William Harris Stahl (New York: Columbia University Press, 1952), III, 7.
7. *Patrologiae Cursus Completus*; Series Latina, ed. J. P. Migne (Paris: Garnier, 1880), 176, 211.
8. *The Lives of St. Francis of Assisi* (London: Methuen, 1908), XC, 127.

Machiavelli, Montaigne, and the Problem of External Address in Renaissance Ethics (pp. 236–253)

1. A. Grafton, "On the Scholarship of Politian and Its Contexts," *JWCI* 40 (1977):150–88.
2. F. Petrarca, *Le Familiari*, ed. V. Rossi (Florence: Sansoni, 1937), XIII, 4, 7: "cum multa quidem congregent occupati homines, tempus effundunt, et cum agere omnia videantur, unum idque optimum semper omittunt, vivere; ubique sunt preterquam apud semet ipsos; loquuntur sepe cum aliis, nunquam secum." Cf. IX, 5, 14.
3. See my "Lorenzo Valla: Humanist Rhetoric and the Critique of the Classical Languages of Morality," in *Renaissance Florence*, ed. J. J. Murphy (Berkeley: U of California Press, 1982), pp. 191–206; and "Metaphoric Morals: Ethical Implications of Cusanus's Use of Figure," in *L'Archéologie du signe*, ed. L. Brind'Amour and E. Vance (Toronto: Pontifical Institute of Medieval Studies, 1982), pp. 305–41.
4. Within the scope of this paper, I am able to present only parts of a longer argument about the perspicacious connections between discipline and address that will constitute the last section of a study of Renaissance ethics.
5. K.-H. Stierle, "Histoire comme Exemple; Exemple comme Histoire," *Poétique* 10 (1972):176–98.
6. C. Guillén, "Towards a Definition of the Picaresque," *Literature as System* (Princeton: Princeton University Press, 1971), pp. 71–106.
7. Machiavelli, *Lettere*, ed. F. Gaeta, in *Opere* (Milan: Feltrinelli, 1981), vol. 6, p. 451 to F. Guicciardini, Jan. 3, 1526: "Sempre, mentre che io ho di ricordo o e' si fece guerra, o e' se ne ragionò; hora se ne ragiona, di qui a un poco si farà, et quando la sarà finita se ne ragionerà di nuovo, tanto che mai sarà tempo a pensare a nulla . . ."; trans. by A. Gilbert, *The Letters of Machiavelli* (New York: Capricorn, 1961), p. 223.
8. *Lettere*, p. 454, to Guicciardini, March 15, 1526: ". . . et disputai tre conclusioni, l'una, che non obstante l'accordo il re non sarebbe libero; l'altra, che se il re fosse libero osserverebbe lo accordo; la terza, che non osserverebbe. Non dissi già quale di queste tre io mi credessi, ma bene conclusi che in qualunque di esse l'Italia haveva da havere guerra, et a questa guerra non detti remedio alcuno"; trans. Gilbert, *Letters*, p. 224.
9. On "possible worlds" semantics, see J. Hintikka, "The Intentions of Intentionality," in *The Intentions of Intentionality and Other New Models for Modalities* (Dordrecht: Reidel, 1975), pp. 192–222.

10. See J. Pinborg, "Introduction," to Sigerus de Contrarco, *Summa modorum significandi; sophismata* (Amsterdam: Benjamins, 1977); "A *sophisma* takes as its starting point a proposition which for some reason or another is odd and has odd consequences," (p. xv); they are sometimes mere pretext, quickly dismissed, to discuss some other problems; "they are important as exercises in the technique of argumentation," (p. xv).

11. Mark Miller, "Courtliness in the English Renaissance," unpublished dissertation, Johns Hopkins, 1977.

12. On the presuppositional nature of language, see P. Henry, *Le mauvais outil; Langue, sujet et discours* (Paris: Klincksieck, 1977).

13. B. Croce, *Elementi di politica* (Bari: Laterza, 1925), p. 62; cited by F. Chiappelli, *Studi sul linguaggio del Machiavelli* (Florence: Le Monnier, 1952), pp. 113–14.

14. Davidson, "How Is Weakness of the Will Possible?" in *Essays on Action and Events* (Oxford: Oxford University Press, 1980), pp. 21–22, 34.

15. D. Sperber, "Rudiments de rhétorique cognitive," *Poétique* 23 (1975): 389–415; Sperber holds that certain concepts are essential to a description of the rhetorical mechanism: "Ceux de savoir partagé, de savoir partagé mobilisé, de champ (large ou restreint), de la pertinence, d'informativité et de pertinence relative."

16. *Les Essais de Montaigne*, ed. P. Villey (Paris: P.U.F., 1965), vol. 1, pp. 635, 648; citations hereafter will be to the volume and page numbers of this edition. On the "web of belief," see W. V. Quine and J. S. Ullian, *The Web of Belief* (New York: Random House, 1978), chap. 2, "Belief and Change of Belief," pp. 9–19.

17. P. Ricoeur, "La Problématique de la croyance; opinion, assentiment, foi," in *On Believing; Epistemological and Semiotic Approaches*, ed. H. Parret (Berlin: de Gruyter, 1983), pp. 292–301.

18. H. Parret, "Introduction; Beliefs and Believing: The Web and the Spinning," in *On Believing*, p. 13. There are parallels between Montaignian belief and Wittgenstein's "common sense certainty," the acceptance of regulative grounds that make life possible; see Parret, "Common Sense and Basic Beliefs," as well as his "Introduction," in *On Believing*, pp. 221, 4.

19. Thus, in 2.809: "Le pris de l'ame ne consiste pas à aller haut, mais ordonneement"; in 1.658: "La recommandation que chacun cherche, de vivacité et promptitude d'esprit, je la pretends du reglement; d'une action esclatante et signalée, ou de quelque particuliere suffisance, je la pretends de l'ordre, correspondance, et tranquillité d'opinions et de meurs"; in 2.1110: "La grandeur de l'ame n'est pas tant tirer a mont et tirer avant comme sçavoir se ranger et circonscrire." Montaigne's formalization has its analogues in Quintilian's simple formal definition of prudence as self-consistency in doing and not doing, while discursive virtue is self-consistency in speaking and not-speaking: ". . . si consonare sibi in faciendis ac non faciendis virtus est, quae pars eius prudentia vocatur, eadem in dicendis ac non dicendis erit," *Institutio Oratoria*, trans. H. E. Butler (Cambridge, Mass.: Harvard University Press, 1963), II, xx, 5.

20. B. Pascal, *Pensées*, ed. L. Lafuma (Paris: Editions du Luxembourg, 1951); see especially fragments 577, 680, 863, 872.

21. On Montaigne's practices of citation, see A. Compagnon, *La Seconde*

Main; ou le travail de la citation (Paris: Seuil, 1979); on the gloss as practice see A. Tournon, *Montaigne: La glose et l'essai* (Lyon: Presses Universitaires de Lyon, 1983).

22. J. Shklar, *Ordinary Vices* (Cambridge, Mass.: Belknap Press, 1984); the source of the title is revealed in the epigraph of the introduction: "Treachery, disloyalty, cruelty, tyranny . . . are our ordinary vices," [*Essais* 1.210].

23. M. de Certeau, "Une pratique sociale de la Différance: Croire," in *Faire Croire* (*Collection de l'Ecole Française de Rome*, no. 51 [Rome: Palazzo Farnese, 1981], pp. 363–83).

24. Montaigne, of course, does not overvalue the opinion of the multitude: "Il y a du malheur d'en estre là que la meilleure touche de la verité ce soit la multitude des croians, en une presse où les fols surpassent de tant les sages en nombre" (2.1028). Although Pascal claims that Montaigne is wrong, he simply refines rather than confutes Montaigne when he attributes the force of custom not to reason or justice but to belief: ". . . le peuple la suit par cette seule raison qu'il la croit juste" (525).

25. B. Williams, *Ethics and the Limits of Philosophy* (Cambridge, Mass.: Harvard University Press, 1985).

26. Cf. 1.657: the three audiences are characterized as "les sçavans," "les ames communes et populaires," and "les ames reglées et fortes d'ellesmesmes."

27. F. Villey, *Les Sources et l'évolution des Essais de Montaigne* (1933, Osnabrück: Otto Zeller, 1976), pp. 149–50; Villey makes the point as well that there are certain discursive similarities between the *Discorsi* and the *Essais*—e.g., short units, with tenuous interrelations (p. 30). The tendency of the older scholarship was to look for Machiavelli's "influence" on Montaigne; see, for example, A. Nicolai, "Le Machiavellisme de Montaigne," *Bulletin de la Société des Amis de Montaigne*, 3rd ser., 1.4 (1957):11–15 ff.

28. M. Fumaroli, of course, maintains the continuity of the Humanist tradition between Petrarch's letters and Montaigne's essays: "Genèse de l'épistolographie classique; Rhétorique humaniste de la lettre, de Pétrarque à Juste Lipse," *Revue d'histoire littéraire de la France* 78 [1978]; 886–918.

29. *Institutio oratoria*, V,viii,1; V,x,8; cf. Cicero, *Brutus*, l. 187, trans. G. L. Hendrickson (Cambridge, Mass.: Harvard University Press, 1952), p. 159, "fidem facit oratio."

30. Cf. Petrarch, *Fam.*, XX, 15, 27–28, where he decries friends who are rapacious of counsel, preempting discourse; cf. XVI, 3, 14–15, where Petrarch finds them addicted to "degeneres sententias."

31. For Machiavellian awareness of disjunction, recall the preface to Book II of the *Discorsi*: "Perché gli è offizio di uomo buono, quel bene che per la malignità de' tempi e della fortuna tu non hai potuto operare, insegnarlo ad altri, acciò che, sendone molti capaci, alcuno di quelli più amato dal Cielo possa operarlo" [For it is the duty of a good man to teach others about whatever good he has been unable to perform on account of the malignity of the times and of Fortune, so that, among the many thus informed, someone more beloved of Heaven than the others may be able to perform that good (trans. W. S.)], *Discorsi*, ed. S. Bertelli (Milan: Feltrinelli, 1971), p. 274.

Contributors

Albert Russell Ascoli is associate professor of French and Italian at Northwestern University and author of *Ariosto's Bitter Harmony: Crisis and Evasion in the Italian Renaissance* (1987).

Kevin Brownlee is professor of romance languages and literature at the University of Pennsylvania. He is the author of *Poetic Identity in Guillaume de Machaut* (1984), and coeditor of *Romance: Generic Transformation from Chrétien de Troyes to Cervantes* (1985).

Marina Scordilis Brownlee is professor of romance languages and literature at the University of Pennsylvania. She is the author of *The Poetics of Literary Theory: Lope de Vega's Novelas a Marcia Leonarda and their Cervantine Context* (1981), *The Status of the Reading Subject in the* Libro de buen amor (1985), and coeditor of *Romance: Generic Transformation from Chrétien de Troyes to Cervantes* (1985).

James F. Burke is professor of Spanish and Portuguese at the University of Toronto and author of *History and Vision: The Figural Structure of the* Libro del Cavallero Zifar (1972).

David F. Hult is associate professor of French at the Johns Hopkins University and author of *Self-Fulfilling Prophecies: Readership and Authority in the first* Roman de la rose (1986).

William J. Kennedy is professor of comparative literature at Cornell University. He is the author of *Rhetorical Norms in Renaissance Literature* (1978) and *Jacopo Sannazaro and the Uses of Pastoral* (1983).

Giuseppe Mazzotta is professor of Italian at Yale University. He is the author of *Dante, Poet of the Desert* (1979) and *The World at Play in Boccaccio's Decameron* (1986).

François Rigolot is Meredith Howland Pyne Professor of French Literature at Princeton University. He is author of *Les Langages de Rabelais* (1972), *Le Texte de la Renaissance* (1982), and *Les Métamorphoses de Montaigne* (1988).

Walter Stephens is associate professor of French and Italian at Dartmouth College and author of *Giants in Those Days: Folklore, Ancient History, and Nationalism* (1989).

Nancy S. Struever is professor of humanities and history at the Johns Hopkins University. She is author of *The Language of History in the Renaissance: Rhetoric and Historical Consciousness in Florentine Humanism* (1970), and coeditor of *Rhetoric and the Pursuit of Truth: Language Change in the Seventeenth and Eighteenth Centuries* (1985).

Donald Phillip Verene is professor of philosophy at Emory University. His books include Vico's *Science of the Imagination* (1981) and *Hegel's Recollection: A Study of Images in the Phenomenology of Spirit* (1985).

Nancy J. Vickers is professor of French and Italian at the University of Southern California. She is coeditor of *The Dialectic of Discovery: Essays on the Teaching and Interpretation of Literature Presented to Lawrence E. Harvey* (1984) and *Rewriting the Renaissance: The Discourses of Sexual Difference in Early Modern Europe* (1986).

Index